# HOW TO COLLECT
# STAMPS

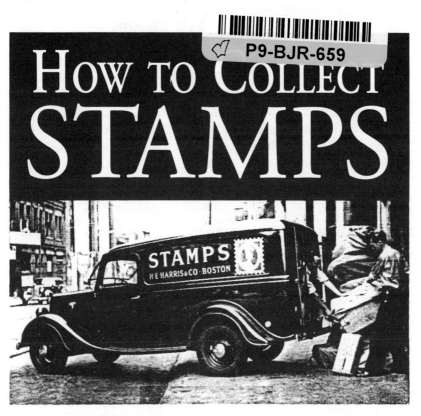

*H.E.Harris & Co.* ®

*Collectors serving collectors since 1916*

International Standard Book Number (ISBN): 937458-29-5

Copyright 1993 by H. E. Harris & Co.

Florence, AL 35631-0817

All Rights Reserved

Printed in USA

# CONTENTS

# COLLECTING IS
# THE OLDEST HOBBY!

Man is a born collector — since time immemorial, he has been collecting all sorts of things, for all sorts of different reasons. The first collector was probably a caveman who found some unusually attractive rocks and decided to take them home. Or it may have been some bones to which he attached some supernatural significance, or some shell, or feathers — no matter. What is important is that today, more people are collectors than any other type of hobbyist; and more people by far collect stamps than any other object.

Why stamps? Think of all the different things that people collect — antiques, magazines, bottles, coins, rocks, automobiles, works of art, even autographs — and the reasons why they collect them — aesthetic appeal, cultural or historical significance, curiosity, nostalgia value, pride of ownership, or just plain whimsy — and you'll find that stamp collecting offers all these attractions combined and more!

Aesthetic appeal? You would need a museum larger than the fabulous Louvre to house all the marvelous paintings, magnificent statues, and other great works of art to be found on stamps. The Mona Lisa, Venus de Milo, Rodin's "The Thinker," Rembrandts, Michelangelos, Picassos, Van Goghs—they're all here. And many collectors consider stamps themselves, with their finely executed designs and exquisite details, to be miniature works of art in their own right.

Cultural and historical significance? Through stamps you'll gain knowledge about the manners, customs, dress, traditions, and folklore of people in all parts of the globe. You'll witness events which shaped the world as it is today, meet heroic figures of the past, and catch futuristic glimpses of things to come.

Curiosity? Nothing will whet your curiosity like the hundreds of strange and unknown people, events, and other subjects

you'll find on stamps. You'll delve through history, geography, science, sports, every subject known to man seeking the answers to questions posed by your stamps.

Nostalgia? Antique autos, people dressed as they were years ago, old buildings long since torn down, figures from the past — they're all on stamps. Pride of ownership? Just watch a stamp collector beam as he regards a new acquisition, or straightens out the volumes in his collection. Whimsy? There are stamps picturing scenes from fairy tales, cartoon characters, imaginary space creatures, and more.

And stamp collecting has other virtues, too. It offers relaxation, rejuvenation of the spirit, an escape from the cares of the everyday world. It offers the excitement of the hunt, the unknown, as you pore through a pile of stamps hoping to find something of value, perhaps even great rarity!

Through stamp collecting, too, you can make new friends, and strengthen existing relationships. One of the pleasures of stamp collecting is meeting with other collectors, to swap stamps, discuss finer philatelic points, and in general share your interest in the hobby. Families find that stamp collecting offers an excellent way to spend time together; and stamp collectors in their

neighborhood, city, state, other states, even other countries. Stamp collecting provides a common ground for understanding between peoples, near and far. As stamp collector Lily Pons, the famed opera star said, "Stamp collecting — like music — makes one part of a great world-wide fraternity knowing no bounds of nationality."

It is no wonder, then, that famous people from every walk of life — presidents, kings and queens, businessmen, movie stars, religious leaders — have all been avid stamp collectors.

As president Franklin D. Roosevelt said, "Stamp collecting dispels boredom, enlarges our vision, broadens our knowledge, makes for better citizens, and in innumerable ways enriches our life."

# A BRIEF HISTORY
# OF STAMP COLLECTING

Who was the first stamp collector? No one knows for sure, but it can't have been too long after the first stamps were issued that someone thought it would be a grand idea to collect these little bits of postal paper as novelties or souvenirs. As more and more countries adopted the new postal system, and the number of different stamps from different countries began to grow, other people took interest, and the hobby of philately was under way.

Of course, it was easier to collect stamps then. There were no decisions that had to be made over what countries or topics to collect — nearly everyone was a worldwide collector. Ten years after the introduction of the Penny Black, only 153 more stamps had been introduced; in 1860, the total number of stamps was still under 1,000. But the number of stamps and stamp-issuing countries and colonies increased rapidly thereafter, and today there are well over 200,000 different stamps — not including all the minor varieties, errors, reprints, and so forth.

Then, as today, people gathered stamps for many different reasons: one woman advertised for used Penny Blacks to paper her walls; another wanted to use the stamps to decorate lampshades. The first known advertisement for stamps for actual hobby-collecting purposes appeared in the London *Family Herald* in 1851. It was probably through such advertisements that stamp collectors first made contact with each other, and formed the first stamp clubs and philatelic societies. The very first philatelic society on record was called the Omnibus Club, and was formed in the United States in 1856. Today, there are many different philatelic societies in many countries, and an international society called **FIP** — the Federation Internationale de Philatelie, founded in 1926.

As for the use of the word "philately" to describe stamp collecting, it first appeared in an article written in 1864 by a French stamp collector named Herpin for a French stamp magazine. Derived from two Greek roots, "philo," meaning "love," and "atelos," meaning something exempt from "taxes," i.e., a letter with postage stamps. The term gained such widespread popularity — many people must have thought it described exactly the way they felt — that it was incorporated into common usage.

Some people in those early days of philately may have thought that stamp collecting was just a passing fancy, a short-lived fad — time has proven them very wrong. Interest in stamp collecting has grown steadily through the years until today countless people throughout the world — and more than 16 million in the United States alone — turn to stamp collecting for both recreation and pleasure, making it truly "The World's Most Popular Hobby."

# A BRIEF HISTORY OF
# POSTAGE STAMPS

The first organized system for carrying written messages was established by the Persians under Darius, who created a network of mounted couriers stationed at various points throughout his vast empire, ready to speed letters to any part of the country. These early "Pony Express" riders were so efficient that they inspired the ancient Greek historian Herodotus to coin the famous phrase which appears on the facade of the New York City post office building: "Neither snow nor rain nor heat nor gloom of night stays these couriers from the swift completion of their appointed rounds."

Darius' system was adopted and expanded upon by Caesar Augustus, whose "Cursus Publicus" included couriers on foot, on horseback, and in carriages, traveling well-maintained highways connecting Rome with every outlying territory of the Roman Empire. The "Cursus Publicus" was known familiarly as the "post" system because of the way-stations, or posts, established at regular intervals along each route to provide the couriers with food and fresh horses.

The first postal system open to the public (the earlier ones had all been exclusively for royal use) was established in 1505 by the Thurn and Taxis families of Austria, who offered to carry letters and parcels anywhere in continental Europe for anyone who could pay the fee. Organized under a royal license, the Thurn and Taxis system survived for more than 350 years, well into the modern postal era.

The Thurn and Taxis system was privately-owned, and so was the London Penny Post when it was inaugurated in 1680 by a businessman named William Dockwra. But the Penny Post proved to be so profitable that the government, seeing in it an

6

ideal source of internal revenue, decided to take over its operation for itself. Thus was born, in 1698, the first postal system.

Dockwra's Penny Post was a model of Postal efficiency, and
it remains so even to this day. Letterboxes were posted at hundreds of points throughout London, and branch offices were established in every district. For one penny, a letter or parcel deposited at a letter box or branch station would be picked up, hand
stamped to indicate the time of collection and certify that the
postage had been paid, and delivered to any address in the city.
Deliveries were made every hour in the business district and from
four to eight times a day in the outlying sections.

In colonial America, meanwhile, the first post office had been
established at Boston in 1639, and by 1691 a uniform postal service was in operation throughout the colonies. The first postal
system of the new government of the United States went into
operation in 1775, with Benjamin Franklin as the first Postmaster General.

Until 1840, however, all these systems operated without the
benefit of a postage stamp. Items were hand stamped mostly to
show receipt at a post office, and postage was collected from the
addressee upon delivery. Many people developed secret codes
by which they could cheat the postal services: secret marks on
the outside of the envelope conveyed the sender's message, and
all the addressee had to do was to read the secret message on the
envelope, then refuse to accept the letter and pay the fee.

To counter this trend, Sir Rowland Hill, the British Postmaster General, created the first adhesive postage stamp in 1840 —
and the modern postal era was born. The stamps were to be bought
beforehand by the person wishing to send a letter, then affixed to
the letter, indicating that the postage had been paid. The stamps
were designed by Hill himself, and bore a profile likeness of the
Queen Victoria, who had just come to the throne three years before. Because they were printed in black, the one-cent stamps
became known as "Penny Blacks" — and were the first govern-
ment-printed postage stamp.

This new postal system of collecting the postage in advance
proved immensely popular, and it was not long before all the
civilized countries in the world had instituted like systems. The

United States itself issued its first stamps in 1847, a 5¢ Franklin and a 10¢ Washington.

As more and more nations joined the postal fraternity, the frontiers between them began to cause numerous difficulties. Different nations had different postal rates, transportation fees, and internal conditions, so the delivery of mail over international boundaries involved the negotiation of complicated and confusing bilateral written treaties. Mail from Spain to Germany, for example, had to travel from Spain to France under one treaty, and from France to Germany under another — and might be stopped altogether if the treaty expired while the mail was en route. An obvious need existed for a broad international postal system to replace the multitude of bilateral treaties.

One of the early leaders in the movement for an international postal organization was Montgomery Blair, the U.S. Postmaster General. It was mostly through Blair's efforts that the first international postal conference was convened in Paris in 1863, attended by the United States and 15 European Nations. Though an international postal organization was not founded in Paris, many of the proposals forwarded at the conference, such as standardization of postal weights and rates, influenced the agreement which finally emerged 12 years later.

In the following years, the initiative in the international movement was taken over by the German Postmaster General, Dr.

Heinrich von Stephan, who worked hard to draft proposals which would make the flow of mail between countries as simple and efficient as the flow of mail within countries. His years of labor bore fruit in October, 1874, when 22 countries met in the first Postal Congress in Berne, Switzerland, and founded the Universal Postal Union. The final agreement, which took place in July, 1875, included such principles as a unified rate for letters, the principle that the postage is paid by the sender, standardized delivery and transportation fees, etc.

Today, all civilized nations of the world belong to the U.P.U. In addition to expediting the world-wide distribution of mail, the U.P.U. also regulates international organizations, the U.P.U. is the one body which comes closest to successfully fulfilling its original goals.

# FAMOUS RARITIES

Mention stamp collecting to the average non-collector, and chances are the first thing that will come to his mind will be some story he has heard in the past about a rare stamp being sold for a fabulous amount of money. And in truth, such tales are as much a part of the hobby as are the stamps themselves.

For example, practically every collector (and many non-collectors as well) knows the story of the 1856 British Guiana one cent magenta, the world's rarest stamp. Found in the attic by an English schoolboy in 1873, and sold to a friend for a $1.50, this one stamp is valued at $500,000.

Other famous rarities include the 1847 Mauritius 1¢ and 2¢ issues accidentally printed "Post Office" instead of "Post Paid," and worth $350,000 apiece (all values given here are 1993 Standard Catalog prices); the 1851 2¢ Hawaiian Missionary stamp, valued at $250,000, Spain's 1851 2 reale stamp, printed in blue instead of red and worth $110,000, and another color error, the 1851 Baden 9 kreuzer green (it should have been red), valued at $60,000.

Famous United States rarities include most of the 1846-47 Postmaster's Provisionals, particularly the Alexandria, VA 5¢ "Blue Boy" worth $125,000, the Boscawen, NH 5¢, and the Lockport, NY 5¢, valued at $150,000 apiece; the 1869 "Landing of Columbus," 1869 "Shield, Eagle, and Flags" 30¢ stamp with inverted Flags, worth $165,000; and the most famous U.S. rarity of all, the 1918 "Curtis Jenny" 24¢ airmail with inverted center, valued at $135,000.

What makes these little pieces of paper worth so much money? The answer lies in the age-old law of supply and demand: in the more than 100 years since the 1856 British Guiana was discovered, no other copy has come to light. Meanwhile the number of collectors in the world has grown into the tens of millions, all of whom would like to own this one stamp. It's no wonder, then that the price has risen to such astonishing heights!

Of course, the chance of finding any of the really old rare stamps grow slimmer each day, with so many millions of collectors engaged in the search; but important philatelic finds are still being made, usually as they have always been made in the past: by someone browsing through a collection of old letters, cleaning out an attic, thumbing through a pile of old documents, etc.

The best place to look for valuable stamps is anywhere mail has been saved or accumulated for many years. Attics, basements, storage rooms, etc., often yield old trunks or bundles containing letters from grandparents or even great-grandparents. Among these letters there is always the possibility that a valuable stamp will be found.

Many businesses, banks, and other financial concerns, schools, country courthouses, churches, etc., store their correspondence and records for years; some of the greatest stamp finds have been made among such ancient papers.

A stamp does not necessarily have to be very old, however, to be extremely valuable — the law of supply and demand applies to modern stamps as well as to ancient ones.

In 1954, for example, a copy of the newly-minted Kenya 5¢ stamp picturing the Owen Falls Dam was found to have a picture of the dam inverted. Millions of "correct" copies of this stamp were printed in 100-stamp sheets, four sheets to a pane. But no other copy of the stamp with the "upside-down dam" has ever turned up, the one-of-a-kind stamp was eventually purchased by a wealthy Indian maharajah for a price estimated to be around $10,000, and its value today is considered to be many times that sum.

*CORRECTLY PRINTED*                    *ERROR*

Again, as recently as 1962, a sheet of Canal Zone "Thatcher Ferry Bridge" 4¢ stamps was found which had the picture of the bridge erroneously omitted. Eighteen years later, these stamps were valued at $10,000 a piece.

This last case, incidentally, was one of great importance to all collectors. The Thatcher Ferry Bridge find was made by H.E. Harris, founder of the stamp firm which bears his name, and one of the great pioneers of the stamp hobby. When Canal Zone postal authorities learned of Harris' discovery, they proposed to print millions of additional stamps with the bridge omitted — deliberate "errors" which would have rendered Harris' copies worthless as rarities.

Harris went to court to protect his find, and in a landmark decision, the postal authorities were enjoined from any action which would devalue genuine errors. This decision set a legal precedent which assures every collector who even dreams of finding a valuable error that any such discovery cannot be rendered worthless through deliberate government interference.

This hope of someday discovering a rare stamp, no matter how remote the chances may be, adds much to the excitement of stamp collecting — but it is still only a small part of the large pleasures the hobby has to offer. What makes a stamp valuable is the fact that, though millions of people may want one, only a very select few collectors will ever be privileged to own a copy of it, thus, a collector whose only interest in the hobby lies in the acquisition of great rarities is almost certain to be disappointed.

Obviously, then, the millions of people in the world today who collect stamps must do so for some reason other than the simple acquisition of rarities. And, although much has been said time and again about the many virtues of the hobby — it is educational, it brings people together, it is relaxing, it teaches good habits, etc. — the one overriding fact that remains is this: stamp collecting is fun!

# HOW TO BEGIN

Stamps can be obtained from any sources. First of all, save them from your own incoming mail, and have your friends, relatives, and business acquaintances do the same. Servicemen and others visiting foreign countries can bring back many interesting stamps. You can swap stamps with friends or "pen pals," exchanging your duplicates for others that you do not have.

The best way to obtain a goodly number of all-different stamps for a reasonable price is by purchasing a large stamp packet at a local stamp or hobby store or department store. Bags or boxes of "mixture" — that is, stamps still on paper, unpicked and unsorted — are very different; their cost per stamp is much less but you will probably receive many duplicates of very common stamps, although you will probably also find a few good commemorative stamps or others to add to your collection.

As your collection grows, you may wish to add more packets — available for many different countries and topics — or stamps purchased from a reputable mail-order house such as Harris. Through mail-order catalogs and stamp retail stores, you can buy stamps in sets, packets, and individually.

You will probably want to keep your stamps in an album, and you will find helpful hints as to album selection in the section on "Albums" in this book. Duplicate stamps and those you have not yet mounted in your album are usually kept in glassine envelopes or stock books (see "Accessories" section.)

NEVER paste, glue or tape stamps down in an album, always use an approved stamp mounting such as hinges.

In the earliest years of stamp collecting, stamps were merely glued down, often with their own gum. Then collectors began to preserve most of the original gum by using "stamp hinges," little gummed pieces of paper or glassine that are folded in the middle and act like a hinge, one part attached to the back of the stamp, the other to the album page, as described under "Hinges." In recent years however, the majority of collectors prefer to keep the gum on mint stamps intact by using the so-called "hingeless" mounts, which protect the stamp completely, but from which the stamp can be removed, if desired. (Note: Most **mounts** are **not** peelable, while better grades of stamp hinges **are** peelable and can be removed from the album page and stamp with very little trace.)

Very old and rare stamps, such as found once in a blue moon on old correspondence, plus those with special postal markings such as "First Day of Issue," are likely to be worth more if left on their original envelopes. But nearly all stamps — and especially those which the beginning collector is likely to acquire through buying "mixture" lots or from his own current mail — should be cleanly separated from any attached paper before being mounted in the collection.

Place the stamps in cold or luke-warm (but not hot) water for five or ten minutes, and you will find that the paper peels off easily. Then place the stamp face down on a clean blotter and let it dry thoroughly before you mount it in your album. If the stamps curl, they may be straightened by drying them between blotters on which a book has been placed, or by using a "stamp press." NOTE: A few stamps have ink which will run or disintegrate when placed in water. The best guide to these stamps is the Scott Standard Postage Stamp catalog, which may be purchased from almost any stamp dealer or can be found in the reference section of most public libraries. If you buy, or have access to, a Scott Catalog, you will find a wealth of information at the beginning of each volume as to how stamps are printed, the various types of paper, printing, etc.

Most collectors acquire duplicate stamps; many wonder what to do with them. First of all, you will want the best possible copy of each stamp for your collection, so if you acquire a second copy, check with the one you already have and mount the best one in your album. (Some collectors even maintain two collections, one for unused and one for used stamps.) Duplicate stamps may be used for trading with other collectors, while a small packet of one's duplicates and an inexpensive album make a wonderful gift for a youngster who has not yet started this fascinating hobby. Veteran's hospitals, prisons and orphanages often welcome donations of stamps.

After collecting stamps of the world for a while, enjoying the romance of acquiring these fascinating and colorful little pieces of paper that move the world's mail, many enthusiasts begin to narrow their collecting interests to a particular country or topic, and here is where stamp collecting can become truly personal, for there are almost as many ideas about collecting as there are collectors. Some people keep right on collecting stamps of the whole world, others may specialize in airmails, or British Empire stamps, or those of some particular country. Perhaps they choose art on stamps, or sports on stamps, or animals, birds or flowers; or any one of a thousand or more other topics. Whatever appeals to you — whatever strikes your fancy — that's what **you** should collect, for that is what will surely give you the most pleasure.

There is also a whole fascinating micro-world in stamps — secret marks, minor varieties and the like, as seen through a magnifying glass (see U.S. Identifier section for examples.) There are stamps that can be told apart only by their perforations as measured in a space of two centimeters, or by whether they are printed on watermarked or unwatermarked paper. (See further information elsewhere in this book.) You can spend hours, like Sherlock Holmes with his magnifying glass, tracking down the identity of a single stamp, or you can let your imagination roam the whole world as you leaf through your stamp album. The choice is **yours**!

# HOW TO COLLECT STAMPS

The "Ten Commandments" of Stamp Collecting are:

1. NEVER PASTE, GLUE OR TAPE A STAMP DOWN. Always use stamp hinges or other approved stamp mounts.
2. ALWAYS USE STAMP TONGS TO HANDLE MINT STAMPS. In fact, it is a good idea to use tongs when handling all stamps.
3. HANDLE YOUR STAMPS CAREFULLY AT ALL TIMES. Don't cram them into a box so that they may become torn, creased or otherwise damaged and thus destroy their value.
4. USE VERY LITTLE MOISTURE WHEN USING ANY KIND OF STAMP MOUNT. This applies to all mounts — hinges or any other type of mounting.
5. BEWARE OF HUMIDITY. Stamp gum is made to stick, and stamps with gum will stick to almost anything if moisture is introduced, and there is no absolutely sure way to unstick them. If you are in a humid area, keep your stamp collection in as cool and dry a place as possible.
6. ONCE YOU HAVE DECIDED WHAT YOU WILL COLLECT, BUY THE BEST (Largest) ALBUM YOU CAN AFFORD. Buying a too-small album will only require transferring stamps to new album pages later — a time-consuming and expensive process.
7. NEVER SEAL A STAMP MOUNT COMPLETELY. Paper may disintegrate if kept absolutely air-tight.
8. DO NOT SOAK A STAMP OFF A COVER (ENVELOPE) UNTIL YOU FIND OUT WHETHER IT HAS ANY SPECIAL POSTAL MARKINGS OR OTHER REASON THAT WOULD MAKE IT MORE VALUABLE IF LEFT "ON COVER." For instance, a cover stamped "First Day of Issue" would be more desirable than the stamp by itself. Generally speaking, common, ordinary stamps may be soaked off without any further checking; older covers should generally be checked with the Scott Standard Postage Stamp Catalog first, or better yet, with a qualified cover expert.
9. REMEMBER THAT A FEW STAMPS HAVE "FUGITIVE" INKS, AND THESE INKS WILL RUN IF PUT IN WATER OR IN WATERMARK DETECTION FLUID. If in doubt, check the Scott Catalog first.
10. ENJOY YOUR HOBBY TO THE FULLEST! It can bring you a whole lifetime of enjoyment.

# HISTORY OF
# FIRST DAY COVERS

If you are a stamp collector, you probably have a few First Day Covers (FDC's) in an album or shoe box. For most collectors a FDC is a cacheted envelope with a new stamp and a "First Day of Issue" postmark. Some might also have a First Day Program, outlining the Ceremony held on the First Day in the official First Day city.

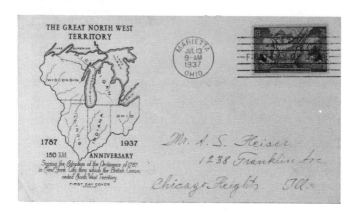

*First Use of First Day Issue
cancellation*

First Day Cover collecting as we know it today did not start until the 1920's and 30's. Between July, 1922, and Sept. 1923, the first official First Day of Issue, the First Day Ceremony and program and the first commercial FDC cachet all appeared.

It wasn't until 1937 that the familiar "First Day of Issue" slogan was first used. Since then these basic elements of FDC collecting have changed very little.

When considering FDC's before 1922, all the rules change. Collectors accustomed to an official First Day for each new stamp will be surprised to learn there were only nineteen Designated First Days for all U.S. stamps issued before 1922. These official dates were designated by the Post Office in either PO instructions for stamp sale, with the PO announcement of the new issue, or by the Congress in the bill which authorized the stamps.

Even with these few cases, First Day Covers do not exist for all issues with Designated First Days. Often the stamp was not available for sale until after Designated First Day, and in at least one case there is evidence that a stamp sold before the Designated First Day.

*"Earliest Dated Cover" without cachet*

First Day Covers for most issues before 1922 are more properly called "Earliest Dated Covers." An Earliest Dated Cover is one with the earliest known postmark for the particular issue on cover.

The history of First Day Cover collecting changed when the USPOD designated the first official First Day of Issue on July 12, 1922. This was the First Day of E12, the 10¢ Special Delivery stamp.

The next stamp issued with an official First Day was the 11¢ Hayes regular issue, on October 4, 1922, in Washington, D.C., and Fremont, OH. This FD included several new firsts: the first FD city outside Washington, D.C., the FD ceremony and the FD program.

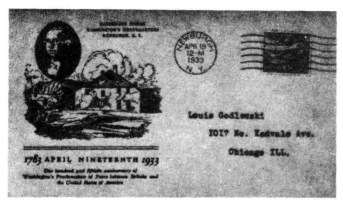

*Linprint cachet*

On September 1, 1923, George Linn serviced the first commercially produced US FDC cachet. Linn printed a simple five line cachet on a black bordered, mourning envelope. Several hundred of these cacheted FDC's were prepared and offered for sale in philatelic journals of the period: *Collector's Club Philatelist, MeKeel's Weekly Philatelic Gossip,* as well as his own paper, *Linn's Weekly Stamp News.*

From a simple start of one cachet in 1923, cachet making grew in popularity to over thirty different cachets per issue for the Clark and Sullivan commemoratives of 1929, and nearly 100 different cachets per issue for many of the three cent purples of the 1930's.

*Cover addressed to Adam Bert*

Cacheted FDC's before 1935 were made in very small quantities and they are getting harder to find every year. Because of this, many collectors are happy to have uncacheted covers in this period.

Covers with addresses of prominent FDC enthusiasts, Adam Bert, C.E. Nickles, Heny Hammelman, Philip Ward and Edward Worden are highly sought after by many FDC specialists.

## Introduction to Cachet Collecting

Today, many FDC collectors are really cachet collectors. The thrill of the hobby is in finding a scarce cachet for their collection. Up to one hundred different cachets exist for many stamp issues from mid-1930's up to the present.

Some collectors enjoy the challenge of collecting different cachets for a stamp or a set that they will like. Some will collect by topic, such as U.S. history, Masonic history or a professional topic. Topical collections can be researched, written up and mounted on pages to produce a personalized album or exhibit. Others collect by cachet, trying to put together a collection of all the cachets produced by a cachetmaker they like.

# CACHETS

*Grimsland cachet*

**ENGRAVED CACHETS** have always been very popular with collectors. Four popular engraved cachets are Grimsland, House of Farnam, ArtCraft and Artmaster. Henry Grimsland of Chicago, Illinois produced engraved cachets from 1933 until 1951. Most are one color cachets, with many in the color of the stamp. Most are signed "Grimsland" in the design.

House of Farnam cachets have been produced for every issue from the TIPEX Souvenir sheet of 1936 up to the present. Farnam cachets are engraved usually in one color; many are signed "House of Farnam" or "HF."

ArtCraft Cachets have been continually produced by Washington Stamp Exchange since 1939. The first ArtCraft, prepared for the World's Fair issue of 1939, is an unsigned engraved design, in blue. Most ArtCraft cachets are black, signed with the ArtCraft pallet and brushes trademark.

Artmaster Cachets have been produced for all new U.S. stamps since the Honorable Discharge Commemorative of 1946. Artmaster cachets are engraved cachets usually in a dark green or gray color, and are signed "Artmaster."

**COLORED CACHETS** appeal to many FDC collectors. Ioor, Grandy, Staehle and Boll all produced colored cachets. Harry Ioor produced two-colored cachets from 1929 until 1951. In the 1940's and early 50's most Ioor cachets were signed, but before 1940 they were unsigned.

W.M. Grandy produced one or more cachet designs per issue from 1935 until 1957. They are all two color cachets, usually signed "W.M. Grandy," or "WMG."

*Ludwig W. Staehle cachet*

Ludwig W. Staehle was one of the most prolific U.S. cachet makers, usually producing three or more cachet designs for each issue. Staehle cachets are known for the vivid use of color, often with three or more colors on the design. Staehle produced designs from the late 30's until the early 50's.

Cachet Craft produced from the late 1930's until the early 1970's. During the 1940's Cachet Craft produced attractive two color cachet designs by both L.W. Staehle and Ken Boll. Several popular lines of cachets have been produced from original artwork. C. Stephen Anderson designed cachets from 1933 until his death in 1978. Anderson cachets are usually one color line drawings, with an illustration above, and historical text below. Most are signed "C. Stephen Anderson" or "CSA."

Aristocrat Cachets have been continually produced since 1936. Most Aristocrat cachets will capture the interest of FDC collectors. Fulton, Fluegel, Crosby and "Silk" cachets are very popular for these reasons.

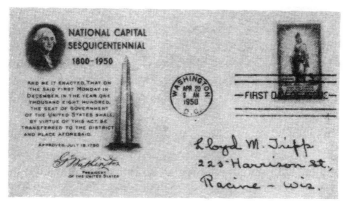

*Fulton cachet*

Fulton Cachets are finely engraved cachets, usually printed in color rather than black. Because Fultons were produced only from 1947 to 1950, they offer an opportunity to assemble a complete collection of very attractive cachets. While many Fultons can be located with some persistence, a few, such as the foreign issues and the U.S. Utah cachet, are quite difficult to find.

*House of Farnam cachet*

*Fluegel cachet*

Fluegal Covers are attractive, multicolored cachets produced from 1945 until 1968. Attractive use of color is being appreciated more and more by the cachet collector, and all Fluegal cachets are becoming harder and harder to find.

*Crosby cachet*

One of the most intriguing cachetmakers of the 1930's and 40's is W.G. Crosby. Crosby produced cachets using a raised print, with a space in the printed design for a small photo to be posted on the cover. Crosby produced many varieties of his cachet by changing the printed design and the photo. Over twenty-five different Crosby cachet varieties are known to exist on the Navy issue of 1945.

"Silk" Cachets have been produced in the United States only since 1971. However, since that time, they have become the most popular and fastest growing cachet on the market. As new collectors have gone back to buy the early "Silk" Cachets, the demand has far exceeded the supply. Today many early "Silk" Cachets are bringing high prices when they appear on the market.

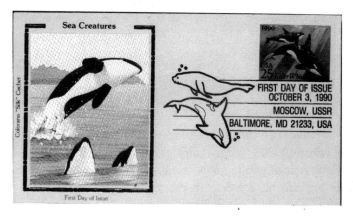

*"Silk" cachet*

Another very popular area of FDC collecting is First Cachets. A First Cachet is the very first cachet produced by any cachetmaker. Very often the first cachets were produced in small quantities. First cachets by the popular cachetmakers such as ArtCraft, Colorano, Farnam, Fluegel, Fulton and others are difficult to locate, and sell for ten to fifty times the price of a common cachet on the same issue.

# ACCESSORIES

## STAMP TONGS

To avoid getting your stamps soiled or creased, you should never handle them with your fingers, or with anything other than a clean pair of good quality stamp tongs. These handy tweezer-like instruments are easy to use, and come in several different styles, allowing you to choose according to your own personal preference. A good pair of stamp tongs should be thin enough to pick a stamp up from a flat surface, and should have slightly rounded ends and highly polished edges and surfaces to avoid damaging the stamp.

PERFORATION GAUGE

Measuring the number of perforation holes in a two-centimeter space along the edge of a stamp is often the only way to tell the difference between two stamps that may look exactly alike, but actually belong to different issues. By placing a stamp on a perforation gauge, and moving the stamp up and down until the dots on the gauge perfectly fit the holes along the edge of the stamp, you can tell exactly what the "perf. number" is.

## MAGNIFIERS

Magnifying glasses enable you to examine stamps closely and identify details too small to be seen easily with the naked eye. Magnifiers come in many different styles, ranging from small, folding pocket magnifiers to large battery-powered "flashlight" types and stand-type magnifiers which leave both hands free.

## WATERMARK TRAY AND FLUID

Watermarks on stamps (see pg. 158) are often very difficult to see clearly, so stamp collectors use various methods to make them easier to detect. The most common method is to place the stamp face down in a black tray or dish and pour a few drops of detector fluid onto the stamp, making the watermarked design stand out against the black background.

CAUTION: Watermark detection fluids may react unfavorably with some inks and dissolve them, so extreme care should be taken in their use.

### STAMPLIFT

The stamplift is a nonchemical device used to remove old hinges and separate stuck-together or stuck-down mint stamps without destroying the original gum.

### UV LAMP

Ultraviolet lamps are used to make phosphor tags (see pg. 151) visible, and can be obtained either as complete units, or as ultraviolet bulbs which will fit into regular fluorescent or incandescent fixtures. Direct ultraviolet light can damage the eyes, so you should take care not to look directly into an ultraviolet lamp.

### STAMP PRESS

A stamp press is used to flatten out folds and creases in stamps, and to prevent them from curling while they are drying after having been soaked.

# HOW TO COLLECT STAMPS

## GLASSINE ENVELOPES

Many collectors use glassine envelopes to keep their stamps sorted, identified, clean, and undamaged prior to mounting them in an album, or to package and prepare them for sale or trading. Glassines are translucent and come in a wide range of sizes.

## STOCK BOOKS

Stock books are temporary albums used to keep stamps for preliminary sorting or accumulation prior to mounting, or to keep duplicates for sale or trade. The pages have long, shallow pockets into which stamps can be slipped; they are then held reasonably secure, but can be quickly and easily removed when necessary. Stock books may have either stiff manila pocket pages or transparent plastic pockets on black backing, to show off your stamps better; they may be inexpensive, and small enough to fit into your pocket or purse, or as large and luxurious as any standard stamp album.

# HOW TO COLLECT STAMPS

## HINGES

Stamp Hinges are small pieces of gummed glassine paper used to mount stamps in your album. The shiny side is gummed; keep it outside as you fold the hinge.

Just moisten the upper half of the gummed side of the hinge and attach it to the back of the stamp; then moisten the other half and attach it to the album page. It's easy! (Remember to leave the stamp, where it is hinged in the album, until dry; otherwise if you try to remove the stamp, you may damage it.)

## MOUNTS

1. Insert stamp in tube.
2. Trim tube close to stamp with scissors.
3. Moisten gum, and fasten to album.
4. Fold back upper part of tube and crease so stamp will lie flat.

Another method of mounting stamps in an album is to use plastic strips or tubes, which can be cut to an exact fit. Stamps thus mounted are well-protected by the tough plastic shell, but remain completely visible. Use of plastic mounts instead of hinges also means that the original gum on mint stamps remains intact. There are many different mounts available.

# CATALOGUES

A catalogue is basically an illustrated list of stamps, usually arranged in sets according to face value, and listed in order of the date of issue. Besides helping to identify stamps and giving the current market values, catalogues also provide other information: color and design variations, watermarks, perforation numbers, type of printing used, etc. Both general world-wide and specialized catalogues are available.

## WORLD-WIDE CATALOGUES

The world-wide catalogue most widely used in the United States is the Scott Standard Postage Stamp Catalogue (U.S.). Other highly regarded world-wide catalogues include the Minkus (U.S.), Stanley Gibbons (Great Britain), Michel (Germany), and Yvert & Tellier (France).

In the catalogues, the individual stamps in the set are listed, with the index, or catalogue, number, design-type number (referring to the illustration with that number), denomination, color

Reproduced at left is part of a page from the Scott Standard Catalogue. Under the illustration of the stamp and description of the other designs in the set are given the date of issue, type of printing process used and perf. number.

Reproduced at right is a page from the specialized 1994 Harris US/BNA Catalogue. Under each illustration is a listing by Scott Catalogue number of the individual stamps having that design.

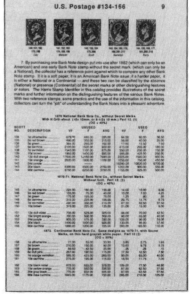

(if two or more colors are used, the color of the frame or border is given first, then the colors of the central, or vignette portion of the design), and the prices for unused and canceled copies of the stamp. Minor variations are denoted by a lowercase alphabet letter.

## SPECIALIZED CATALOGUES

Specialized catalogues deal with specific topics, countries, or types of issues. The largest selling catalog for U.S. and Canada stamps is the Harris Reference Catalog of Postage Stamp Prices of the United States, Canada and Provinces. Other prominent specialized catalogues include the Scott U.S. Specialized Catalogue, Sanabria's World Airmail Catalogue (for collectors who specialize in airmail issues), and many country and regional catalogues. It is also possible to get listings of issues on specific topics from some of the topical collecting societies.

# ALBUMS

The best way to keep your stamp collection organized, well protected, and beautifully displayed is to mount your stamps in an album.

In choosing an album, consider carefully your own interests and needs — are you interested in collecting stamps from around the world, or from one specific country; or are you interested in a specific topic, like sports or flowers, or a specific type of stamp, like air mails or special deliveries? Whatever your interests, albums come in such a wide range of classes, prices, sizes and types that there is bound to be one that is just right for you.

Choice of an album is a very personal matter, but there are some helpful guidelines. If the user is to be a youngster, then the amount of time and money he or she will be able to spend on the hobby, and whether or not there will be adult supervision, should be considered. A youngster "on his own" or carrying a heavy school and extra-curricular schedule would become frustrated by a too-large album for which he has too little time. If his stamp collecting will be aided by an adult, or better yet, if it is going to be a real "family hobby," then a larger album is desirable. An adult may wish to start with a moderate-sized or larger album.

Most collectors start with a world-wide album and then, later on — sometimes many years later — narrow their collecting interests too a single country or topic, at which time they can choose one of the many excellent specialized albums on the market.

Loose-leaf albums, especially, are virtually a must because they allow you to add or rearrange pages whenever it becomes necessary. Most album manufacturers publish annual supplements for their loose-leaf albums, allowing you to keep your collection up-to-date with the latest issues.

There are two general classes of albums, those in which the pages have ruled spaces for the stamps (often illustrated), and those in which the pages are blank. Within the ruled-space category one finds the general world-wide albums, plus most single-country specialized albums; blank albums are generally for collectors with very specialized interests, or very advanced collectors who wish to design their own albums.

World-wide albums can range in size and comprehensiveness from the very smallest beginner's album costing about $3.00 to the huge 20+ Volume International, costing more than $2,500.00. The larger the album, of course, the more complete it will be, but all world-wide albums, regardless of size, are by necessity abridged to some degree. To be truly complete, an album would have to include every stamp ever issued by every country in the world since Great Britain issued the first adhesive postage stamp, the famous "Penny Black," back in 1840. This would not only require many, many volumes, but would also mean providing spaces for many rare stamps which are today essentially unobtainable to all but the very wealthiest collectors — if they are obtainable at all. The most popular world-wide albums today are those which concentrate on the easily-obtainable low- and medium-priced stamps which the average collector is most likely to have in abundance.

Specialized albums concentrate on stamps from specific areas — individual countries, like the United States or France, or groups of countries, like the British Commonwealth; individual topics, like sports, space, or flowers; and individual types of issues, like air-mails, special deliveries, or postage dues. Individual country albums usually have spaced and illustrated pages; other specialty albums usually have blank pages with simple titles.

*Plate Block Heirloom*                    *Canada Heirloom*

Some excellent examples of specialized single-country albums, all loose-leaf, are pictured here. The U.S. Liberty Album is 100% illustrated and virtually complete for issues of the United States and Confederate States. It includes not only regular postage and air-mails, but also special deliveries, postage dues, hunting stamps, etc. For beginning U.S. collectors, the Independence Album offers many of the same features as the larger, much more comprehensive Liberty, with spaces for more than 2,000 stamps, 100% illustrated. The 2-Volume U.S. Plate Block Album is 100% illustrated, and is specifically designed for collectors of United States plate blocks.

Blank albums are primarily for collectors who cannot find exactly what they want in a standard ruled-space album, or who want to arrange their stamps themselves, rather than mount them according to a pre-arranged order or pattern. They are particularly suitable for topical collectors.

The pages themselves may be entirely blank, or they may have a faint blue or gray quadrille-type ruled background, to help the collector arrange the stamps in a balanced pattern. The ruling may be standard 1/4-, 1/5-, or 1/8-inch squares; also available are the Harris "Speed-rille" ruled pages, which have faint gray lines dividing the pages into various equal sections — fifths, sixths, sevenths, etc. — to make it easier to evenly space out a row of stamps.

Often, the pages will also have decorative ruled borders, and may come with separate printed titles which are gummed and may be affixed to the pages as the collector desires. In the case of blank albums designed for specific topics or countries, the pages may not only have decorative ruled borders, they may also have fancy titles and illustrations.

Blank albums for topical collections will usually come in matched sets of binder and pages, with extra pages available separately; but you can also select a binder and pages separately, to suit your own tastes. There is a wide variety of binders available, in different sizes and of different constructions, as well as many different styles and sizes of blank pages.

If you decide to mount your collection in a blank album, some accessories you may find helpful are: stamp positioner to help you space out your stamps on non-ruled pages; stencil guides, for writing descriptive captions for the stamps; and decorative gummed flags of various countries and states, to add a colorfully attractive touch to your blank pages.

Special albums are also available for collectors of first day covers and mint sheets. Cover albums have cover-sized transparent plastic pockets into which the covers are slipped, while mint sheet albums have whole pages made of sheets of plastic, open at the top and one side, and closed at the bottom and the binder side, so the sheets can easily be inserted and removed, yet will not fall out.

Most of the larger stamp companies today produce large, highly illustrated supply catalogues and would be pleased to send you their latest catalogue.

# WORLDWIDE STAMP IDENTIFIER

By picking out a word, sign or symbol on a stamp of unknown origin and looking it up in the index, the collector will be guided at once, in most cases, to the stamp's correct country name.

Only the relatively difficult-to-classify stamps have been indexed. If the country name in its English form appears anywhere on the stamp, no identifying words are necessary and none have been included here.

Likewise, such words as "postage" and "pence", for example, which appear on the stamps of dozens of countries, would be of little or no value as guides. For this reason, *if you do not find the first words you look up, try other words on the stamp* until the indexing word is found.

Some stamps — early Afghanistan and Egypt, certain of the Indian Native States, and others — are printed entirely in Arabic or other Oriental characters and therefore cannot be indexed. To help you with these stamps, see the illustrated section, "OTHER HARD-TO-IDENTIFY STAMPS" at the end of the regular listings.

**A.B.** on stamps of Russia: **Far Eastern Republic.**

**АВИОПОУТА : Russia.**

**A.C.C.P. : Azerbaijan.**

**AÇORES: Azores.**

**A.D. HALL: United States — Gainsville, Alabama.**

**A.E.F.** ("Afrique Equatorial Francaise") on stamps inscribed "Centenaire du Gabon": **French Equatorial Africa.**

**ΛΕΓΤΑ: Greece.**

**ΛΕΗΤΑ: Epirus.**

**AFGAN, AFGHANES: Afghanistan.**

**AFRICA CORREIOS: Portugese Africa.**

**AFRICA OCCIDENTAL ESPANOLA: Spanish West Africa.**

**AFRICA ORIENTALE ÌTALIANA: Italian East Africa.**

**AFRIQUE EQUATORIAL FRANÇAISE: French Equatorial Africa:** on stamps inscribed "Moyen Congo": **Middle Congo;** plus "Tchad": **Chad;** With bars through "Gabon" and value: **French Equatorial Africa;** on stamps of Gabon: **Gabon.**

**AFRIQUE EQUATORIALE GABON: Gabon.**

**AFRIQUE OCCIDENTALE FRANÇAISE: French West Africa.**

**ΑΗΜΝΟΣ: on stamps of Greece: Greece — Aegean Islands — Lemnos.**

**AITUTAKI** on stamps of New Zealand or Cook Islands: **Aitutaki.**

**ALAOUITES** on stamps of France and Syria: **Alaouites.**

**ALBANIA** on stamps of Italy: **Italy — Offices in Turkey — Albania.**

**ALBANY GA.: United States — Albany, Georgia.**

**ALDERNEY: Great Britain — Alderney.**

**ALECHA: on stamps of Peru: Peru — Ancachs.**

**ALEXANDRIA: United States — Alexandria, Virginia.**

**ALEXANDRIE: France — Offices in Egypt — Alexandria.**

**ALGERIE:** on stamps of France: **Algeria.**

**ALLEMAGNE DUITSCHLAND** on stamps of Belgium: **Germany — Belgian occupation.**

**A.M.G. - F.T.T.** on stamps of Italy: **Trieste — Zone A.**

**A.M.G. - V.G.** on stamps of Italy: **Italy — Venezia Giulia — Allied occupation.**

**A.M. POST: Germany — Allied occupation.**

**ANDERSON C.H.S.C.: United States — Anderson Court House, South Carolina.**

**ANDORRA** on stamps of Spain: **Andorra — Spanish Administration.**

**ANDORRE** on stamps of France: **Andorra — French Administraton.**

**ANNA: British East Africa, India, Indian States, Mesopotamia, Pakistan, Zanzibar.**

**ANNAPOLIS: United States — Annapolis, Maryland.**

**ANTIGUA: Antigua & Barbuda.**

**ANTIOQUIA: Colombia — Antioquia.**

**A.O.** on stamps of Congo Democratic Republic (ex-Belgian): **German East Africa.**

**A.O.F.** on stamps of France: **French West Africa.**

**A.O.I.** on stamps of Italy: **Italian East Africa.**

**A PAYER TE BETALEN** ("postage due"): **Belgium.**

**A PERÇEVOIR: Belgium, France,** many **French Colonies.**

**APURIMAC** on stamps inscribed "Franqued": **Peru — Apurimac.**
: **Yugoslavia.**

**A.R.: Colombia, Montenegro, Panama, Chile.**

**ARABIE SAOUDITE: Saudi Arabia.**

**ARCHIPEL DES COMORES: Comoro Islands, Grand Comoro.**

**A RECEMBER: Portugal, Portugese Colonies.**

**ARRIBA** on stamps of Spain: **Spain — San Sebastian.**

**ASCENSION** on stamps of St. Helena: **Ascension.**

**ASSISTENCIA D.L. on 72** on war tax stamps of Portugese India: **Timor.**

**ATHENS S.A.: United States — Athens, Georgia.**

**ATLANTA GA.** or **GEO.: United States — Atlanta, Georgia.**

**ATT, ATTS: Siam.**

**A & T** on stamps of French Colonies: **Annam and Tonkin.**

**AUNUS** on stamps of Finland: **Russia — Finnish occupation.**

**AUR: Iceland.**

**AUSTIN, MISS.: United States — Austin, Mississippi.**

**AUSTIN, TEX.: United States — Austin, Texas.**

**AUSTRALIAN ANTARCTIC TERRITORY: Australia — Australian Antarctic Territory.**

**AVISPORTO: Denmark.**

**AVO, AVOS: Macao, Timor.**

**A.W. McNEEL P.M.: United States — Autaugaville, Alabama.**

**AYACUCHO: Peru — Ayacucho.**

**ATTONOMOΣ: Epirus.**

**AZERBAIDJAN: Azerbaijan.**

# B

**B** in an oval, on stamps with no country name: **Belgium** — parcel post stamps; on stamps of Straits Settlements: **Bangkok.**

**BADEN: Germany — Baden — French occupation.**

**B.A. ERITREA, B.A. SOMALIA,** or **B.A. TRIPOLITANIA** on stamps of Great Britain: **Great Britain — Offices in Africa — Eritrea, Somalia, Tripolitania.**

**BAGHDAD** on stamps of Turkey: **Mesopotamia.**

**BAHAWALPUR: Pakistan — Bahawalpur.**

**BAHRAIN:** on stamps of Great Britain or India: **Bahrain.**

**BAHT: Siam.**

БАНДЕРОЛЬНОЕ       ОТУРАВЛЕНIЕ : **Russia — Offices in Turkey**

**BAJAR PORTO: Indonesia.**

**BAMRA: India — Bamra.**

**BÁNÁT BÁCSKA** on stamps of Hungary: **Hungary — Serbian occupation — Banata, Bacaska.**

**BANI: Romania;** on stamps of Austria: **Romania — Austrian occupation.**

**BARANYA** on stamps of Hungary: **Hungary — Serbian occupation.**

**BARBUDA** on stamps of Antigua or Leeward Islands: **Barbuda.**

**BARCELONA: Spain.**

**BARWANI: India — Bawani.**

**BASEL: Switzerland — Basel.**

**BASUTOLAND** on stamps of South Africa: **Basutoland.**

**BATAAN** on stamps with inscriptions in oriental characters: **Phillipines — Japanese occupation.**

**BATON ROUGE, LA.: United States — Baton Rouge, Louisiana.**

БАТУМ.Об., БАТУМОбЯАС, БАТУМСКАЯ ПОЧТА, БАТУМбОбЛ  on stamps of Russia: **Batum.**

**BAYERN, BAYR: Bavaria.**

**B.C.A.** on stamps inscribed "British South Africa Company": **British Central Africa.**

**B.C.M., BRITISH CONSULAR MAIL: Madagascar — British Consulate.**

**B.C.O.F.—JAPAN 1946** on stamps of Australia: **Australia.**

**B. DPTO. ZELAYA: Nicaragua — Zelaya.**

**BEAUMONT: United States — Beaumont, Texas.**

**BECHUANALAND** on stamps of South Africa: **Bechuanaland.**

**BECHUANALAND PROTECTORATE** on stamps of Great Britain: **Bechuanaland Protectorate.**

ВЕНДЕНСКАЯ: **Russia — Wenden.**

**BELGIAN EAST AFRICA: Ruanda — Urundi.**

**BELGIE: Belgium.**

**BELGIEN** on stamps of Germany: **Belgium — German Occupation.**

**BELGIQUE: Belgium.**

**BELGISCH CONGO: Belgian Congo.**

**BELIZE: British Honduras.**

**BENADIR: Somalia.**

**BENGASI** on stamps of Italy: **Italy — Offices in Africa — Bengasi.**

**BENIN** on stamps of French Colonies: **Benin.**

**BERLIN** on stamps of Germany: **Germany — Berlin.**

**BEYROUTH** on stamps of Russia: **Russia — Offices in Turkey.**

**BHOPAL: India — Bhopal.**

**BHOR: India — Bhor.**

**BIAFRA** on stamps of Nigeria: issued by revolutionary forces in 1968-69.

**B.I.O.T.** on stamps of Seychelles: **British Indian Ocean Territory.**

**BISHOP'S: United States — Cleveland, Ohio.**

**B.M.A. ERITREA, B.M.A. SOMALIA,** or **B.M.A. TRIPOLITANIA** on stamps of Great Britain: **Great Britain — Offices in Africa — Eritrea, Somalia,** or **Tripolitania.**

**BMA MALAYA: Straits Settlements.**

**ВОСТОЧНАЯ       КОРРЕСПОНДЕНЦІЯ : Russia — Offices in Turkey.**

**BOFTGEBIET** on stamps of Germany: **Lithuania — German occupaton.**

**BOGCHAN, BOGACHES: Yemen.**

**BOHMEN ŮND MAHREN: Czechoslovakia — Bohemia and Moravia.**

**ВОНΘΕΙΤΕ: Greece.**

**BOLIVAR: Columbia — Bolivar.**

**BOLLODELLA DI SICINA: Two Sicilies — Sicily.**

**BOLLO POSTALE: San Marino.**

**BOSNIEN—HERAEGOVINA** or **BOSNIEIHERZEGOWINA: Bosnia and Herzegovina.**

**BOYACA: Columbia — Boyaca.**

**BRASIL: Brazil.**

**BRATTLEBORO VT.: United States — Brattleboro, Vermont.**

**BRAUNSCHWIG: Brunswick.**

**BRIEFPOST: Germany — French occupation.**

**BRITISH BECHUANALAND** on stamps of Cape of Good Hope or Great Britain: **Bechuanaland.**

**BRITISH EAST AFRICA COMPANY** on stamps of Great Britain: **British East Africa.**

**BRITISH NEW GUINEA: Papua New Guinea.**

**BRITISH OCCUPATION** on stamps of Russia: **Batum.**

**BRITISH PROTECTORATE OIL RIVERS** on stamps of Great Britain: **Niger Coast Protectorate.**

**BRITISH SOMALILAND** on stamps of India: **Somaliland Protectorate.**

**BRITISH SOUTH AFRICA COMPANY: Rhodesia.**

**BRITISH VICE CONSULATE: Madagascar — British Consulate.**

**BR.** or **BRITISH VIRGIN ISLANDS: Virgin Islands.**

**BROWN & McOILLS: United States — Louisville, Kentucky.**

**BRUNEI** on stamps of Labuan: **Brunei.**

**BRUXELLES, BRUSSEL: Belgium.**

**BUENOS ARIES: Argentina — Buenos Aires;** with "Agosto de 1921": **Argentina.**

**BUITEN BEZIT** on stamps inscribed "Netherlandsch — Indie": **Dutch Indies.**

**BULGARIE: Bulgaria.**

**BUNDI: India — Bundi.**

**BURKINA FASO: Upper Volta** or **Burkina Faso.**

**BURMA** on stamps of India: **Burma.**
**BUSHIRE** on stamps of Persia: **Bushire.**
**BUSSAHIR: India — Bussahir.**

# C

C preceded by numeral of value, on stamps with Japanese characters: **Ryukyu Islands.**
**CABO: Nicaragua — Cabo Gracias a Dios.**
**CABO JUBI, CABO JUBY** on stamps of Rio de Oro, Spain, or Spanish Morocco: **Cape Juby.**
**CABO VERDE: Cape Verde.**
**CACHES** on stamps of France or French Colonies: **French India.**
**CADIZ** on stamps of Spain: **Spain — Cadiz.**
**САНАТОРИУМЬ: Bulgaria.**
**CAIMO: Puerto Rico — Caimo.**
**CALCHI on** stamps of Italy: **Italy — Calimno.**
**CAMBODGE: Cambodia.**
**CAMEROONS U.K.T.T.** on stamps of Nigeria: (British) **Cameroons.**
**CAMEROUN** on stamps of Gabon or Middle Congo: **Cameroun.**
**CAMPECHE: Mexico — Campeche.**
**CAMPIONARIA DE TRIPOLI: Tripolitania, Libya.**
**CANAL ZONE** on stamps of Columbia, Panama, or United States: **Canal Zone.**
**CANARIAS** on stamps of Spain: **Spain — Canary Islands.**
**CANTON** on stamps of Indo-China: **France — Offices in China — Canton.**
**CARCHI** on stamps of Italy: **Italy — Aegean Islands — Karki.**
**CASTELLORISO, CASTELLORIZO or CASTELLOROSSO** on stamps of France, French Colonies, or Italy: **Castellorizo.**
**CAUCA: Columbia — Cauca.**
**CAVALLE: France — Offices in Turkey — Cavalle.**
**C C C P** (abbreviation for "Union of Soviet Socialist Republics"): **Russia.**
**C. CH.** on stamps of French Colonies: **Cochin China.**
**C. or CS. DE PESO: Phillipines.**
**CECHY A MORAVA: Czechoslovakia — Bohemia and Moravia.**
**C.E.F.** (Cameroon Expeditionary Force) on stamps inscribed "Kamerun": (British) **Cameroons;** (Chinese Expeditionary Force) on stamps of India: **India — military stamps.**
**CENT or CENTS** on stamps of France: **France — Offices in China;** on stamps of Russia: **Russia — Offices in China;** with crowns in a circle: **Mongolia.**
**CENTENAIRE ALGERIE** ("Algerian Centenary"): **France.**
**CENTENAIRE DU GABON: French Equatorial Africa.**
**CENTESIMI: Italy,** many Italian Colonies, **San Marino, Vatican City;** on stamps of Austria or Bosnia and Herzegovina: **Italy — Austrian occupation.**
**CENTESIMI DI CORONA** in serif letters on stamps of Italy: **Austria — Italian occupation;** in sans-serif letters on stamps of Italy: **Dalmatia.**

# HOW TO COLLECT STAMPS

**CENTIMES** on stamps of Germany: **Germany — Offices in Turkey;** on stamps of Austria: **Austria — Offices in Crete.**

**CENTIMOS** with no country name: **Spain;** on stamps of France: **French Morocco.**

**CESKOSLOVENSKA, CESKOSLOVENSKO:** Czechoslovakia.

**CESKO — SLOVENSKO:** Czechoslovakia — Slovakia.

**C F A** on stamps of France: **Reunion.**

**C.G.H.S.:** Upper Silesia.

**CH** followed by oriental characters: **Korea.**

**CHALA:** Peru — Chala.

**CHAMBA:** India — Chamba.

**CHAPEL HILL, N.C.:** United States — Chapel Hill, North Carolina.

**CHARKHARI:** India — Charkhari.

**CHARLESTON S.C.:** United States — Charleston, South Carolina.

**CHATTANOOGA, TEN.:** United States — Chattanooga, Tennessee.

**CHEMINS DE FER SPOORWEGEN:** Belgium.

**CHIFFRE TAXE** with no country name: **France, French Colonies.**

**CHINA** on stamps of Hong Kong: **Great Britain — Offices in China;** on stamps of Germany: **Germany — Offices in China.**

**CHINE** on stamps of France: **France — Offices in China.**

**CHRISTMAS ISLAND** on stamps of Australia: **Christmas Island.**

**CIHS** on stamps of Germany: **Upper Silesia.**

**CILICIE** on stamps of France or Turkey: **Cilicia.**

**CINQUANTENAIRE 24 SEPTEMBRE** on postage due stamps of French Colonies: **New Caledonia** — postage due stamps.

**CIRENNICA** on stamps of Italy or Tripolitania: **Cyrenaica.**

**CITY DISPATCH POST:** United States — New York, New York.

**CITY POST:** United States — Charleston, South Carolina.

**C.M.T.** on stamps of Austria: **Western Ukraine — Romanian occupation.**

**CN** (for "cheun"): **Korea.**

**COCHIN, COCHIN ANCHAL:** India — Cochin.

**CO. Ci.** on stamps of Yugoslavia: **Yugoslavia — Ljubljana.**

**COLIS POSTAL or POSTAUX** on stamps with no country name: **Belgium.**

**COLOMBIA** on stamps showing a map of Panama: **Panama — Colombian dominion.**

**COLONIA DE RIO DE ORO:** Rio de Oro.

**COLONIA ERITREA** on stamps of Italy or Somalia: **Eritrea.**

**COLONIE or COLOLIALI ITALIANE:** Italian Colonies.

**COLONIES DEL'EMPIRE FRANCAISE:** French Colonies.

**COMMISSION DE GOUVERNEMENT HAUTE SILESIE:** Upper Silesia.

**COMMISSION INTERALLIEE MARIENWERDER** on stamps of Germany: **Marienwerder.**

**COMORES:** Comoros Islands.

**COMP. or COMPANHAI DE MOÇAMBIQUE:** Mozambique Company: on stamps of Mozambique: **Mozambique Company.**

**COMUNICAÇIONES:** Spain.

**CONFEDERATE STATES or CONFEDERATE STATES OF AMERICA:** United States — Confederate States.

# HOW TO COLLECT STAMPS

**CONFEDERATO HELVETICA** ("Helvetic Confederation"): **Switzerland.**

**CONGO** on stamps with Portugese inscriptions: **Portugese Congo;** with "Belge": **Congo Democratic Republic** (ex-Belgian); with "Francaise": **French Congo;** with "Francaise Gabon": **Gabon;** with "Republic du": **Congo Democratic Republic** (ex-Belgian) or **Congo People's Republic** (ex-French).

**CONGRESO DE LOS DIPUTADOS: Spain.**

**CONSTANTINOPLE** on stamps of Russia: **Russia — Offices in Turkey.**

**CONSTANTINOPOLI** on stamps of Italy: **Italy — Offices in Turkey — Constantinople.**

**COO** on stamps of Italy: **Italy — Aegean Islands — Coo.**

**COOK ISLANDS—NIUE: Niue.**

**CORDOBA:** Argentina — Cordoba.

**COREE, COREAN: Korea.**

**CORFU** on stamps of Greece or Italy: **Corfu — Italian occupation.**

**CORONA: Dalmatia:** on stamps of Italy: **Austria — Italian occupation.**

**CORREIO** with no country name: **Portugal.**

**CORREO AEREO** with no country name: **Spain.**

**CORREO ESPANOL MARRUECOS** on stamps of Spain: **Spanish Morocco.**

**CORREO ESPANOL TANGER: Spanish Morocco — Tangier.**

**CORREO URBANO DE BOGOTA: Colombia — Bogota.**

**CORREOS** with no country name and denomination in CUATOS, REALES, CS, or CTOS., (i.e. CENTIMOS): **Spain; with "Real": Dominican Republic.**

**CORREOS** with no country name: **Cuba, Peru, Philippines, Dominican Republic, Spain, Uruguay.**

**CORREOS ARGENTINOS: Argentina.**

**CORREOS DE COLOMBIA: Columbia.**

**CORREIOS, CORREIOS E TELEGRAPHOS: Portugal.**

**CORREOS INTERIOR: Philippines.**

**CORREOS MEXICO GOBIERNO REVOLUCIONARO: Mexico — Yeatan.**

**CORREOS NAÇIONALES: Columbia.**

**CORREOS NALES: Columbia.**

**CORREOS OXACA: Mexico — Oaxaca.**

**CORREOS SONORA: Mexico — Sonora.**

**CORREOS Y TELEGs: Spain.**

**CORRESPONDENCIA URGENTE: Spain.**

**CORRIENTES:** Argentina — Corrientes

**COS** on stamps of Italy: **Italy — Aegan Islands — Coo.**

**COSTA ATLANTICA B: Nicaragua — Zeleya.**

**COSTA ATLANTICA C: Nicaragua — Cabo Gracias a Dios.**

**COTE DE SOMALIS** or **COTE FRANÇAIS: Somali Coast.**

**COTE D'IVOIRE: Ivory Coast.**

**COURTLAND AL: United States — Courtland, Alabama.**

**СРБИЈА: Serbia.**

**СРБСКА: Serbia.**

**CRUZ ROJA DOMINICA: Dominican Republic.**

**CRUZ ROJA HONDURENA: Honduras.**

**CRVENI KRST** on stamps of Yugoslavia: **Yugoslavia — Offices Abroad, Montenegro — German Occupation.**

**CROISSANT ROUGE TURC: Turkey.**

**CRUZ VERMELHA PORTUGUESA: Portugal.**

**C.S.** or **C.S.A. POSTAGE: United States — Confederate States.**

**СТ., СТОТ., СТОТИНКИ, СТ., СТОТ.: Bulgaria.**

**CUAUTLA: Mexico — Cuautla.**

**CUBA** on stamps of United States: **Cuba — U.S. Administration.**

**CUERNAVACA: Mexico — Cuernavaca.**

**CUNDINAMARCA: Columbia — Cundinamarca.**

**CURAÇAO: Netherlands Antilles.**

**CUZCO** on stamps inscribed "Peru" or "Franqued": **Peru — Cuzco.**

**C.X.C.** ("Serbs, Croats, and Slovenes"): **Yugoslavia.**

**CYPRUS** on stamps of Great Britain: **Cyprus.**

**D** (for "dinar") on stamps with Arabic writing: **Persia.**

**d** (pence)/(shilling) or **£** (pound) preceded by a numeral, on stamps with king or queen's head but no country name: **Great Britain.**

**d/** on stamps of Cape of Good Hope: **Griqualand West.**

**DAI NIPPON** on stamps of Straits Settlements: **Malaya — Japanese occupation;** on various Malaya states: **Malaya States — Japanese occupation** of state overprinted on.

**DALTON GA.: United States — Dalton, Georgia.**

**DANMARK: Denmark.**

**DANSK-VESTINDISKE** or **VESTINDIEN: Danish West Indies.**

**DANVILLE, VA.: United States — Danville, Virginia.**

**DANZIG** on stamps of Germany: **Danzig.**

**DARDANELLES** on stamps of Russia: **Russia — Offices in Turkey.**

**D.B.L.** in script letters on stamps of Russia: **Far Eastern Republic;** with three bars: **Siberia.**

**DDR: Germany — German Democratic Republic.**

**DEDDAHG: France — Offices in Turkey.**

**DEFICIT: Peru.**

**DELEGACOES: Portugal.**

**DEL GOLFO DE GUINEA: Spanish Guinea.**

**DENWAISEN SIROTAM** on stamps of Italy: **Yugoslavia — Ljubljana — German occupation.**

**DEUTFCHES REICH** on stamps of Bavaria: **Bavaria.**

**DEUTFCHES REICH: Germany.**

**DEUTFCHOFTERREICH: Austria.**

**DEUTSCHLAND: Germany —Allied occupation.**
**DEUTSCH:** ("German") followed by **NEU-GUINEA: German New Guinea;** by
  **OSTAFRIKA: German East Africa;** by **SUDWEST AFRIKA: German**
  **South West Africa.**
**DEUTSCH DEMOKRATISCHE REPUBLIK: Germany — German Democratic**
  **Republic.**
**DEUTSCHE BUNDESPOST: Germany;** inscribed **BERLIN: Germany — Berlin.**
**DEUTSCHE FELDPOST: Germany** — military parcel post stamps.
**DEUTSCHE MILITAER—VERWALLUNG MONTENEGRO** on stamps of
  Yugoslavia: **Montenegro — German occupation.**
**DEUTSCHE NATIONAL VERSAMMLUNG: Germany.**
**DEUTSCHE POFT** or **POST: Germany, Germany — Berlin, Germany —**
  **German Democratic Republic.**
**DEUTSCHE POST OSTEN** on stamps of Germany: **Poland — German occupa-**
  **tion.**
**DEUTSCHES REICH: Germany.**
**DEUTSCHES REICH GENERAL GOUVERNEMENT: Poland — German**
  **occupation.**
**DEUTSCHES REICHS—POST: Germany.**
**DHAR: India — Dhar.**
**D.H. GHASS P.M.: United States — Lynchburg, Virginia.**
**DIEGO—SUAREZ** on stamps of French Colonies: **Diego — Suarez.**
**DIENST** on stamps inscribed "Nederlandsch—Indie": **Dutch Indies.**
**DIENSTMARKE: Bavaria, Danzig, Germany, Prussia, Saar.**
**DIENST SACHE: Wurttemberg** — Official stamps.
**DILIGENCIA: Uraguay.**
**DINAR** or **DINARS: Persia.**
**DINERO: Peru.**
**DIOS, PATRIA, REY: Spain.**
**DISTRITO: Peru — Cuzco.**
**DJ** or **DJIBOUTI** on stamps of Obock: **Somali Coast.**
**DOLLAR** on stamps of Russia: **Russia — Offices in China.**
**DOLLATA: Central Lithuania, Poland.**
**DOPLATIT** or **DOPLATNE** with no country name: **Czechoslovakia.**
**DRZAVA, DRZAVNA** on stamps of Bosnia and Herzegovina: **Yugoslavia — Bosnia**
  **and Herzegovina.**
**DUC. DL. PARMA: Parma.**
**DUITSCH OOST AFRIKA BELGISCHE BEZETTING** on stamps of Congo
  Democratic Republic (ex-Belgian): **German East Africa — Belgian**
  **occupation.**
**DURAZZO** on stamps of Italy: **Italy — Offices in Turkey — Durazzo.**
**DUTTIA: India — Duttia.**

# E

**E.A.** on stamps of Algeria: on stamps of Greece: **Greece — Aegean Islands — Chio.**

**E.A.F.** on stamps of Great Britain: **Great Britain — Offices in East Africa — Somalia.**

**ΣΑΜΟΤ: Greece — Aegean Islands — Samos.**

**EAST AFRICA & UGANDA PROTECTORATES** with portrait of King George V: if watermarked Multiple Crown and C.A.: **East Africa and Uganda;** if watermarked Multiple Crown and Script C.A.: **Kenya, Uganda, and Tanzania.**

**EAST INDIA POSTAGE: India;** on stamps with Crown and new denominations: **Straits Settlements.**

**EATONTON GEO.: United States — Eatonton, Georgia.**

**ECUADOR** on stamps of Columbia: **Ecuador.**

**E.E.F.** ("Egyptian Expeditionary Force"): **Palestine.**

**EESTI** on stamps of Russia: **Estonia.**

**EE. UU. DE C.: Colombia — Tolima.**

**EGEO** on stamps of Italy: **Italy — Aegean Islands.**

**EGYPTE: Egypt.**

**EINZUZIEHEN: Danzig** — Postage due stamps.

**EIRE: Ireland.**

**EJERCITO RENOVADOR: Mexico — Sonaloa.**

**EL PRLAMENTO A CERVANTES: Spain** — Official stamps.

**Elsab** (Alsace) on stamps of Germany: **France — German occupation.**

**EL SALVADOR: Salvador.**

**ELUAKENTA: Hawaii.**

**EMORY: United States — Emory, Virginia.**

**EMP. OTTOMAN: Eastern Rumelia, Turkey.**

**EMPIRE CENTRAFRICAIN: Central Africa.**

**EMPIRE FRANC: France, French Colonies.**

**ΕΝΑΡΙΘΜΟΝ: Greece.**

**ΕΘΝΙΚΗ: Greece.**

**ЕРМАКδ : South Russia.**

**EQUATEUR: Ecuador.**

**E.R.** ("Elizabeth Regina") on stamps with queen's head: **Great Britain.**

**ESCUELAS: Venezuala.**

**ESPANA SAHARA: Spanish Sahara.**

**ESPANA, ESPANOLA: Spain.**

**ESPANS: Spain.**

**ESTADO DA INDIA: Portugese India.**

**ESTADO ESPANOL** ("Spanish State"): **Spain.**

**ESTADOS UNIDOS DE NUEVA GRENADA: Colombia.**

**EST AFRICAIN ALLEMAND OCCUPATION BELGE** on stamps of Congo Democratic Republic (ex-Belgian): **German East Africa.**

**50**

**ESTERO** on stamps of Italy: **Italy — Offices Abroad.**

**ÈTABLISSEMENTS DANS L'INDÈ or DE L'INDE:** French India.

**ÈTABLISSEMENTS DE L'OCEANIE:** French Polynesia.

**ÈTAT DU CAMEROUN:** Cameroun.

**ÈTAT FRANÇAIS:** France.

**ETAT IND. DU CONGO** ("Independent State of Congo"): **Congo Democratic Republic (ex-Belgian).**

**ETIOPIA, ETHIOPIE, ETHIOPIENNES:** Ethiopia.

**ETS. FRANCS. DE L'OCEANIE:** French Polynesia.

**E.U. DE COLOMBIA** ("United States of Columbia"): **Colombia.**

**EUPEN or EUPEN & MELMEDY** on stamps of Belgium: **Germany — Belgian occupation.**

**EXPED. SCIENT.** on stamps with oriental characters: **China.**

**EXPOSIÇION DE BARCELONA, EXPOSIÇION GENERAL ESPANOLA** or **EXPOSIÇION GRAL SEVILLA BARCELONA: Spain.**

**EXPOSITION COLONIALE INTERNATIONALE PARIS 1931** with no country name: **France.**

**EXPOSITION INDUSTRIELLE DAMAS 1929** ("Damascus Industrial "Exhibition"): **Syria.**

ΕΛΛΑΧ, ΕΛΛΑΣ ("Hellas") **Greece;** on stamps of Italy: **Italy — Ionian Islands — German occupation;** on stamps of Crete: **Crete.**

ΕΛΛΗΝΙΚΗ on stamps of Bulgaria: **Greece — Aegean Islands — Cavilla, Dedaegatch, North Epirus, and Occupied Territories.**

ΕΛΛΗΝΙΚΗ: **Greece.**

ΕΛΛΗΚΙΚΗ ΔΙΟΚΣΙΣ on stamps of Greece: **Greece — Aegean Islands — Icaria.**

ΕΛΛνμωη Καραρχη Μυτιληυησ on stamps of Greece: **Greece — Aegean Islands — Mytilene.**

ΕΛΕΤΟΕΠΑ **VONITEIA:** Greece — Aegean Islands — Icaria.

ΕΔΔ on stamps of Greece: **Greece — Aegean Islands — Dodecanes Islands.**

**FACTAJ** on stamps of Romania: **Romania** — Parcel post stamps.

**FARIDKOT: India — Faridkot.**

**FCFA: Reunion.**

**FDO. POO: Fernando Po.**

**FEDERATA DEMOKRATIKE MDERKOMETORE: Albania.**

**FEDERATED MALAY STATES: Malaya.**

**FEDERATION OF MALAYA: Malay.**

**FEDERATION OF MALI: Mali.**

**FELDPOST** on stamps of Germany: **Germany** — Military stamps.

**FEN, EN: Manchukuo; FEN** on stamps of Poland: **Poland.**

**FERANADO POO: Fernando Po.**

**FEZZAN or FEZZAN GHADAMES: Libya — French occupation.**

**FIERA DI TRIESTE** on stamps of Italy: **Trieste.**

**FILIPAS, FILIPINAS: Philippines.**

**FILLÈR: Hungary.**

**FILS** on stamps with no country name: **Iraq, Jordan.**

**FINCASTLE: United States — Fincastle, Virginia.**

**FIUME** on stamps of Hungary: **Fiume.**

**FLUCHTINGSHIFE MONTENEGRO** on stamps of Yugoslavia: **Montenegro — German occupation.**

**FLUGPOST** ("Airmail"): **Austria, Danzig, Germany.**

**FORCES FRANCAISE LIBRES-LEVANT: Syria — Free French Administration.**

**fr.** on stamps of Sengal: **French West Africa.**

**FØROYAR: Faroe Islands.**

**FRANC** on stamps of Austria: **Austria — Offices in Crete.**

**FRANCA** on stamps of Peru: **Peru — Ancanch, Chiclayo.**

**FRANÇAISE: France.**

**FRANCE D'OUTRE—MER: French Colonies.**

**FRANCO: Philippines, Spain, Switzerland.**

**FRANCO BOLLO** with no country name on perforated stamps: **Italy;** on imperforated stamps: **Sardinia.**

**FRANCO BOLLO DI STATO: Italy — Official stamps.**

**FRANCO BOLLO POSTALE** with denominations in BAJ, SCUDO, CENT. or CENTESIMI: **Roman States.**

**FRANCO SCRISOREI: Romania — Modavia —Walachia.**

**FRANK: Austria.**

**FRANKLIN, N.C.: United States — Franklin, North Carolina.**

**FRANQUICIA: Spain.**

**FREDERICKSB'G: United States — Fredericksburg, Virginia.**

**FREI DURCH ABLOSUNG** ("Free because of prepayment"): **Germany.**

**FREIE STADT DANZIG: Danzig.**

**FREIMARKE** with no country name: **Baden, Prussia, Thurn and Taxis, Wurttemberg.**

**FREISAAT BAYERN** on stamps of Germany: **Bavaria.**

**FRIMARKE KGL POST: Denmark.**

**FUNF GROTE: Bremen.**

**FURSTENTTUM or FVERSTENTUM LIECHTENSTEIN: Liechtenstein.**

G or GW on stamps of Cape of Good Hope: **Griqualand West.**

GAB. or GABON on stamps of French Colonies: **Gabon.**

GALVESTON TEX.: **United States — Galveston, Texas.**

GARCH: **Saudi Arabi.**

GARZON: **Colombia — Tolima.**

**G.E.A.** on stamps of East Africa and Uganda: **German East Africa — British occupation;** on stamps of Kenya: **Tanganyika.**

**GENERAL GOVERNMENT: Poland — German occupation.**

**GENEVA: Switzerland — Geneva.**

**GEN—GOUV. WARSCHAU** on stamps of Germany: **Poland — German occupation.**

**GEORGIE, GEORGIENNE: Georgia.**

**GEORGETOWN S.C.: United States — Georgetown, South Carolina.**

**GERUSALEMME** on stamps of Italy: **Italy — Offices in Turkey — Jerusalem.**

**GHADAMES: Libya — French occupation.**

**GHANA** on stamps of Gold Coast: **Ghana.**

**GIBRALTAR** on stamps of Bermuda: **Gibraltar.**

**GILBERT & ELLICE PROTECTORATE** on stamps of Fiji: **Gilbert and Ellice Islands.**

**GIORNALI STAMPE: Sardinia.**

**GOLFE DE BENIN: Benin.**

**GOLIAD: United States — Goliad, Texas.**

**GONZALES TEXAS: United States — Gonzales, Texas.**

**GOVERNMENT CITY DISPATCH: United States — Baltimore, Maryland.**

**GOVERNO MILTARE ALLEATO** on stamps of Italy: **Italy — Allied occupation.**

**GOYA: Spain.**

**G.P.E.** or **G.&D.** on stamps of French Colonies: **Guadeloupe.**

**GRAHAMLAND** on stamps of Falkland Islands: **Falkland Islands — Grahamland.**

**GRANA: Two Sicilies.**

**GRANADINE: Colombia.**

**GRANDE COMORO: Grand Comoro.**

**GRAND LIBAN: Lebanon.**

**GREENSBORO ALA.: United States — Greensboro, Alabama.**

**GREENSBORO N.C.: United States — Greensboro, North Carolina.**

**GREENVILLE, ALA.: United States — Greenville, Alabama.**

**GREENVILLE C.H.S.C.: United States — Greenville Court House, South Carolina.**

**G.R.I.** on stamps inscribed "Deutsch New Guinea": **New Britain;** on stamps of Samoa: **Samoa — German Administration.**

**GRIFFIN GA.: United States — Griffin, Georgia.**

**GRONLAND: Greenland.**

**GROSSDEUTSCHES REICH** ("Great Germany"): **Germany;** with **BOHMEN UND MAHREN: Czechoslovakia — Bohemia and Moravia.**

**GROSSDEUTSCHES REICH GENERALGOVERNMENT: Poland — German occupation.**

**GROUCH: Turkey.**

**GROVE HILL ALA.: United States — Grove Hill, Alabama.**

**GUADEL: Mexico — Guadel.**

**GUADELOPE** on stamps of French Colonies: **Guadeloupe.**

**GUAM** on stamps of United States: **Guam.**

**GUANACASTE: Costa Rica — Guanacaste.**

**GUERNSEY: Great Britain — Guernsey.**

**GUINE** or **GUINE PORTUGUESA: Cape Verde, Portugese Guinea.**

**GUINE BISSAU: Guinea — Bissau.**

**GUINEA** followed by **CONTINENTAL, CORREOS,** or **ESPANOLA: Spanish Guinea;** by **ECUATORIAL: Equatorial Guinea.**

**GUINEE** or **GUINEE FRANÇAIS: French Guinea.**

**GULTIG 9 ARMEE** on stamps of Germany: **Romania — German occupation.**

**GUYANA** on stamps of British Guinea: **Guyana.**

**GUYANE FRANÇAISE: French Guiana.**

**GWALIOR: India — Gwalior.**

**G.ЛÍ.O. ONZ** on stamps of Russia: **Russia — Offices in Turkey.**

**HABILADO** on stamps of Cuba: **Cuba — U.S. Administration.**

**HALLETTSVILLE TEX.: United States — Hallettsville, Texas.**

**HAMBURG S.C.: United States — Hamburg, South Carolina.**

**HASHMITE KINGDOM OF JORDAN: Jordan.**

**HATAY DEVLETI: Hatay.**

**HAUTE SILESIE: Upper Silesia.**

**HAUTE VOLTA: Upper Volta.**

**HAUT—SENEGAL—NIGER: Upper Senegal and Niger.**

**H.E.H. THE NIZAN'S: India — Hyderabad.**

**HEJAZ & NEID, HEDJAZ & NEDJDE: Saudi Arabia.**

**HELENA: United States — Helena, Texas.**

**HELLER: Austria, Bosnia — Herzegovina, Liechtenstein.**

**HELVETIA: Switzerland.**

**H.H. NAWAB SHAH JAHANBECAM: India — Bhopal.**

**H.I.** or **HAWAIIAN ISLANDS POSTAGE: Hawaii.**

**H.I. & U.S.: Hawaii.**

**HIRLAPJEGY: Hungary.**

**НОВЧ, НОВЧИЧ: Montenegro.**

**HOI HAO** on stamps of Indo-China: **France — Offices in China — Hoi Hao.**

**HOLKAR STATE: India — Indore.**

**HOLSTEIN: Schleswig — Holstein.**

**HONDOUR'S: United States — Charlestown, South Carolina.**

**HOUSTON TXS.: United States — Houston, Texas.**

**H.P. Á: Bulgaria.**

**HRVATSKA: Croatia, Yugoslavia.**

**HRZGL.: Schleswig — Holstein.**

**HT SENEGAL-NIGER: Upper Senegal and Niger.**

**HUNGARIC REPUBLICA: Hungary.**

**HUNTSVILLE TEX.: United States — Huntsville, Texas.**

**HYDERABAD: India — Hyderabad.**

**НΓΙΕΙΡΟΣ: Epirus.**

# I

**ICC** on stamps of India: **India — International Commission in Indochina — Laos and Vietnam.**

**IDAR: India — Idar.**

**I.E.F.** ("Indian Expeditionary Force"): **India.**

**I.E.F.'D'** on stamps of Turkey: **Mesopotamia.**

**IERUSALM** on stamps of Russia: **Russia — Offices in Turkey.**

**ILE DE LA REUNION: Reunion.**

**ILE ROUAD** on stamps of French offices in the Levant: **Rouad.**

**ILES WALLIS ET FUTUNA: Wallis and Futuna Islands.**

**IMPERIAL BRITISH EAST AFRICA COMPANY: British East Africa.**

**IMPERIAL CHINESE POST, CHINESE IMPERIAL POST or CHINESE EMPIRE: China.**

**IMPERIAL JAPANESE POST: Japan.**

**IMPERIAL KOREAN POST: Korea.**

**IMPERIO COLONIAL PORTUGUES** with no colony name: **Portugese Africa.**

**IMPTO** or **IMPUESTO DE GUERRA: Spain.**

**INCI YIL DONUMU: Turkey.**

**INDE, INDIE: French India.**

**INDEPENDENCE, TEX.: United States — Independence, Texas.**

**INDIA** with inscriptions in Portuguese or words REIS, TANGAS, or RUPIA: **Portugese India.**

**INDO CHINE: Indo-China.**

**INDONESIA** not preceded by "REPUBIK": **Dutch Indies — Indonesia.**

**INDORE: India — Indore.**

**INDUSTRIELLE KRIEGSWIRTSCHAFT: Switzerland.**

**INHAMBANE** on stamps of Mozambique: **Inhambane.**

**INKERI: North Ingermanland.**

**INLAND: Liberia.**

**INSELPOST** on stamps of Germany: **Germany** — military stamps.

**INSTRUCAO** on stamps of Portuguese India: **Timor.**

**INSTRUCCION: Venezuela.**

**INSUFFICIENTLY PREPAID POSTAGE DUE: Zanzibar.**

IONIKAPATOΣ: **Ionian Islands.**

**I.O.V.R.: Romania.**

**IRAN: Persia.**

**IRANIENNES** ("Iranien"): **Persia.**

**IRAQ** on stamps of Turkey: **Mesopotamia.**

**IRIAN BARAT: West New Guinea.**

**I.R. OFFICIAL** on stamps of Great Britain: **Great Britain** — Official stamps.

**ISLAND: Iceland.**

**ISLAS GALAPAGOS: Ecuador — Galapagos Islands.**

**ISLE OF MAN: Great Britain — Man, Isle of.**

**ISOLE ITALIANE DELL'EGEO** on stamps of Italy: **Italy — Aegean Islands.**

**ISOLE JONIE** on stamps of Italy: **Ionian Islands — Italian occupation.**

**ISTRA** or **ISTRIA: Yugoslavia** — Issues for Istria and the Slovene Coast.

ΙΤΑΑΙΑΣ–ΕΛΛΑΔΟΣ–ΤΟΤΡΚΙΑ: **Greece.**

**ITA-KARJALA** on stamps inscribed "SUOMI—FINLAND": **Karelia — Finnish administration.**

**ITALIA, ITALINE, ITALIANO: Italy.**

**ITALIAN SOMALILAND: Somalia.**

**ITALIA OCCUPAZONE MILTARE ITALIANA ISOLE CAFALONIA E ITACA** on stamps of Greece: **Ionion Islands — Italian occupation.**

**I-U-KA: United States — Iuka, Mississippi.**

**IZMIR HIMAYEIETFAL: Turkey.**

**JAFFA** on stamps of Russia: **Russia — Offices in Turkey.**

**JAIPUR: India — Jaipur.**

**JAM. DIM. SOOMAALIYA: Somalia.**

**JAMES M BUCHANAN: United States — Baltimore, Maryland.**

**JAMHURIZANZIBAR TANZANIA: Zanzibar.**

**JANINA** on stamps of Italy: **Italy — Offices in Turkey — Janina.**

**JAPANESE EMPIRE: Japan.**

**JAVA** on stamps inscribed "Nederlandsch—Indie": **Dutch Indies.**

**J.D. SOOMAALIYEED: Somalia.**

**JEEND STATE: India — Jhind.**

**JERSEY: Great Britain — Jersey.**

**JERUSALEM** on stamps of Russia: **Russia — Offices in Turkey.**

**JIND, JHIND: India — Jhind.**

**JOHORE, JOHOR: Malay States — Johore.**

**JONESBORO T.: United States — Jonesboro, Tennessee.**

**JOURNAUX DAGBLADEN** on stamps of Belgium: **Belgium** — Newspaper stamps.

**J.P. JOHNSON, P.M.: United States — Pittsylvania Court House, Virginia.**

**JUBILE DE L'UNION POSTALE UNIVERSELLE: Switzerland.**

ЈУГОСЛАВИЈА : **Yugoslavia.**

**JUGOSLAVIJA: Yugoslavia.**

# K

**K** with no country name (abbreviation for Krone): **Bosnia and Herzegovina.**

**KAISKON: Austria.**

**KALAALLIT NUNAAT: Greenland.**

**KALAYAAN NANG PLIPINAS: Philippines — Japanese occupation.**

**KALIPEDIA: Memel — Lithuanian occupation.**

**KAMERUN: Cameroun.**

**KAP: Latvia.**

КАРПАТСЬКА−УКРАÏНА on stamps inscribed "Cesko-Slovensko": **Czechoslovakia — Carpath-Ukraine.**

**KARJALA: Karelia.**

**KARKI** on stamps of Italy: **Italy — Aegean Islands — Karki.**

**KARLFONDS: Austria, Bosnia & Herzegovina.**

**KARNTEN ABSTIMMUNG** ("Carinthian Plebisite") on stamps of Austria: **Austria.**

**KAROLINEN: Caroline Islands.**

К.С. ПОUТА or КСГбСКА: **Serbia.**

**KEDAH: Malay States — Kelantan.**

**KEMAHKOTAAN** or **KETAHKOTAAN** on stamps inscribed "Johore": **Malay States — Johore.**

**KENTTA-POSTI** or **KENTTA-POSTIA: Finland** — Military stamps.

**KENYA & UGANDA: Kenya, Uganda, and Tanzania.**

**KERASSUNDE** on stamps of Russia: **Russia — Offices in Turkey.**

**K.G.L.** or **KONGELIGT: Danish West Indies, Denmark.**

**KHMER REPUBLIC: Cambodia.**

**KHOR FAKKAN: Sharjah and Dependencies.**

**KIAUTSCHOU: Kiauchau.**

**KIBRIS CUMHURIYETI: Cyprus.**

**KINGSTON GA.: United States — Kingston, Georgia.**

**KIONGA** on stamps of Lourenco Marques: **Kionga.**

**KISHANGARH: India — Kishengarh.**

**K.K.** or **KAISERLICHE KONIGLICHE OSTERREICHISCHE POST** ("Imperial and Royal Austrian Post"): **Austria.**

**KK-POST-STEMPEL** with values in KREUZER: **Austria;** with values in CENTES: **Austria — Lombardy — Venetia.**

**K-numeral-K** on stamps of Russia: **Far Eastern Republic.**

**K 60 K** on stamps of Russia: **Armenia.**

**KNOXVILLE: United States — Knoxville, Tennessee.**

КОН, КОП, КON: **Batum, Far Eastern Republic, Finland, Latvia, Russia, South Russia.**

**KOP: Finland.**

**KORCA** or **KORCE: Albania.**

**KOREAN POST: Korea.**

**KORONA: Hungary.**

# HOW TO COLLECT STAMPS

**KOUANG-TCHEOU** or **KOUANGTCHEOUWAN** on stamps of Indo-China: **France — Offices in China — Kwangchowan.**

**КРАЈЬЕВСТВО|C.X.C.:** Yugoslavia.

**KPALJEVSTO** or **KRALJEVINA SRBA, HRVATA I SLOVENACA** ("Kingdom of the Serbs, Croats and Slovenes"): **Yugoslavia.**

**KPHTH: Crete.**

**KR., KREUZER: Austria, Baden, Bavaria, Germany, Hungary, Wurttemburg.**

**КRAIЬ. УВНАГОРА : Montenegro.**

**KRONE, KRONEN: Austria.**

**K.S.A.:** (Kingdom of) **Saudi Arabia.**

**K.U.K.** ("Imperial and Royal"): **Austria, Bosnia and Herzegovina.**

**K-U-K-FELDPOST: Austria;** with values in "BANI" or "LEI": **Romania.**

**K-U-K-MILITARPOST: Bosnia and Herzegovina.**

**K. UND K. FELDPOST: Austria.**

**KUWAIT** on stamps of India or Great Britain: **Kuwait.**

**K. WURTT: Wurttemburg.**

**КИТАИ** on stamps of Russia: **Russia — Offices in China.**

# L

**LA AGUERA: Aguera.**

**LABUAN** on stamps of North Borneo: **Labuan.**

**LA CANEA** on stamps of Italy: **Italy — Offices in Crete.**

**LA GEORGIE: Georgia.**

**LA GRANGE TEX.: United States — La Grange, Texas.**

**LAIBACH: Yugoslavia — Ljubljana — German occupation.**

**LAKE CITY FLA.: United States — Lake City, Florida.**

**LANSA: Columbia.**

**L.A.R.** (Libyan Arab Republic): **Libya.**

**LAS BELA: India — Las Bela.**

**LATTAQUIE** on stamps of Syria: **Latakia.**

**LATVIJA, LATWIJA: Latvia.**

**LAVACA: United States — Port Lavaca, Texas.**

**LAVANTE** on stamps of Italy: **Italy — Offices in Turkey.**

**LEI** on stamps of Austria: **Romania — Austrian occupation.**

**LENOIR N.C.: United States — Lenoir, North Carolina.**

**LEROS** or **LERO** on stamps of Italy: **Italy — Aegean Islands — Leros.**

**LESTHO** on stamps of Basutoland: **Lestho.**

**LEVA: Bulgaria.**

**LEVANT: France — Offices in Turkey;** on stamps of Great Britain: **Great Britain — Offices in Turkey;** on stamps of Poland: **Poland — Offices in Turkey.**

**LEXINGTON, MISS.: United States — Lexington, Mississippi.**

58

**LIBAN, LIBANAISE: Lebanon.**

**LIBAUD** on stamps of Germany: **Latvia — German occupation.**

**LIBIA, LIBYE: Libya;** on stamps of Cyrenaica: **Libya.**

**LIETUVA, LIETVOS: Lithuania;** on stamps of Russia: **Lithuania — South District.**

**LIGNES AERIENNE F.A.F.L.** or **LIGNES AERIENNE DE LA FRANCE LIBRE: Syria — Free French Administration.**

**LIMA: Peru.**

**LIMBAGAN—1543-1943** on stamps of Philippines: **Philippines.**

**LIPSO, LISSO** on stamps of Italy: **Italy — Aegean Islands — Lisso.**

**LIRE** on stamps of Austria: **Italy — Austrian occupation.**

**LISBOA: Portugal.**

**LITAS: Lithuania.**

**LITWA SRODKOWA, LITWY SRODKOWEI: Central Lithuania.**

**LIVINGSTON: United States — Livingston, Alabama.**

**LJUBLJANSKA: Yugoslavia — Ljubljana — German occupation.**

**L. MARQUES** on stamps of Mozambique: **Louenco Marques.**

**LOCKPORT N.Y.: United States — Lockport, New York.**

**LOSEN: Sweden.**

**LOTHRIGEN** on stamps of Germany: **France — German occupation.**

**L.P.** on stamps of Russia: **Latvia.**

**LTSR** on stamps of Lithuania: **Lithuania — Russian occupation.**

**LUBIANA** on stamps of Yugoslavia: **Yugoslavia — Ljubljana — Italian occupation.**

**LUFTELDPOST: Germany** — Military air post stamps.

**LUXEMBURG: Luxembourg;** on stamps of Germany: **Luxembourg — German occupation.**

**MACAU** or **MACAV: Macao.**

**MACON: United States — Macon, Georgia.**

**MADIERA** on stamps of Portugal: **Madeira.**

**MADRID: Spain.**

**MAGYAR** ("Hungarian"): **Hungary.**

**MAGYAR KIR.: Hungary.**

**MAGARKIRALY** or **MAGY. KIR: Hungary.**

**MAGYAR NEMZEMI KORMANY SZEGED** on stamps of Hungary: **Hungary — Serbian occupation — Szeged.**

**MAGYARORZÁG: Hungary.**

**MALACCA: Malay States — Malacca.**

**MALAGA** on stamps of Spain: **Spain — Malaga.**

**MALAGASY:** Madagascar.

**MALAYA** with no further inscriptions, over portrait of Sultan: **Malaya States —
        Kelantan, Negri Sembilan, Pahang, Perak, Perlis, Selangor,
        Trengganu;** over picture of mosque: **Selangor;** over picture of state arms:
        **Negri Sembilan.**

**MALGACHE:** Madagascar.

**MALDIVES: Maldive Islands.**

**MALMEDY** on stamps of Belgium: **Germany — Belgian occupation.**

**MANAMA: a dependency of Ajman.**

**MAPKA: Finland, Russia, Serbia.**

**MARCA DA BOLLO: Italy.**

**MARIAM: Mariana Islands.**

**MARIANS ESPANOLAS** on stamps inscribed "Filipinas": **Mariana Islands —
        Spanish Dominion.**

**MARIETTA: United States — Marietta, Georgia.**

**MARION VA.: United States — Marion, Virginia.**

**MARK, MARKKAA: Finland.**

**MARKA: Estonia.**

**MAROC: French Morocco, Morocco.**

**MAROCCO, MAROKKO** on stamps of Germany: **Germany — Offices in
        Morocco.**

**MARREUCOS: Morocco — Northern Zone, Spanish Morocco.**

**MARSHALL-NSELN: Marshall Islands.**

**MARTINIQUE** on stamps of French Colonies: **Martinique.**

**MAURITANIE: Mauritania.**

**M.B.D.** on stamps inscribed "Raj Nandoan": **India — Nandgoan.**

**MBLEDHAJA** on stamps of Albania: **Albania — Italian dominion.**

**MBRENTNIJA SHQUPTARE, MBLEDHJEA KUSTETUE, MBR. SHIQTAR,
        MBRETNIA SHGYPTARE: Albania.**

**M.C. GALLAWA: United States — Memphis, Tennessee.**

**MECKLEMB. SCHERIN: Mecklenburg — Schwerin.**

**MEDELLIN: Colombia, Colombia — Antioqua.**

**MEDIA ONZA: Spain.**

**MEDIO REAL: Dominican Republic.**

**M.E.F.** on stamps of Great Britain: **Great Britain — Offices in Africa.**

**MEJICO: Mexico.**

**MELAKA: Malay States — Malacca.**

**MEMELGEBIET** ("Memel Territory"): **Memel.**

**MEMPHIS TENN.: United States — Memphis, Tennessee.**

**METELIN** on stamps of Russia: **Russia — Offices in Turkey.**

**MEXICANO** ("Mexican"): **Mexico.**

**MICANOPY FLA.: United States — Micanopy, Florida.**

**MILIT** or **MILITARPOST PORTOMARKE** or **ELLMARKE: Bosnia and
        Herzegovina.**

**MILL., MILLIEMES** on stamps of France: **France — Offices in Egypt.**

**MILLEDGEVILLE GA.: United States — Milledgeville, Georgia.**

**M. KIR.** ("Magyar Kirly"): **Hungary.**

**MN: Korea.**

**MOBILE ALA.: United States — Mobile, Alabama.**

**MOÇAMBIQUE: Mozambique.**

**MONGTZE, MONGTSEU** on stamps of Indo-China: **France — Offices in China — Mongtseu.**

**MONROVIA: Liberia.**

**MONT ATHOS** on stamps of Russia: **Russia — Offices in Turkey.**

**MONTENEGRO** on stamps of Austria: **Montenegro — Austrian occupation;** on stamps of Yugoslavia: **Montenegro — Italian occupation.**

**MONTEVIDEO: Uruguay.**

**MONTGOMERY: United States — Montgomery, Alabama.**

**MONTSERRAT** on stamps of Antigua: **Montserrat.**

**MOQUEGRA, MOQUEA** on stamps inscribed "Peru" or "Fraqued": **Peru — Moquegua.**

**MOГA: Ukraine.**

**MOROCCO AGENCIES** on stamps of Great Britain: **Great Britain — Offices in Morocco.**

**MORVI: India — Morvi.**

**MOYEN CONGO: Middle Congo.**

**MQE** on stamps of French Colonies: **Martinique.**

**MULTA: Portugal and Portuguese Colonies** — Postage due stamps.

**MUSCAT & OMAN: Oman.**

**M.V.I.R.** on stamps of Germany or Romania: **Romania — German occupation.**

**NABAH: India — Nabha.**

**NACIONES UNIDAS: United Nations.**

**NANADGAON: India — Nandigaon.**

**ПAPA: Serbia.**

**NAPOLETANA: Two Sicilies.**

**NASHVILLE: United States — Nashville, Tennessee.**

**NA SLASK: Central Lithuania.**

**NATIONALER VERWAILTUGSAUSSCHUSS** on stamps of Montenegro: **Montenegro — German occupation.**

**NATIONS UNIES: United Nations** or **United Nations — Offices in Geneva.**

**NAURU** on stamps of Great Britain: **Nauru.**

**N.C.E.** on stamps of French Colonies: **New Caledonia.**

**N.D. HRVATSKA: Croatia.**

**ДЕВА, ДЕВb : Bulgaria.**

**NEDERLAND: Netherlands.**

**NED-INDIE, NEDERL-INDIE, NEDERLANSCH-INDIE: Dutch Indies.**

**NED** or **NEDERLANDSE ANTILLEN: Netherlands Antilles.**

**NED** or **NEDERLANDS NIEUW GUINEA: Netherlands Dutch New Guinea.**

**NEGERI SEMBILAN: Malay States — Negri Sembilan.**

**NEW HAVEN CT.: United States — New Haven Connecticut.**

**NEW HEBRIDES CONDOMINUM** on stamps of Fiji: **New Hebrides.**

**NEW ORLEANS** or **N.O.P.O.: United States — New Orleans, Louisiana.**

**NEW YORK: United States — New York, New York.**

**NEZAVISNA DRZAVA HRVATSKA: Croatia.**

**NEZ. DRZ. HRVATSKA: Croatia.**

**N.F.** on stamps of Nyasaland Protectorate: **German East Africa — British occupation.**

**NIEUW GUINEA: Dutch New Guinea.**

**NIEUW REPUBLIK: New Republic.**

**NIPPON: Japan.**

**NISIROS** or **NISIRO** on stamps of Italy: **Italy — Aegean Islands — Nisiro.**

**NIUE** on stamps of New Zealand: **Niue.**

**NILLE CALEDONIE: New Caledonia.**

**NO HAY ESTAMPILLES: Colombia — many states.**

ПОРТО МАbКА ("postage due"): **Serbia.**

**NORDDEUTSCHER POST—BEZIRK** ("North German Postal District"): **Germany — North German Confederation.**

**NOREG: Norway.**

**NORTHERN COOK ISLANDS: Penrhyn Island.**

**NOSSI-BE** on stamps of French Colonies: **Nossi-Be.**

**NOUVELLE CALEDONIE: New Caledonia.**

**NOUVELLES HEBRIDES: New Hebrides** (French Issues).

ПОЩАВЪРОПЖИЯ: **Romania — Bulgarian occupation.**

**NOWANUGGUR: India — Nowanuggur.**

ПОЩТА: **Serbia.**

ПОЧТА ("postage"): **Russia.**

ПОЧТ МАРКА on stamps with no country name: **Azerbaijan.**

ПОЧТОВАЯ МАРКА: **Finland.**

ΠΡΟΣΩΡΙΝΟΝ or ΠΡΟΕΩΡΤΑΧΤΔΡ: **Crete.**

**N.S.B.** on stamps of French Colonies: **Nossi-Be.**

**N. SEMBILAN: Malay States — Negri Sembilan.**

**N.S.W.: New South Wales.**

**N.W. PACIFIC ISLANDS** on stamps of Australia: **North West Pacific Islands.**

**NYASALAND: Nyasaland Protectorate.**

**NYASSA** on stamps of Mozambique: **Nyassa.**

**N.Z.: New Zealand.**

**ОДНА МАКА**: Finland.

**OAXACA: Mexico — Oaxaca.**

**OBOCK** on stamps of French Colonies: **Obock.**

**OCCUPATION FRANCAISE** on stamps of Hungary: **Hungary — French occupation.**

**OCEANIE: French Polynesia.**

**OESTERR POST: Austria;** with name Liechetenstein: **Liechtenstein — Austrian postal administration.**

**OEUVRES DE SOLIARITE FRANCAISE: French Colonies.**

**OFFENTIG SAK: Norway.**

**OFFICIAL** on stamps of Kenya, Uganda, and Tanzania: **Tanganika.**

**OFFISIEEL** ("Official"): **South Africa, South West Africa.**

**OFF. SAK.: Norway** — Official stamps.

**OFTERREICH: Austria.**

**OIL RIVERS: Niger Coast Protectorate.**

**ОКСА**: Russia — Army of the North.

**OLTRE GIUBA** on stamps of Italy: **Oltre Giuba.**

**O.M.F. SYRIE** on stamps of France: **Syria.**

**ORANGE RIVER COLONY** on stamps of Cape of Good Hope: **Orange River Colony.**

**ORANGE VRIJ STAAT** ("Orange Free State"): **Orange River Colony.**

**ORCHA: India — Orcha.**

**ORE: Denmark, Norway, Sweden;**

**ORTS-POST: Switzerland.**

**O.S.: Norway.**

**OSTERREICH: Austria.**

**OSTERR-POST, OSTERREICHISCHE POST: Austria.**

**OSTLAND** ("Eastland") on stamps of Germany: **Russia — German occupation.**

**OTVORENIE SLOVENSKENO** on stamps of Czechoslovakia: **Czechoslovakia — Slovakia.**

**OUBANGUI—CHARI: Ubangi.**

**O.W. OFFICIAL** on stamps of Great Britain: **Great Britain — Official stamps.**

ОΛТМ., ОΛТМΠΙΑΚΟΙ ("Olympic"): **Greece.**

ОΔТМΠ: **Greece.**

# P

**P** on stamps of Strait Settlements: **Malay States — Perak.**

**p** (pence) or **£** (pound) preceded by a numeral, on stamps with king's or queen's head but no country name: **Great Britain.**

**PACCI POSTALI** ("Parcel Post"): **Italy;** with value in diagonal band: **San Marino;** with star and crescent emblem: **Somalia.**

**PACKHOI** or **PAK-HOI** on stamps of Indo-China: **France — Offices in China — Packhoi.**

**PAHANG: Malay States — Pahang.**

**PAID** with value in cents: **United States** — various provisionals.

**PAIS, PICE: Nepal.**

**PAITA** on stamps of Peru: **Peru — Paita.**

**PAKISTAN** on stamps of India: **Pakistan.**

**PAKKE-PORTO: Greenland.**

**PALESTINE** on stamps of Egypt: **Egypt — Palestine occupation.**

**PAPUA** on stamps of British New Guinea: **Papua New Guinea.**

**PAPUA & NEW GUINEA: Papua New Guinea.**

**PARA** or **PARAS: Egypt, Mesopotamia, Turkey;** on stamps of Austria: **Austria — Offices in Turkey;** on stamps of Germany: **Germany — Offices in Turkey;** on stamps of Great Britain: **Great Britain — Offices in Turkey;** on stamps of Romania: **Romania — Offices in Turkey;** on stamps of Russia: **Russia — Offices in Turkey;** on stamps of France: **France — Offices in Turkey;** on stamps of Italy: **Italy — Offices in Turkey.**

**PASCO** on stamps of Peru: **Peru — Pasco.**

**PATIALA: India — Patiala.**

**PATMOS** or **PATMO** on stamps of Italy: **Italy — Aegean Islands — Patmo.**

**P.C.Ф.C.P.** (abbreviation for "Russia Soviet Socialist Republic"): **Russia.**

**P.E.** inscribed on stamps with arabic overprints: **Egypt.**

**PECHINO** on stamps of Italy: **Italy — Offices in China — Peking.**

**PEN, PENNI, PENNIAS: Finland.**

**PENNY: United States** — various provisionals.

**PENRHYN ISLAND** on stamps of Cook Islands or New Zealand: **Penrhyn Island.**

**PEOPLE'S DEMOCRATIC REPUBLIC OF YEMEN: Yemen, People's Democratic Republic.**

**PERAK: Malay States — Perak.**

**PERLIS: Malay States — Perlis.**

**PERSANE: Persia.**

**PERSEKUTAN TANAH MELAYU: Malaya.**

**PERUANA: Peru.**

**PERV-AERO: Peru** — air post.

**PESA** on stamps of Germany: **German East Africa.**

**PESETAS** with no country name: **Spain.**

**PETERSBURG VIRGINIA: United States — Petersburg, Virginia.**

**PF** or **PFG** on stamps of Germany: **Germany — Offices in China, Kaiuchau;** on stamps of Russia: **Estonia — German occupation.**

**PFENNIG: Bavaria, Germany, Wurttemberg.**

**P.G.S.** on stamps of United States: **Philippines — U.S. Administration.**

**PIASTER: Austria — Offices in Turkey; Germany — Offices in Turkey.**

**PIASTRA, PIASTRE, PIASTRES** on stamps of Italy: **Italy — Offices in Crete or in Turkey;** on stamps of Great Britain: **Great Britain — Offices in Turkey;** on stamps of Russia: **Russia — Offices in Turkey;** on stamps of France: **France — Offices in Turkey.**

**PIASTRO** on stamps of Italy: **Italy — Offices in Crete.**

**PIES: India.**

**PILGRIM TERCENTENARY** with no country name: **United States.**

**PILIPINAS: Philippines.**

**PINSIN: Ireland.**

**PISCO** on stamps of Peru: **Peru — Pisco.**

**PISCOPI** on stamps of Italy: **Italy — Aegean Islands — Piscopi.**

**PIURA** on stamps of Peru: **Peru — Piura.**

**PLEASANT SHADE: United States — Pleasant Shade, Virginia.**

**PLEBISCITE OLSZTYN ALLENSTEIN** on stamps of Germany: **Allenstein.**

**PLEBISCIT SLESVIG: Schleswig.**

**P.M.** on stamps of Italy: **Italy** — Military stamps.

**РОССІЯ: Russia, South Russia.**

**POCZTA: Poland.**

**POCZTA POLSKA** ("Polish postage"): **Poland;** on stamps of Germany: **Germany — Polish occupation;** on stamps of Austria: **Poland;** on stamps inscribed "Waszara": **Poland.**

**POHJOIS INKERI: North Ingermanland.**

**POLSKA: Poland.**

**POLYNESIE FRANCAISE: French Polynesia.**

**PONCE, P.R.: Puerto Rico — Ponce.**

**Р.О.П.И.Т.** on stamps of Russia: **Russia — Offices in Turkey, Ukraine.**

**PORTEADO: Portugal.**

**PORTE DE CONDUCCION: Peru.**

**PORTE DE MAR: Mexico.**

**PORTE FRANCO: Peru, Portugal.**

**PORT GDANSK** on stamps of Poland: **Poland — Offices in Danzig.**

**PORT LAGOS** on stamps of French colonies: **France — Offices in Turkey — Port Lagos.**

**PORTO** on stamps with no country name: **Austria;** with "piastre": **Austria — Offices in Turkey.**

**PORTO GAZETEI: Romania — Moldavia.**

**PORTOMARK: Bosnia & Herzegovina.**

**PORTO RICO** on stamps of United States: **Puerto Rico.**

**PORT-SAID: France — Offices in Egypt — Port Said.**

**POSTA CESKOSLOVENSKA** on stamps of Austria: **Czechoslovakia.**

**POSTAGE** with value in pies, annas or rupees: **India — Hyderabad;** with **CAMB.**

# HOW TO COLLECT STAMPS

**AUST. CIGILLUM NOV** in a circle: **New South Wales.**

**POSTAGE, POSTAGE & REVENUE** with denominations in d or p (pence)/ (shilling) or £ (pound) and portraits of a king or queen, but no country name: **Great Britain;** with denominations in annas: **India — Kishengarh.**

**POSTAGE I.E.F.'D'** on stamps of Turkey: **Mesopotamia.**

**POSTAGE DUE** with denominations in d or p (pence)/(shilling), or £ (pound): **Australia, Great Britain.**

**POSTAGE TWO CENTS** with portrait of Andrew Jackson, and initials C.S. in lower corners: **United States — Confederate States.**

**POSTALI: Italy;** with value in diagonal band: **San Marino;** with star and crescent emblem: **Somalia.**

**POSTA ROMANA CONSTANTINOPOL** on stamps of Romania: **Romania — Offices in Turkey.**

**POSTAS LE NIOC** or **N'LOC: Ireland.**

**POSTE AERIEO** or **POSTE AERIENNE** on stamps with no country name: **Persia.**

**POSTE** followed by **EGYPTIENES: Egypt;** followed by **HEDJAZ AND NEJDE: Saudi Arabia;** followed by **OTTOMANES: Mesopotamia, Turkey;** followed by picture of crescent: **Afghanistan.**

**POSTE CENTIME** with numeral in center of stamp covered with a network of colored lines: **France — Alsace and Lorraine — German occupation.**

**POSTE ESTENSI: Modena.**

**POSTEK NEDEUIERGIZIANNE** or **POSIEXHEDEVIEECIZANE: Egypt.**

**POSTE LOCAL: Switzerland** — various cantons.

**POSTES: Belgium, France, French Colonies, Luxembourg.**

**POSTES PERSANES: Bushire, Persia.**

**POSTE VATICANE: Vatican City.**

**POSTGEBIET OB. OFT** on stamps of Germany: **Lithuania — German occupation.**

**POST OFFICE DISPATCH: United States — Baltimore, Maryland.**

**POSTZEGEL** with no country name: **Netherlands.**

**POUL: Afghanistan.**

**PREUSSEN: Prussia.**

**PRINCE FAROUK: Egypt.**

**PRINCIPAUTE DE MONCO** ("Principality of Monaco"): **Monaco.**

**PRO TACNA Y ARICA, PLEBISCITO TACNAYRICA: Peru.**

**PROJECT MERCURY: United States.**

**PROTECTORADO ESPANOL** or with **EN MARRUECOS** on stamps of Spain: **Spanish Morocco.**

**PROTECTORATES** on stamps of Becuananaland: **Becuananaland Protectorate.**

**PROTECTORAT FRANCAIS** on stamps inscribed "Chiffre Taxe": **French Morocco.**

**PRO TUBERCULOSOS POBRES: Spain.**

**PRO UNION IBEROAMERICANA** ("For the Spanish American Union"): **Spain.**

**PROVINCE MODONES: Modena.**

**PROVINZ LAIBACH: Yugoslavia — Ljubljana — German occupation.**

**PROVISIONAL 1881-1882** on stamps inscribed "Peru" or "Franqued": **Peru — Arequipa.**

**PROV. R.I.: United States — Providence, Rhode Island.**

**PS.: Colombia — Cauca.**
**P.S.N.C.** letters on four corners: **Peru.**
**PTO. RICO, PUERTO RICO: Puerto Rico.**
**PUL: Afghanistan.**
**PUNO** on stamps inscribed "Peru" or "Franqued": **Peru — Puno.**
**PUTTIALA** on stamps of India: **India — Patiala.**
**РУВ** or **РУЬ: Finland, Russia, Siberia, South Russia.**
**РУССКАЯПОУТА, РУССОИ АРМІН** on stamps of Russia or Ukraine: **Russia**
       **— Offices in Turkey — Wrangel Issues.**

**QATAR** on stamps of Great Britain: **Qatar.**
**QARKU: Albania.**
**QINDAR, QINTAR: Albania.**
**QUELIMANE** on stamps of various Portugese Colonies: **Quelimane.**

# R

R on stamps covered with Arabic writing: **India — Jhind.**
R on stamps of Colombia: **Panama.**
R (for "rial") on stamp with Arabic lettering, but no country name: **Persia.**
**RAJASTHAN** on stamps of Jaipur: **India — Rajasthan.**
**RALEIGH N.C.: United States — Raleigh, North Carolina.**
**RAPPEN: Switzerland.**
**RECARGO: Spain.**
**RECUEROD DEL I'DE FEBRERO: Honduras.**
**REGATUL ROMANIEI** ("Roumanian Kingdom") on stamps of Hungary: **Hungary**
       **— Roumanian occupation.**
**R.H.** (Abbreviation for "Republic of Haiti"): **Haiti.**
**RHEATOWN: United States — Rheatown, Tennessee.**
**RHEINLAND-PFALZ: Germany — Rhine Palatinate — French occupation.**
**RIAL** or **RIALS: Persia.**
**RIALTAR SEALDAC NA HEIREANN** ("Provisional Government of Ireland") on
       stamps of Great Britain: **Ireland.**
**RIAU** on stamps ofIndonesia: **Indonesia — Riouw Archipelago.**

**RICHMOND TEXAS:** United States — **Richmond, Texas.**

**RINGGOLD GEORGIA:** United States — **Ringgold, Georgia.**

**RIN, RN:** Japan.

**RIO DE ORO** on stamps inscribed "TERRITORIOS ESPANDLES DEL AFRICA OCCIDENTAL": **Rio de Oro.**

**RIS** on stamps of Dutch Indies: **Indonesia.**

**RIZEH** on stamps of Russia: **Russia — Offices in Turkey.**

**RL. PLATA F.:** Cuba, Philippines.

**RO** on stamps of Turkey: **Eastern Rumelia.**

**REGENCE DE TUNIS:** Tunisia.

**REGNO D'ITALIA** ("Kingdom of Italy"): **Italy;** on stamps of Austria with words VENEZIA GIULIA or with TRENTINO: **Austria — Italian occupation;** on stamps inscribed FIVME or FIUME: **Fiume.**

**REICH, REICHPOST:** Germany.

**REIS** with no country name: **Portugal.**

**REP. DI S. MARINO:** San Marino.

**REPUBLIKA MALAGASY:** Madagascar.

**REPUBBLICA ITALIANA:** Italy.

**REPUBBLICA SOCIALE ITALIANA:** Italy — Italian Socialist Republic.

**REPUBLICA DE COLOMBIA:** Colombia, Panama.

**REPUBLICA DOMINICANA:** Dominican Republic.

**REPUBLICA ESPANOLA:** Spain.

**REPUBLICA ORIENTAL** ("Eastern Republic"): **Uruguay.**

**REPUBLICA PERUANA:** Peru.

**REPUBLICA POPULARA ROMANIA:** Romania.

**REPUBLICA PORTUGUESA:** Portugal.

**REPUBLICA QUELIMANE** on stamps of various Portuguese Colonies: **Quelimane.**

**REPUBLICA TETE** on stamps of various Portuguese Colonies: **Tete.**

**REPUBLIC OF BOTSWANA** on stamps of Bechuanaland Protectorate: **Botswana.**

**REPUBLIC OF CHINA:** China — Taiwan.

**REPUBLIEK VAN SUID-AFRIKA:** South Africa.

**REPUBLIKA NG. PILINAS:** Philippines — Japanese occupation.

**REPUBLIKA POPULLORE E SHQIPERISE:** Albania.

**REPUBLIK INDONESIA:** Indonesia.

**REPUBLIQUE ARABE SYRIENNE:** Syria.

**REPUBLIQUE ARAB UNIE:** Syria — United Arab Republic.

**REPUBLIQUE AUTONOME DU TOGO:** Togo.

**REPUBLIQUE CENTRAFRICANE:** Central African Republic.

**REPUBLIQUE d'AZERBAIJAN:** Azerbaijan.

**REPUBLIQUE DA GUINE—BISSAU:** Guinea — Bissau.

**REPUBLIQUE DE COTE D'IVOIRE:** Ivory Coast.

**REPUBLIQUE DE DJIBOUTI:** Djibouti.

**REPUBLIQUE DE GUINEE:** Guinea.

**REPUBLIQUE DE HAUTE VOLTA:** Upper Volta.

**REPUBLIQUE DEMOCRATIQUE DU CONGO:** Congo Democratic Republic (ex-Belgian).

# HOW TO COLLECT STAMPS

**REPUBLIQUE DEMOCRATIQUE POPULAIRE LAO: Laos.**

**REPUBLIQUE D'HAITI: Haiti.**

**REPUBLIQUE DU CAMEROUN: Cameroun.**

**REPUBLIQUE DU CONGO: Congo Democratic Republic** (ex-Belgian), **Congo People's Republic** (ex-French).

**REPUBLIQUE DU DAHOMEY: Dahomey.**

**REPUBLIQUE DU MALI: Mali.**

**REPUBLIQUE DU NIGER: Niger.**

**REPUBLIQUE DU SENEGAL: Senegal.**

name: **France, French Colonies**

**REPUBLIQUE DU TCHAD: Chad.**

**REPUBLIQUE DU TOGO: Togo.**

**REPUBLIQUE DU ZAIRE: Congo Democratic Republic** (ex-Belgian).

**REPUBLIQUE FEDERALE ISLAMIQUE DES COMOROS: Comoro Islands.**

**REPUB. FRANC or REPUBLIQUE FRANÇAISE** if perforated: **France;** if imperforated: **French Colonies.**

**REPUBLIQUE GABONAISE: Gabon.**

**REPUBLIQUE ISLAMIQUE DE MAURITANIE: Mauritania.**

**REPUBLIQUE LIBANAISE: Lebanon.**

**REPUBLIQUE MALGACHE: Madagascar.**

**REPUBLIQUE POPULAIRE DU BENIN: Benin.**

**REPUBLIQUE POPULAIRE DU CONGO: Congo People's Republic** (ex-French).

**REPUBLIQUE RWANDAISE: Rwanda.**

**REPUBLIQUE TOGOLAISE: Togo.**

**REPUBLIQUE TUNISIENNE: Tunisia.**

**RETYMNO: Crete.**

**REUNION** on stamps of French Colonies: **Reunion.**

**R. COMMISSARIATO,** etc. on stamps of Yugoslavia: **Yugoslavia — Ljubljana — Italian occupation.**

**R.F.** (Abbreviation for "Republic of France") with no country.

**RODI: Italy — Aegean Islands — Rhodes.**

**ROMAGNE: Romagna.**

**ROMANA or ROMINA: Romania.**

**ROSS DEPENDENCY: New Zealand — Ross Dependency.**

**ROUMELIE ORIENTALE** on stamps of Turkey: **Eastern Rumelia.**

**ROYAUME DE L'ARABIE SAOUDITE: Saudi Arabia.**

**ROYAUME DE YEMEN: Yemen.**

**ROYAUME DU BURUNDI: Burundi.**

**ROYAUME DU CAMBODGE: Cambodia.**

**ROYAUME DU LAOS: Laos.**

**ROYAUME DU MAROC: Morocco.**

**RP.** (rappen): **Liechtenstein, Switzerland.**

**R.P.E. SHQIPERISE: Albania.**

**RPF** on stamps of Luxembourg: **Luxembourg — German occupation.**

**R.P. ROMANIA: Romania.**

**R.R.** with value in opposite corners: **Switzerland — Zurich.**

**R.S.A.: South Africa.**

**R.S.M.: San Marino.**
**RUANDA** on stamps inscribed "CONGO": **German East Africa — Belgian occupation.**
**RUANDA-URUNDI** on stamps of Congo Democratic Republic (ex-Belgian): **Ruanda-Urundi.**
**RUMANIEN** on stamps of Germany: **Romania — German occupation.**
**RUSSISCH-POLEN** on stamps of Germany: **Romania — German occupation.**
**RUTHERFORDTON N.C.: United States — Rutherfordton, North Carolina.**
**RYUKYUS: Ryukyu Islands.**

# S

**S** on stamps of Straits Settlements: **Malay Straits — Selangor.**
**S.A.: Saudi Arabia.**
**SAARE** on stamps of Germany: **Saar.**
**SAARGEBIET** ("Saar Territory"): **Saar.**
**SAARLAND, SAARPOST: Saar.**
**SABAH** on stamps of North Borneo: **Sabah.**
**SACHSEN: Saxony.**
**SAHARA ESPANOL** or **SAHARA OCCIDENTAL: Spanish Sahara.**
**ST. CHRISTOPHER-NEVIS-ANGUILLA: St. Kitts — Nevis.**
**SAINT LOUIS: United States — St. Louis, Missouri.**
**SAINT-PIERRE ET MIQUELON: ST. Pierre and Miquelon.**
**S.A.K.: Saudi Arabia.**
**SALEM N.C.: United States — Salem, North Carolina.**
**SALISBUY N.C.: United States — Salisbury, North Carolina.**
**SALONICCO** on stamps of Italy: **Italy — Offices in Turkey — Salonic.**
**SALONIQUE** on stamps of Russia: **Russia — Offices in Turkey.**
**SAMOA** on stamps of Germany or New Zealand: **Samoa.**
**SAN ANTONIO TEX.: United States — San Antonio, Texas.**
**SANDJAK D'ALEXANDRETTE** on stamps of Syria: **Alexandretta.**
**SANTANDER: Colombia — Santander.**
**SAORSTAT ERIEANN** ("Free State of Ireland") on stamps of Great Britain: **Ireland.**
**SARKARI: India — Soruth.**
**SASENO** on stamps of Italy: **Saseno.**
**SAURASHTRA** or **SOURRASHTRA: India — Soruth.**
**SCARPANTO** on stamps of Italy: **Italy — Aegean Islands — Scarpanto.**
**SCHLESWIG: Schleswig — Holstein.**
**SCINDE DISTRIC DAWK: India — South District.**
**SCTARI DI ALBANIA** on stamps of Italy: **Italy — Offices in Turkey — Scutari.**
**SCUDO: Roman States.**
**SEGNA TASSA** or **SEGNATASSE** with no country name: **Italy — Postage due.**

**SEJM WILNIE: Central Lithuania.**

**SELANGOR: Malay States — Selangor.**

**SEN, SN.: Japan, Ryukyu Islands.**

**SENEGAL** on stamps of French Colonies: **Senegal.**

**SENEGAMBIE ET NIGER: Senegambia and Niger.**

**SERBIEN** on stamps of Austria or Bosnia: **Serbia — Austria occupation.**

**SERVICE:** Official stamps of **India,** various Indian states, **Nepal, Pakistan.**

**SERVICO POSTAL MEXICANA: Mexico.**

**SEVILLA-BARCELONA: Spain.**

**S.H.: Schleswig-Holstein.**

**SHANGHAI** on stamps of United States: **United States — Offices in China.**

**SHQIPENA, SHQIPENIAE, SHQIPENIE, SHQIPERIA, SHQIPERIE, SHQIPERIJA, SHQIPERISE, SHQIPTARE, SHQIPNI, SHQIPNIJA, SHQIPONIES, SHQYPNIS, SHQYPAARE: Albania.**

**S.H.S.** (Abbreviation for "Serbs, Croats, Slovenes"): **Yugoslavia.**

**SIEGE DE LA LIGUE ARABE: Morocco.**

**SIEGE OF MAFEKINF: Cape of Good Hope.**

**SIMI** on stamps of Italy: **Italy — Aegean Islands — Simi.**

**SINGAPORE MALAYA: Singapore.**

**SIRMOOR: India — Sirmoor.**

**SKILLING: Denmark, Norway.**

**SLD.: Austria — Offices in Turkey.**

**SLESVIG: Schleswig.**

**SLOVENSKA POSTA** or **SLOVENSKO: Czechoslovakia — Slovakia.**

**SLOVENSKY STAT, SLOVENSKO** on stamps of Czechoslovakia: **Czechoslovakia — Slovakia.**

**S. MARINO: San Marino.**

**SMIRNE** on stamps of Italy: **Italy — Offices in Turkey — Smyrna;** on stamps of Russia: **Russia — Offices in Turkey.**

**S.O. 1920** on stamps of Czechoslovakia or Poland: **Eastern Silesia.**

**SOBRETASA AREA: Colombia.**

**SOCIALIST PEOPLE'S LIBYAN ARAB JAMAHIRIYA: Libya.**

**SOCIEDAD COLOMBIA—ALEMANA DE TRANSPORTES AEROEOS: Colombia.**

**SOCIEDAD DE GEOGRAPHIA DE LISBOA: Portugal.**

**SOCIETE DES NATIONS** ("League of Nations"): **Switzerland — Official Stamps for the League of Nations.**

**SOL: Peru.**

**SOLDI: Austria—Lombardy—Venetia.**

**SOLIDARITE FRANÇAISE: French Colonies.**

**SOMALIA** on stamps of Italy: **Somalia.**

**SOMALIA ITALIANA** on stamps of Italy: **Somalia.**

**SOMALI DEMOCRATIC REPUBLIC: Somalia.**

**SONORA: Mexico.**

**SOOMAALYA: Somalia.**

**SORUTH: India — Soruth.**

**SOUDAN** on stamps of Egypt: **Sudan;** on stamps of French Colonies: **French Sudan.**

**SOUDAN FRANÇAIS: French Sudan.**

**SOURASHTRA: India — Soruth.**

**SOUTHERN RHODESIA** on stamps of Great Britain: **Southern Rhodesia.**

**SOUTH GEORGIA** on stamps of Falkland Islands: **Falkland Islands Dependencies.**

**SOUTH ORKNEYS** on stamps of Falkland Islands: **Falkland Islands Dependencies.**

**SOUTH SHETLANDS** on stamps of Falkland Islands: **Falkland Islands Dependencies.**

**SOUTH WEST AFRICA** on stamps of South Africa: **South West Africa.**

**SOWJETISCHE BESATZUGS ZONE** on stamps of Germany: **Germany — Russian occupation.**

**SPARTA GEO.: United States — Sparta, Georgia.**

**SPARTANBURO S.C.: United States — Spartanburg, South Carolina.**

**SPM** on stamps of French Colonies: **St. Pierre and Miquelon.**

**S.Q. TRSTA—UVJA: Trieste — Zone B.**

**SRODKOWA LITVA: Central Lithuania.**

**ST, STG** ("stang"): **Siam.**

**STAMPALIA** on stamps of Italy: **Italy — Aegean Islands — Stampalia.**

**STATE OF SINGAPORE: Singapore.**

**STATI PARM,** or **PARMEASI: Parma.**

**S. THOME E PRINCIPE: St. Thomas and Prince Islands.**

**STOCKHOLM: Sweden.**

**Á    : Bulgaria.**

**ST.PIERRE M-ON** on stamps of French Colonies: **St. Pierre and Miquelon.**

**STRAITS SETTLEMENTS** on stamps of Labuan: **Straits Settlements.**

**S.T. TRSTA-VUJA: Trieste — Zone B.**

**STT UVJA: Trieste — Zone B;** on stamps of Yugoslavia: **Trieste — Zone B.**

**S.U.** on stamps of Straits Settlements: **Malay States — Sungei Ujong.**

**SUIDAFRIKA: South Africa.**

**SUIDWES AFRIKA: South West Africa.**

**S. UJONG: Malay States — Sungei Ujong.**

**SUL BOLLETTINO** or **SULLA RICEVUTA: Italy,** unless additionally overprinted for the various Italian Colonies; on stamps with star and crescent emblem: **Somalia.**

**SULTANT D'ANJOUAN: Anjouan.**

**SULTANATE OF OMAN** on stamps of Muscat and Oman: **Oman.**

**SUNGEI UJONG: Malay States — Sungei Ujong.**

**SUOMI: Finland.**

**SURINAME: Surinam.**

**SVERIGE: Sweden.**

**S.W.A.: South West Africa.**

**SWAZIELAND: Swaziland.**

**SWAZILAND** on stamps of South Africa: **Swaziland.**

**SYRIAN ARAB REPUBLIC: Syria.**

**SYRIE, SYRIENNE: Syria.**

# T

**T: Belgium;** in four corners of stamp, with numeral in center: **Dominican Republic;** enclosed in a circle: **Peru — Huacho.**

**TAHITI** on stamps of French Colonies: **Tahiti.**

**TAKCA: Bulgaria.**

**TAKSE: Albania.**

**TALBOTTON GA.: United States — Talbotton, Georgia.**

**TANGANYIKA, KENYA, UGANDA: Kenya, Uganda and Tanzania.**

**TANGANYIKA ZANZIBAR: Tanzania.**

**TANGER** with "Correo Espanol": **Spanish Morocco — Tangier;** on stamps of France: **French Morocco;** on stamps of Great Britain: **Great Britain — Offices in Morocco.**

**TANZANIA, KENYA, UGANDA: Kenya, Uganda and Tanzania.**

**TASE GAZZETTE: Modena.**

**TAXA DE GUERRA** ("War tax") with value in AVOS: **Macao;** with value in OS: **Portugese Africa;** with values in RP: **Portuguese India;** with values in REIS: **Portuguese Guinea.**

**TAXE: Albania.**

**TC** on stamps of India or Cochin: **India — Travancore — Cochin.**

**T.C.E.K.: Turkey.**

**TCHAD: Chad.**

**TCHONGKING** on stamps of Indo-China: **France — Offices in China — Tchong King.**

**T.C. POSTALARI: Turkey.**

**TE BETALEN: Dutch Indies, Netherlands, Netherlands Antilles, Suriname;** preceded by "A PAYER": **Belgium.**

**TE BETALEN PORT** on red or carmine stamps: **Dutch Indies;** on vermillion stamps: **Dutch New Guinea;** on blue stamps: **Netherlands;** on green stamps: **Netherlands Antilles;** on lilac or purple stamps: **Surinam.**

**TELLICO PLAINS TENN.: United States — Tellico Plains, Tennessee.**

**T.E.O.** ("Occupied Territories of the Enemy") with denominations in Millemes on stamps of France: **Syria;** on stamps of **France — Offices in Turkey: Cilicia.**

**TERRES AUSTRALES ET ANTARCTIQUES FRANÇISES: French Southern and Antarctic Territories.**

**TERRITOIRE DE IFNI** on stamps of Spain: **Ifni.**

**TERRITOIRE DE'ININI: Inini.**

**TERRITOIRE DU FEZZAN: Libya — Fezzan — French occupation.**

**TERRITOIRE DU NIGER: Niger.**

**TERRITOIRE FRANÇAIS DES AFARS ET ISSAS: Afars and Issas.**

**TERRITORIO DE IFNI (ESPANA): Ifni.**

**TERRITORIOS DEL AFRICA OCCIDENTAL ESPANOLA: Spanish West Africa.**

**TERRITORIOS or TERRS. ESPANOLES DEL GOLFO DE GUINEA: Spanish**

Guinea.

**TETUAN: Spanish Morocco — Tetuan.**

**THAILAND** or **THAI: Siam.**

**THAILAND** with values in cents: **Malaya — Siamese occupation.**

**THOMASVILLE GA.: United States — Thomasville, Georgia.**

**THRACE INTERALLIEE** or **THRACE OCCIDENTAL** on stamps of Bulgaria: **Thrace.**

**TIENTSIN** on stamps of Italy: **Italy — Offices in China — Tien Tsin.**

**TIMBE IMPERIAL JOURNAUX: France.**

**TIMBER POSTE** on stamps of France: **French Morocco.**

**TIMBRE TAXE** with numeral and no country name: **French Colonies.**

**TIMOR** on stamps of Macao or Mozambique: **Timor.**

**TJENESTEFIRMERKE: Norway.**

**TJENEST-FRIMARKE: Denmark.**

**TOGA: Tonga.**

**TOGO** on stamps of Dahomey, Germany or Gold Coast: **Togo.**

**TOLIMA: Columbia — Tolima.**

**TO PAY: Great Britain — Postage due.**

**TOSCONO: Tuscany.**

**TOU.: Persia.**

**TOUVA: Tannu Tuva.**

**TRAITE DE VERSAILLES: Allenstein**

**TRANS-JORDAN: Jordan.**

**TRANSPORTO PACCHI IN CONCESSIONE: Italy** — Authorized delivery stamps.

**TRAVANCORE: India — Travancore.**

**TRAVANCORE—COCHIN: India — Travancore — Cochin.**

**TREBIZONDE** on stamps of Russia: **Russia — Offices in Turkey.**

**TRENGGANU: Malay States — Trengganu.**

**TRIPOLI: Tripolitania;** preceded by "FIERA CAMPIONARIA": **Libya.**

**TRIPOLI DI BARBERIA** on stamps of Italy: **Italy — Offices in Africa — Tripoli.**

**TRIPOLITANIA** on stamps of Italy: **Tripolitania.**

**TRISTAN DA CUNHA** on stamps of St. Helena: **Tristan da Cunba.**

**T. Ta. C.: Turkey.**

**TULLAHOMA TEN.: United States — Tullahoma, Tennessee.**

**TUNIS, TUNISIE: Tunisia.**

**TURKIYE CUMHURIYETI: Turkey.**

**TURKIYE, TURK POSTALARI: Turkey.**

**TUSCUMBIA: United States — Tuscumbia, Alabama.**

**TUSCUMBIA ALA.: United States — Tuscumbia, Alabama.**

**T. WELSH: United States — Montgomery, Alabama.**

**TWO PENCE** under an enthroned queen: **Victoria.**

ЦАРСТВО: **Bulgaria.**

ЦАРСТВО БЪЛГАРИЯ: **Bulgaria.**

**U.A.R.** (United Arab Republic) with values in "M" or "£": **Egypt;** with values in "P": **Syria — United Arab Republic.**

**U.G.: Uganda.**

**UGANDA** on stamps of British East Africa: **Uganda.**

**UGANDA, KENYA, TANGANYIKA: Kenya, Uganda and Tanzania.**

**UGANDA, KENYA, TANZANIA: Kenya, Uganda and Tanzania.**

**UKRAINE** on stamps of Germany: **Russia — German occupation.**

**ULTRAMAR** ("Beyond the Sea") with a year date: **Cuba, Puerto Rico;** with denominations in "AVOS" or "REIS": **Guinea, Macao.**

**UNEF** on stamps of India: **India — Military stamps — Gaza.**

**U.N. FORCE (INDIA) CONGO** on stamps of India: **India — Military stamps — Congo.**

**UNION CITY, TENNESSEE: United States — Union City, Tennessee.**

**UNITED ARAB EMIRATES** on stamps of Abu Dhabi: **United Arab Emirates.**

**UNTEA** on stamps of Dutch New Guinea: **West New Guinea.**

UOPTO OKPИCOPИ: **Romania — Moldavia.**

ЦРНА ГОРА: **Montenegro — Italian occupation.**

**URUNDI** on stamps of Congo Democratic Republic (ex-Belgian): **German East Africa — Belgian occupation.**

**US** or **U.S.A.: United States.**

**U.S. PENNY POST: United States — St. Louis, Missouri.**

**U.S.P.O.: United States.**

**VALDOSTA GA.: United States — Valdosta, Georgia.**

**VALLEES D'ANDORRE: Andorra.**

**VALONA** on stamps of Italy: **Italy — Offices in Turkey.**

**VALPARAISO MULTADO: Chile.**

**VANCOUVER ISLAND: British Columbia and Vancouver Island.**

**VAN DIEMEN'S LAND: Tasmania.**

**VATHY: France — Offices in Turkey.**

**VATICANE or VATICANA: Vatican City.**

**VENEZIA GIULIA, VENEZIA TRIDENTINA** on stamps of Austria or Italy: **Austria — Italian occupation.**

**VENZ, VENSOLANO: Venezuela.**

**VEREINTE NATIONEN:** United Nations — Offices in Vienna.
**VICTORIA:** United States — Victoria, Texas.
**VIET-NAM CONG-HOA:** Viet Nam.
**VIVA ESPANA CORRES AERO** on stamps of Spain: **Spain — various states.**
**VOJNA UPRAVA JUGOSLVENSKE ARMIJE** on  stamps of Yugoslavia:
        **Yugoslavia — Issues for Istria and the Slovene Coast.**
**VOM EMPFANGER EINZUZIEMEN:** Danzig.
**V.R. SPECIAL POST** on stamps of Transvaal: **Cape of Good Hope.**
**VUJA STT or VUJNA STT** on stamps of Yugoslavia: **Trieste — Zone B.**

**WADHWAN:** India — Wadhwan.
**WARRENTON GA.:** United States — Warrenton, Georgia.
**W. AUSTRALIA:** Western Australia.
**W.D. COLEMAN:** United States — Danville, Virginia.
**WENDENSCHNE:** Russia — Wenden.
**WEST AUSTRALIA:** Western Australia.
**WESTERN SAMOA:** Samoa.
**WHARTON'S:** United States — Louisville, Kentucky.
**WILLIAMS:** United States — Cincinnati, Ohio.
**WINNSBOROUGH S.C.:** United States — Winnsborough, South Carolina.
**WN** ("weun"): **Korea.**
**WURTTEMBERG:** Germany — Wurttemberg — French Occupation,
        Wurttemberg.
**WYTHEVILLE VA.:** United States — Wytheville, Virginia.

**ΧΑΡΤΟΣΗΜΟΝ:** Greece.
**ΧΕJΕΡΑ:** Montenegro.
**ΧΕΛΕΡΑ:** Montenegro.
**XII CAMPIONARIA TRIPOLI** ("12th Tripoli Fair"): **Libya.**

# Y

**YCA** on stamps of Peru: **Peru — Yca.**
**Y.C.C.P.: Ukraine;** on stamps of Russia: **Ukraine.**
**YCTAB: Montenegro.**
**YEMEN ARAB REPUBLIC: Yemen.**
**YEMEN PDR: Yemen People's Republic.**
**YEN, YN.: Japan, Manchuko, Ryukyu Islands.**
**YKP** on stamps of Austria: **Western Ukraine.**
**УКРАІНСЬКА : Ukraine.**
**YUNNAN FOU** on stamps of Indo-China: **France — Offices in China — Yunnan Fou.**
**YUNNANSEN** on stamps of Indo-China: **France — Offices in China — Yunnan Fou.**

# Z

**Z. AFR. REPUBLIEK, ZUID AFRIKAANSCHE REPUBLIEK** ("South African Republic"): **Transvaal.**
**ZANZIBAR** on stamps of France: **France — Offices in Zanzibar;** on stamps of British East Africa or India: **Zanzibar.**
**ZANZIBAR TANZANIA: Zanzibar.**
**ZEGELREGT: Transvaal.**
**ZELAYA: Nicaraugua — Zelaya.**
**ZENTRALER KURIERDIENST: Germany — German Democratic Republic.**
**ZONA DE OCUPATIE ROMANIA** on stamps of Hungary: **Hungary — Roumanian occupation.**
**ZONA PROTECTORADO ESPANOL** on stamps of Spain: **Spanish Morocco.**
**ZONE FRANÇAISE: Germany — French occupation.**
**ZRACNA POSTA: Trieste — Zone B.**
**ZUIDWEST AFRIKA: South West Africa.**
**ZULULAND** on stamps of Great Britain or Natal: **Zululand.**
**ZURICH: Switzerland.**

# MISCELLANEOUS

**3.y.H.B.** on stamps of Austria: **Western Ukraine.**
**ПАРА, ПАРЕ: Montenegro, Serbia.**
**ПОРТО МАПКА: Serbia.**
**ПОУТА: Russia.**
**বাংলাদেশ : Bangledesh.**

# OTHER HARD-TO-IDENTIFY STAMPS

A class of stamps very difficult to identify are those which are not inscribed with any recognizable words and therefore cannot be indexed in the preceding word-list. Such stamps should be checked in this section of STAMP IDENTIFIER.

It is impossible, because of limited space to illustrate all stamps of this kind. We have tried to show a sufficient number so that you can identify virtually all of the others.

## AFGHANISTAN

Tiger's head and crudely drawn mosque encircled in wreath or ornament identify many of the early issues.

## ARMENIA

## ARMENIA

Inscription resembling "ZULZ" and "N.F.L." and national emblem — a star, sometimes enclosing a hammer and sickle — identify many stamps of Armenia.

## AUSTRIA

## AZERBAIJAN

## BANGLADESH

## BATUM

## BOSNIA & HERZEGOVINA

These stamps, if imperforate, belong under Bosnia & Herzegovina; if perforate, under Yugoslavia.

ДРЖАВА С.Х.С.
Босна и Херцеговина  ═══  JUGOSLAVIA

## BRAZIL

---

## BULGARIA
## БЪЛГАРИЯ     БЪЛГАРСКА

**overprinted: ROMANIA — Bulgarian Occupation**

Лоша Въ Ромжиия
1916-1917

---

## BURMA
### under Japanese Occupation

**overprinted
under
Japanese Occupation**

## CHINA

The typical Chinese characters, and the sun emblem in a circle, identify many stamps of China.

## CRETE

ΑΕΠΤΑ.ΑΕΠΤΟΝ    ΠΡΟΣΩΡΙΝΟΝ
ΔΡ..ΔΡΑΧΜΗ       ΜΕΤΑΑΛΙΚ
ΕΛΛΑΣ

## CUBA
### under Spanish Occupation

**overprinted: PUERTO RICO**

## NETHERLANDS INDIES
### Under Japanese Occupation

83

## EGYPT

## EPIRUS

ΛΕΠΤΑ.ΛΕΠΤΟΝ
ΗΠΕΙΡΟΣ
ΔΡ..ΔΡΑΧΜΗ

## ETHIOPIA

## FAR EASTERN REPUBLIC

ЦОЧТОВАЯ    МАРКА·

## FAR EASTERN REPUBLIC

**overprinted:**
**SIBERIA**

## FINLAND
## ЦОЧТОВАЯ   МАРКА

## FRENCH COLONIES

**2 CENTS**

— Offices in China

**5**

— French Morocco

## FRANCE

The stamps shown, if perforated, are France, if imperforate, French Colonies. The stamps show are French Colonies.

**85**

## FRENCH COLONIES

Stamps of the type shown were issued for general use in all the French Colonies. To suit local postal needs, varous colonies surcharged these stamps with new denominations. The surcharged issues were thereafter classified under the heading of the colony which surcharged and used them. Each colony's surcharges were printed in a characteristic style of type as shown. In some cases denominations additional to those pictured here were used but the style of type remains constant and makes identification possible.

**overprinted:**

**REUNION**                **Annam and Tonkin**

## GERMANY

**overprinted: FRANCE under German Occupation**

**AUSTRIA**      **Lothringen**      **Elſaß**

**overprinted: POLAND under German Occupation**

**Ruſſiſch-Polen**      **Gen:-Gouv Warſchau**

## GERMANY

**overprinted: ROMANIA under German Occupation**

| | |
|---|---|
| **M.V.i.R** <br> **25 Bani** | **Rumänien** <br> **25 Bani** |

## GEORGIA

## GREAT BRITAIN

**overprinted:**
**IRELAND**

Rialtar
Sealadac
na
hÉireann
1922

Saorstat
Éireann
1922

**overprinted: OMAN**

| $2\frac{1}{2}$ <br> **ANNAS** | **2 RUPEES** | **1** <br> **ANNA** |
|---|---|---|

## GREECE

ΕΛΛΑΣ    ΔΡ..ΔΡΑΧΜΗ
ΛΕΠΤΑ.ΛΕΠΤΟΝ

## GREECE
### overprinted: THRACE

Διοίκησις
Διτικῆς
Θράκης

## HUNGARY

**INDIA - Gwalior**     **INDIA**     **MUSCAT**

गवालियर

सरविस

## INDIA NATIVE STATES

**ALWAR**     **BHOPAL**     **BUNDI**     overprinted: **Rajasthan**

**DHAR**     **FARIDKOT**     **JAMMU & KASHMIR**

# INDIAN NATIVE STATES

### JASDAN    JHALAWAR    KISHANGARH    RAJPEEPLA
### JHIND

### NANDGAON        POONCH        NOWANUGGUR

# IRELAND

# ISRAEL

# JAPAN

A stylized chrysanthemum,. the national emblem of Imperial Japan was included in virtually all stamp designs produced by this country through 1947. Nearly all subsequent issues bear the name of Japan in four Japanese characters, arranged either vertically or horizontally.

**89**

# HOW TO COLLECT STAMPS

## JAPAN

| HONG KONG under Japanese Occupation | NORTH BORNEO under Japanese Occupation | KOREA under U.S. MILITARY Rule |
|---|---|---|
|   |  |  |

## JORDAN

## KOREA

The national emblem of Korea and the characteristic letters under the initials "CH" will enable you to identify most issues.

## LEBANON

## LIBYA

## LOURENCO MARQUES

**Overprinted:**

**10 c.**

**MOZAMBIQUE**

## MALAYA
### under Japanese Occupation

**91**

## MALAY STATES

**Kelantan**

**Pahang**

**Perak**

**Negri Sembilan**

**Selangor**

**Trengganu**

## MANCHUKUO

## MAURITANIA

**5 fr.**  **=**

overprinted:
**FRENCH WEST AFRICA**

## MONGOLIA

## MONTENEGRO

ПОШТЕПРНЕГОРЕ   ПАРА,ПАРЕ
ХЕЛЕР

## NEPAL

93

## PAKISTAN

## PAKISTAN
### Bahawalpur

## PALESTINE

شرقي الاردن

شرق الاردن

**overprinted:
TRANS-JORDAN**

## PANAMA

## PERSIA (IRAN)

The heraldic lion brandishing a sword before the rising sun is the national emblem of Persia and identifies many early issues. Many later issues of Persia may be identified by the Arabic lettering shown in the lower central portion of the last stamp pictured.

## PHILIPPINES
### under Japanese Occupation

## RUSSIA

# ЦОЧТОВАЯ МАРКА Р.С.Ф.С.Р.

All Russian stamps issued since 1922 bear the initials "CCCP", the Russian abbreviation for "Union of Soviet Socialist Republics."

**RUSSIA**
overprinted:

**ARMENIA**

к 60 к

10 г      5 г

**FAR EASTERN REPUBLIC**

Д.        В.
коп 1 коп.
золотом

**SIBERIA**

Прид
Земскій
Край

**GEORGIA**

15.000 ӡ5б

200000
ӡ5б.

**SOUTH RUSSIA**

| 25 | 1 р. | 70 коп. | 10 рублей |
|---|---|---|---|
| —25 | —1 р. | | —70 к. |

5

пять

рублей.

35 коп.

— 3 —
рубля

**TRANSCAUCASIAN FEDERATED REPUBLICS**

700000 РУБ.

| | | |
|---|---|---|
| **Р. О. П. и Т.** | **RUSSIA**<br>**overprinted:**<br>**UKRAINE**<br>**35 к.** |  |

### How to Identify Early
### Issues of Russia and Finland

Stamps of Finland are identical to stamps of Russia except for the dots in circles worked into the background.

Stamps of Finland are lettered for Finnish currency, penna and markaa. Closely similar Russian stamps are lettered in Kopeks and rubles.

## RYUKYU ISLANDS

The country named its own language, arranged horizontally or vertically as shown, and denominations in $ and ¢, will identify most of the issues.

**97**

## SAUDI ARABIA

## SAUDI ARABIA - HEJAZ

## SAUDI ARABIA
### overprinted:
### NEJD

## SAUDI ARABIA overprinted: TRANS-JORDAN

## SAUDI ARABIA - Nejd
**overprinted:**
**TRANS-JORDAN**

| | | |
|---|---|---|
| حكومة | | فن٠ فن٠ ج |
| التنرق العربية | يكرمة | مالك العرب |
| مشنتق | التنرق العربية | اج ١١ |
| ٩ نسان ١٣٤١م | ٥ ثجار ١١٠ | |

حكومة التنرق
العربي
١٣٤٢

---

## SENEGAL overprinted: FRENCH WEST AFRICA

**50 fr.**

=

---

## SERBIA

ИАРА, ИАРЕ     СРЛСКА СРВИЈА

**overprinted: JUGOSLAVIA**

Демократска
Федеративна
Југославија

**+3**     =

99

## SIAM (THAILAND)

## SIBERIA

**overprinted:**
**FAR EASTERN REPUBLIC**

## SOUTH RUSSIA

## SWITZERLAND

## SYRIA

## SYRIA

**overprinted:**
**UNITED ARAB REPUBLIC**

الجمهورية العربية المتحدة
**U . A . R**

## TANNU TUVA

## THRACE  ΘΡΑΚΗΣ. Θραχης

## TRANSCAUCASIAN FEDERATED REPUBLICS

3. C. Ф. C. P.

## TURKEY

Many early issues of Turkey are identified by the "tughra" or sultan's monogram or by the star and crescent, Turkish national emblem. But — caution! — the star and crescent is also the national emblem of Tunisia and of Pakistan; and the tughra appears on some of the early issues of Saudi Arabia.

## TURKEY

**GREECE overprinted: — Mytilene**

Ἑλληνικὴ Κατοχὴ Μυτιλήνης

---

**overprinted: THRACE**

Ὑπότη Ἁρμοστεία
Θραχης
δ Λεπτὰ 5

---

**overprinted: SYRIA**

102

## SAUDIA ARABIA
**overprinted:**
**— Najd**

## UKRAINE
# НАРОДНЯ - РЕСПУБЛІКА

**103**

# The UNITED STATES

# Stamp Identifier

## SHOWS YOU HOW TO DISTINGUISH BETWEEN THE RARE AND COMMON UNITED STATES STAMPS THAT LOOK ALIKE

What does "Grill with points up" mean? "Single line watermark?" How can I tell whether my 15¢ "Landing of Columbus" stamp of 1869 is worth $1,150.00 (Type I), $575.00 (Type II), or the newly discovered Type III.

At one time or another, every collector of United States stamps asks questions like these. For very often, it is a minute difference in design that determines not only whether a stamp is Type I, II, or III, but whether it is a great rarity or just another common variety. The different varieties of the 1¢ Franklin design of 1851-56, for example, range in price from $60.00 to $95,000.00. So it pays to know how to tell

the correct types of your stamps! To enable you to do so easily and quickly is the purpose of this U.S. STAMP IDENTIFIER.

Other seemingly identical, but actually different United States stamps may be told apart by differences in perforations, watermarks, grills or methods in printing. These terms are fully explained in the Guide for Collectors section of this catalog. And charts are included to make it easy for you to quickly identify the many Bank Note varieties and the most troublesome of U.S. stamps — the hard-to-classify regular issues of 1908 to 1932.

*Illustrations and catalog numbers herein are from the Standard Postage Stamp Catalogue, by special permission of the publishers, Scott Publications, Inc.*

## FIRST UNITED STATES POSTAGE ISSUE OF 1847

 #1    #2

 #3    #1,3    #2,4    #4

The first stamps of the United States Government, the 5¢ and 10¢ designs shown to the left above, were placed in use in July 1847, superseding the Postmasters' Provisionals then being used in several cities. In 1875, official reproductions (right above) were made from newly engraved printing plates.

In the original 5¢ design, the top edge of Franklin's shirt touches the circular frame abuot at a level with the top of the "F" of "FIVE", while in the 1875 reproduction it is on a level with the top of the figure "5."

In the original 10¢ design, the left edge of Washington's coat points to the "T" of "TEN", and the right

edge points between the "T" and "S" of "CENTS." In the reproductions, the left and right outlines of the coat point to the right edge of "X" and to the center of "S" in "CENTS" respectively. Also, on the 1875 reprints, the eyes have a sleepy look and the line of the mouth is straighter.

The 1947 "Cipex" Souvenir Sheet, issued on the hundredth anniversary of United States stamps, features reproductions of the two original designs. Stamps cut out of the souvenir sheet are, of course, valid for postage. However, no difficulty in identification should be encountered since the 1947 reproductions are light blue (5¢) instead of the original red brown and browinsh orange (10¢) instead of the original black.

# TYPES OF THE 1¢ FRANKLIN DESIGN OF 1851-60

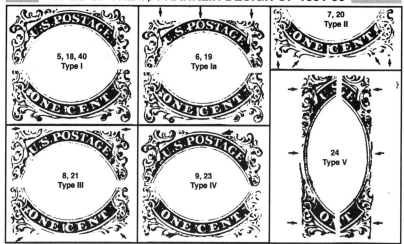

5, 18, 40
Type I

6, 19
Type Ia

7, 20
Type II

8, 21
Type III

9, 23
Type IV

24
Type V

**TYPE I** has the most complete design of the various types of this stamp. At the top and bottom there is an unbroken curved line running outside the bands reading "U.S. POSTAGE" and "ONE CENT." The scrolls at bottom are turned under, forming curls. The scrolls and outer line at top are complete.

**TYPE Ia** is like Type I at bottom but ornaments and curved line at top are partly cut away.

**TYPE Ib** (not illustrated) is like Type I at top but little curls at bottom are not quite so complete nor clear and scroll work is partly cut away 5A.

**TYPE II** has the outside bottom line complete, but the little curls of the bottom scroll, and the lower part of the plume ornaments are missing. Side ornaments are complete.

**TYPE III** has the outside lines at both top and bottom partly cut away in the middle. The side ornaments are complete.

**TYPE IIIa.** (not illustrated) is similar to Type III with the outer line cut away at top or bottom, but not both. 8A, 22.

**TYPE IV** is similar to Type II but the curved lines at top or bottom (or both) have been recut in several different ways, and usually appear thicker than Type II.

**TYPE V** is similar to Type III but has the side ornaments partly cut away. Type V occurs only on perforated stamps.

## TYPES OF 3¢ WASHINGTON DESIGN OF 1851-60

10,11, 25, 41
Type I

26
Type II

26a
Type IIa

**TYPE I** has a frame line around the top, bottom and sides.
**TYPE II** has the frame line removed at top and bottom, while the side frame lines are continuous from top to bottom of the plate.

**TYPE IIa** is similar to Type II, but the side frame lines were recut individually, hence are broken between stamps.

## TYPES OF THE 5¢ JEFFERSON DESIGN OF 1851-60

**TYPE I** is a complete design with projections (arrow) at the top and bottom as well as at the sides.

**TYPE II** has the projections at the top and bottom partly or completely cut away.

**105**

13, 31, 43
Type 1

14, 32
Type II

15, 33
Type II

16, 34
Type IV

35
Type V

**TYPE I** has the "shells" at the lower corners practically complete, while the outer line below "TEN CENTS" is very nearly complete. At the top, the outer lines are broken above "U.S. POSTAGE" and show the "X" in each corner.

**TYPE II** has the design complete at the top, but the outer line at the bottom is broken in the middle and the "shells" are partially cut away.

**TYPE III** has both top and bottom outer lines partly cut away: that is similar to Type I at the top and Type II at the bottom.

**TYPE IV** has the outer lines at the top or bottom of the stam, or at both places, recut to show more strongly and heavily.

**TYPES I, II, and IV** have complete ornaments at the sides and three small circles or pearls (arrow) at the outer edges of the bottom panel.

**TYPE V** has the side ornaments, including one or two of the small "pearls," partly cut away. The outside line over the "X" at the right top has also been partly cut away.

---

## 1851-60 12¢ Issues, plate 1 (Scott #s 17, 36), plate 3 (Scott #36b)

Plate 1 has stronger, more complete outer frame lines than does plate 3. Comes imperforate (#17) or perf 15 (#36)

Plate 3 has uneven or broken outer frame lines that are particulary noticeable in the corners. The stamps are perf 15.

The REPRINT plate (not illustrated) is similar to plate 1, but the Reprint stamps are greenish black and slightly taller than plate 1 stamps (25 mm. from top to bottom frame lines vs. 24.5 mm.) The paper is whiter and the perforations are 12 gauge.

---

## TYPES OF THE 1861 ISSUE, GRILLS & RE-ISSUES

Shortly after the outbreak of the Civil War in 1861, the Post Office demonetized all stamps issued up to that time in order to prevent their use by the Confederacy. Two new sets of designs, consisting of six stamps shown above plus the 24¢ and 30¢ denominations, were prepared by the American Bank Note Company. The first designs, except for the 10¢ and 24¢ values, were not regularly issued and are extremely rare and valuable. The second designs became the regular issue of 1861. The illustrations in the left column on page 5 show the first or (un-issued) designs, which were all printed on thin, semi-transparent paper. The second (or regular) designs are shown at the right.

**63, 85A, 86, 92, 103**

**55**

**63** shows a small dash (arrow) under the top of the ornaments at the right of the figure "1" in the upper left hand corner of the stamp.

**64-66, 74, 79, 82, 83, 85, 85C, 88, 94, 104**

**56**

**64,66, etc.** show a small ball (arrow) at each corner of the design. Also, the ornaments at the corner are larger than in A25a.

**3¢ 1861 PINK** (Scott's #64) — It is impossible to describe a "pink" in words, but it might be helpful to remember that this stamp is usually rather heavily inked, and has a tinge of blue or purple which makes it stand out from the various shades of rose to red brown sometimes mistaken for it.

**67, 75, 76, 80, 95, 105**

**57**

**64, 75, etc.** have a leaflet (arrow) projecting from the scrolled ornament at each corner of the stamp.

**58, 62B**

**58, 62B** has no curved line below the row of stars and there is only one outer line of the ornaments above them.

**68, 85D 89, 96, 106**

These have a heavy curved line below the row of stars (arrow), and the ornaments above the stars have a double outer line.

**69, 85E, 90,97,107**

**59**

**69/107** have an oval and scroll (arrow) in each corner of the design. **59** has no such design and the corners are rounded.

**62**

**62** does not have the row of dashes or spot of color present in **72/111**

**72, 101, 111**

**72/111** have a row of small dashes between the parallel lines of the angle at the top center of the stamp. There is also a spot of color (arrow) in the apex of the lower line of the single.

## TYPES OF THE 15¢ "LANDING OF COLUMBUS" DESIGN OF 1869

**118: Type I**

**119: Type II**

**118, TYPE I** has the central picture without the frame line shown in Type II.

**119, TYPE II** has a frame line (arrows) around the central picture; also a diamond shaped ornament appears below the "T" of "POSTAGE."

**129: Type I, II**

**129: Type III**

**129, TYPE III** is like Type I except that the fringe of brown shading lines which appears around the sides and bottom of the picture on Types I and II has been removed.

**107**

| Description and Identifying Features | 1¢ | 2¢ | 3¢ | 5¢ | 10¢ | 12¢ | 15¢ | 24¢ | 30¢ | 90¢ |
|---|---|---|---|---|---|---|---|---|---|---|
| 1861. National. First Designs. Thin, semi-transparent paper. No grill | 55 | | 56 | 57 | 58[1] 62B | 59 | | 60 | 61 | 62 |
| 1861-62. National. Modified designs.[3] Thicker, opaque paper. No grill. | 63 | | 64[2] 65[2] 66[2] | 67 | 68 | 69 | | 70[2] | 71 | 72 |
| 1861-66. National. Thicker, opaque paper. No grill. a. New designs | | 73 | | | | | 77 | | | |
| b. Same designs, new shades | | | 74[2] | 75[2] 76[2] | | | | 78[2] | | |

1867. National. Grills, all on thick, opaque paper.

| Grills | Pts. as seen from stamp face | Area coveren Horiz X Vert. | # of rows of Pts. | 1¢ | 2¢ | 3¢ | 5¢ | 10¢ | 12¢ | 15¢ | 24¢ | 30¢ | 90¢ |
|---|---|---|---|---|---|---|---|---|---|---|---|---|---|
| A | Up | All over | — | | | | 79 | 80 | | | | 81 | |
| B | Up | 18x15 mm | 22x18 | | | 82 | | | | | | | |
| C | Up | c.13x16 mm | 16-17x 18-21 | | | 83 | | | | | | | |
| D | Down | c.12x14 mm | 15x17-18 | | 84 | 85 | | | | | | | |
| Z | Down | c. 11x14 mm | 13-14x 17-18 | 85A | 85B | 85C | | | 85D | 85E | 85F | | |
| E | Down | c. 11x13 mm | 14x15-17 | 86 | 87 | 88 | | | 89 | 90 | 91 | | |
| F | Down | c. 90x13 mm | 11-12x 15-17 | 92 | 93 | 94 | 95 | 96 | 97 | 98 | 99 | 100 | 101 |

| Description and Identifying Features | 1¢ | 2¢ | 3¢ | 5¢ | 10¢ | 12¢ | 15¢ | 24¢ | 30¢ | 90¢ |
|---|---|---|---|---|---|---|---|---|---|---|
| 1875, National. Re-issues. Hard, white paper. White crackly gum. No grill. | 102 | 103 | 104 | 105 | 106 | 107 | 108 | 109 | 110 | 111 |

Footnotes:
1. #58 does not exist used. Unused, it cannot be distinguished from #62B
2. Different from corresponding 1861-66 issues only in color.
3. See diagrams for design modification.

# TYPES OF THE 1870-71 THROUGH 1887 BANK NOTES

The stamps of the 1870-71 issue were printed by the National Bank Note Company. The similar issue of 1873 was printed by the Continental Bank Note Company. When Continental took over the plates previously used by National, they applied so-called "secret marks" to the designs of the 1¢ through 15¢ denominations by which the two issues can be distinguished as shown below. The illustrations at the left show the original designs of 1870-71; those at the right show the secret marks applied to the issue of 1873.

| ISSUE OF 1870-71 | ISSUES OF 1873-87 | ISSUE OF 1870-71 | ISSUES OF 1873-87 |
|---|---|---|---|
|   |  |  |  |
| **134, 145** | **156, 167, 182, 192** | **135, 146** | **157, 158, 178, 180, 183, 193, 203** |
| **156/192** have a small curved mark in the pearl at the left of the figure "**T**." | | **135 and 146** are red brown. 157 and later numbers have a small diagonal line under the scroll at the left of the "U.S." (arrow). 135, 146, 157, 168 and 193 are various shades of brown. 178, 180, 183 and 203 are shades of vermilion. | |
|   |  |  |  |
| **136, 147** | **158, 169, 184, 194** | **137, 148** | **159, 170, 186, 195** |
| **158** and later numbers have the ribbon under the letters "RE" heavily shaded. | | **159** and later numbers have the first four vertical lines of shading in the lower part of the left ribbon greatly strengthened. | |
|  | |  | |
| **138, 149** | **160, 171, 196** | **139, 150, 187** | **161, 172, 188, 197** |
| **160** and later numbers have two tiny semi-circles drawn around the end of the lines which outlines the ball in the lower right hand corner. | | **161, 172, 188** and **197** have a small semi-circle in the scroll at the right-hand side of the central design. | |
|  |  |  |  |
| **140, 151** | **162, 173, 198** | **141, 152** | **163, 174, 189, 199** |
| **162** and later numbers have the "balls" at the top and bottom of the figure "2" crescent-shaped instead of nearly round as in **140** and **151**. | | **163** and later numbers have strengthened lines (arrow) in the triangle in the upper left-hand corner, forming a "V." | |

The 1¢, 3¢, 6¢ and 10¢ denominations of the 1873 & 1879 issues, shown above were re-engraved in 1881-82. The new plates resulted in four variations described below. The background shading lines in all four of these stamps appear stronger and more heavily inked than in the earlier designs.

**206**

**208**

206 has strengthened vertical shading lines in the upper part of the stamp, making the background appear almost solid. Lines of shading have also been added to the curving ornaments in the upper corners.

208 has only three vertical lines between the edge of the panel and the outside left margin of the stamp. (In the preceding issues there were four such lines.)

**207, 214**

**209**

**207** and **214** have a solid shading line at the sides of the central oval (arrow) that is only about half the previous width. Also a short horizontal line has been cut below the "TS" of "CENTS." **207** and **214** can be told apart by their colors.

**209** has only four vertical lines between the left side of the oval and the edge of the shield. (In the preceding issues there were five such lines.) Also, the lines in the background have been made much heavier so that these stamps appear more heavily inked than previous issues.

## TYPES OF THE REGULAR ISSUES OF 1890-98

**1890-93.** This issue, printed by the American Bank Note Company, consists of a 1¢, 2¢, 3¢, 4¢, 5¢, 6¢, 8¢, 10¢, 15¢, 30¢ and 90¢ denominations.

**1894-98.** This issue — and all subsequent regular United States issues — were printed by the Bureau of Engraving and Printing, Washington, D.C. In more recent years, starting in 1943, some commemorative issues were printed by private firms. The 1894-98 "Bureau" issue is similar in design to the issue of 1890 but triangles (arrows) were added to the upper corners of the stamps and there are some differences in denominations.

## 2¢ "CAP ON 2" VARIETY OF 1890

Cap on left "2"

Cap on right "2"

Plate defects in the printing of the 2¢ "Washington" stamp of 1890 accounts for the "Cap on left 2" and "Cap on both 2s" varieties illustrated above.

| Description and Identifying features | 1¢ | 2¢ | 3¢ | 5¢ | 6¢ | 7¢ | 10¢ | 12¢ | 15¢ | 21¢ | 30¢ | 90¢ |
|---|---|---|---|---|---|---|---|---|---|---|---|---|
| 1870-71, National. No secret marks. White wove paper, thin to medium thick. With grills | 134 | 135 | 136 | | 137 | 138 | 139 | 140 | 141 | 142 | 143 | 144 |
| 1870-71, National. As above, except without grills. | 145 | 146 | 147 | | 148 | 149 | 150 | 151 | 152 | 153 | 154[2] | 155[2] |
| 1873, Continental. White wove paper, thin to thick. No grills. a. With secret marks. | 156 | 157 | 158 | | 159 | 160 | 161 | 162 | 163 | | | |
| b. No secret marks. | | | | | | | | | | | 165[2] | 166[2] |
| 1875, Continental. Special Printing. Same designs as 1873 Continental. Hard, white wove paper. No gum. | 167 | 168 | 169 | | 170 | 171 | 172 | 173 | 174 | 175 | 176 | 177 |
| 1875, Continental New color or denomination. Hard, yellowish wove paper. | | 178 | | 179 | | | | | | | | |
| 1875, Continental. Printing. Same designs as 1875 Continental. Hard, white wove paper. No gum. | | 180 | | 181 | | | | | | | | |
| 1879, American. Same designs as 1873-75 Continental. Soft porous paper. | 182 | 183[3] | 184[3] | 185 | 186[3] | | 187[3] | | 189[3] | | 190[3] | 191[3] |
| a. without secret mark. | | | | | | | 188 | | | | | |
| 1880, American. Special printing. Same as 1879 issue. Soft, porous paper. No gum. | 192 | 193 203[3] | 194[3] | 204 | 195[3] | 196 | 197[3] | 198 | 199[3] | 200 | 201[3] | 202[3] |
| 1881-82. American. Designs of 1873. Re-engraved[4]. Soft, porous paper. | 206 | | 207[5] | | 208 | | 209 | | | | | |
| 1887, American. Same designs as 1881-82. New colors. | | 214[5] | | | | | | | | | 217 | 218 |

**Footnotes:**
1. See diagrams for secret marks.
2. Corresponding denominations differ from each other only in color.
3. Corresponding denominations differ from each other only in color and gum. the special printings are slightly deeper and richer. The lack of gum is not a positive identifier because it can be washed from the 1879 issues.
4. See diagrams for re-engravings.
5. Corresponding denominations differ from each other in color.

## TYPES OF THE
## 2¢ WASHINGTON DESIGN
## OF 1894-98

The triangles in the upper right and left corners of the stamp determine this type.

**248-250, 265
Type I**

**251, 266
Type II**

**252,
267, 279B
Type III**

**TYPE I** has horizontal lines of the same thickness within and without the triangle.

**TYPE II** has horizontal lines which cross the triangle but are thinner within it than without.

**TYPE III** has thin lines inside the triangle and these doe not cross the double frame line of the triangle.

---

## 10¢ WEBSTER DESIGN
## OF 1898

**282C
Type I**

**283
Type II**

**TYPE I** has an unbroken, white curved line below the words "TEN CENTS."

In **TYPE II** the white line is broken by the ornaments at a point just below the "E" in "TEN" and the "T" in "CENTS" (arrows).

*When Quality Counts*
*H.E. HARRIS*
*Since 1916*

## $1 PERRY DESIGN OF
## 1894-95

**261, 276
Type I**

**261A, 276A
Type II**

In **Type I** the circles around the "$1" are broken at the point where they meet the curved line below "ONE DOLLAR" (arrows).

**Type II** shows these circles complete.

## 2¢ COLUMBIAN "BROKEN
## HAT" VARIETY OF 1893

As a result of a plate defect, some stamps of the 2¢ columbian design show a noticeable white notch or gash in the hat worn by the third figure to the left of Columbus. This "broken hat" variety is somewhat less common than the regular 2¢ design.

**231**                 *Broken Hat variety,* **231C**

**4¢ COLUMBIAN BLUE ERROR** — Collectors often mistake the many shades of the normal 4¢ ultramarine for the rare and valuable blue error. Actually, the "error" is not ultramarine at all, but a deep blue, similar to the deeper blue shades of the 1¢ Columbian.

---

## ISSUE OF 1903

**Die I
319, 319G,
320**

**Die II
319F, 320A**

The rounded inner frame line below and to the left "T" in "TWO" has a dark patch of color that narrows, but remains strong across the bottom.

| Perforation | Watermark | Other Identifying Features | | | | | 3¢ thru $1 denominations | 8¢ thru $1 denominations |
|---|---|---|---|---|---|---|---|---|
| PERF. 12 | *USPS* | White Paper | 331 | 332 | | | 333-42 | 422-23 |
| | | Bluish gray paper | 357 | 358 | | | 359-66 | |
| | USPS | White Paper | 374 | 375 | 405 | 406 | 376-82 / 407 | 414-21 |
| COIL 12 | *USPS* | Perf. Horizontal | 348 | 349 | | | 350-51 | |
| | *USPS* | Perf. Vertical | 352 | 353 | | | 354-56 | |
| | USPS | Perf. Horizontal | 385 | 386 | | | | |
| | USPS | Perf. Vertical | 387 | 388 | | | 389 | |
| IMPERF. | *USPS* | | 343 | 344 | | | 345-47 | |
| | USPS | Flat Plate | 383 | 384 | 408 | 409 | | |
| | USPS | Rotary Press | | | | 459 | | |
| | Unwmkd. | Flat Plate | | | 481 | 482-82A | 483-85 | |
| | Unwmkd. | Offset | | | 531 | 532-34B | 535 | |
| COIL 8-1/2 | USPS | Perf. Horizontal | 390 | 391 | 410 | 411 | | |
| | USPS | Perf. Vertical | 392 | 393 | 412 | 413 | 394-96 | |
| PERF. 10 | *USPS* | | | | | | | 460 |
| | USPS | | | | 424 | 425 | 426-30 | 431-40 |
| | Unwmkd. | Flat Plate | | | 462 | 463 | 464-69 | 470-78 |
| | Unwmkd. | Rotary Press | | | 543 | | | |
| COIL 10 | USPS | Perf. Horiz. — Flat | | 441 | 442 | | | |
| | USPS | Perf. Horiz. — Rotary | | 448 | 449-50 | | | |
| | USPS | Perf. Vert. — Flat | | | 443 | 444 | 445-47 | |
| | USPS | Perf. Vert. — Rotary | | | 452 | 453-55 | 456-58 | |
| | Unwmkd. | Perf. Horizontal | | | 486 | 487-88 | 489 | |
| | Unwmkd. | Perf. Vertical | | | 400 | 491-92 | 493-96 | 497 |
| PERF. 11 | *USPS* | | | 519 | | | | |
| | USPS | | | | | 461 | | |
| | Unwmkd. | Flat Plate | | | 498 | 499-500 | 501-07 | 508-18 |
| | Unwmkd. | Rotary Press | | | *544-45 | 546 | | |
| | Unwmkd. | Offset | | 525 | 526-28B | 529-30 | | |
| Perf. 12-1/2 | Unwmkd. | Offset | | | 536 | | | |
| 11 x 10 | Unwmkd. | Rotary | | | 538 | 539-40 | 541 | |
| 10 x 11 | Unwmkd. | Rotary | | | 542 | | | |

\* Design of #544 is 19mm. wide x 22-1/2mm. high.  #545 is 19-1/2 to 20mm. wide x 22mm high.

Size of
Flat Plate
Design

22mm

18-1/2 to 19mm

*Stamps printed by rotary press are always slightly wider or taller on issues prior to 1954. Measurements do not apply to booklet singles.*

## HOW TO USE THIS IDENTIFICATION CHART

Numbers referred to herein are from Scott's Standard Postage Stamp Catalog. to identify any stamp in this series, first check the type by comparing it with the illustrations at the top of the chart. Then check the perforations, and whether the stamp is single or double line watermarked or unwatermarked. With this information you can quickly find out the Standard Catalog number by checking down and across the chart. For example, a 1¢ Franklin, perf. 12, single line watermark, must be Scott's #374.

# TYPES OF THE 2¢ WASHINGTON DESIGN OF 1912-20

During the years 1912 through 1920, the 2¢ Washington design pictured below was issued and re-issued with slight variations which give rise to the many different types of this stamp. Certain of these types, as you will see by consulting the prices in this catalog, are far more valuable than others. The several variations in actual design are pictured and described below. For perforation, watermark and printing variations, see the handy identification chart on the preceding page.

Type I: Between 406 and 499

Type Ia: 482A, 500

Type II: 454, 487,491, 539

Type III: 450, 488, 492, 540, 546

Type IV: 526, 532

Type V: 527, 533

Type Va: 528-534

Type VI: 528A, 534A

Type VII: 528B, 534B

**TYPE I** — The ribbon at left above the figure "2" has one shading line in the first curve, while the ribbon at the right has one shading line in the second curve. Button of toga has a gaint outline. Top line of toga, from button to front of throat, is very faint. Shading lines of the face, terminating in front of the ear, are not joined. Type I occurs on both flat and rotary press printings.

**TYPE Ia** — Similar to Type I except that all of the lines are stronger. Lines of the toga button are heavy. Occurs only on flat press printings.

**TYPE II** — Ribbons are shaded as in Type I. Toga button and shading lines to the left of it are heavy. The shading lines in front of the ear are joined and end in a strong vertically curved line (arrow). Occurs only on rotary press printings.

**TYPE III** — Ribbons are shaded with two lines instead of one; otherwise similar to Type II. Occurs on rotary press printings only.

**TYPE IV** — Top line of toga is broken. Shading lines inside the toga button read "DID." The line of color in the left "2" is very thin and usually broken. Occurs on offset printings only.

**TYPE V** — Top line of toga is complete. Toga button has five vertical shaded lines. Line of color in the left "2" is very thin and usually broken. Nose shaded as shown in illustration. Occurs on offset printings only.

**TYPE Va** — Same as Type V except in shading dots of nose. Third row of dots from bottom has four dots instead of six. Also, the overall height of Type Va is 1/3 millimeter less than Type V. Occurs on offset printings only.

**TYPE VI** — Same as Type V except that the line of color in the left "2" is very heavy (arrow). Occurs on offset printings only.

**TYPE VII** — Line of color in left "2" is clear and continuous and heavier than in Types V or Va, but not as heavy as in Type VI. There are three rows of vertical dots (instead of two) in the shading of the upper lip, and additional dots have been added to the hair at the top of the head. Occurs on offset printings only.

## TYPES OF THE 3¢ WASHINGTON DESIGN 1908-20

**Type I:** Between 333 and 501

**Type II:** 484, 494, 502, 541

**TYPE I.** The top line of the toga is weak as are the top parts of the shading lines that join the toga line. The fifth shading line from the left (arrow) is partly cut away at the top. Also the line between the lip is thin. Occurs on flat and rotary press printings.

**TYPE II.** The top line of the toga is strong and the shading lines that join it are heavy and complete. The line between the lips is heavy. Occurs on flat and rotary press printings.

**Type III:** 529

**Type IV:** 530, 535

**TYPE III.** The top line of the toga is strong, but the fifth shading line from the left (arrow) is missing. The center line of the toga button consists of two short vertical lines with a dot between them. The "P" and "O" of "POSTAGE" are separated by a small line of color. Occurs on offset printings only.

**TYPE IV.** The shading lines of the toga are complete. The center line of the toga button consists of a single unbroken vertical line running through the dot in the center. The "P" and "O" of "POSTAGE" are joined. TYPE IV occurs only on offset printings.

## TYPES OF THE 2¢ WASHINGTON DESIGN OF 1922-29

**Type I:** Between 554 and 634

**Type I** has thin hair lines at top center of head.

**Type II** has three heavy hair lines (arrow) at top.

**Type II:** 599A, 634A

ORIGINAL
(Type I)

REVISED
(Type II)

BOOKLET SINGLE

**ORIGINAL** has the vertical bar of the "¢" symbol pointing to the left part of the "E" in "POSTAGE." In the necktie area, there are complete downward sloping hatch lines which touch the right-hand side of the tie. (1288, 1305E)

**REVISED** has the vertical bar of the "¢" symbol pointing to the center of the "E" in "POSTAGE." In the tie, the downward sloping hatch lines are almost eliminated, while the lines angling upward do not touch the lower right-hand side of the tie. The third line from the bottom is very short, leaving a colorless spot. (1288d, 1305Ei)

**BOOKLET SINGLE** has the vertical bar of the "¢" symbol pointing more toward the "G" of "POSTAGE." The necktie is 4-1/2 millimeters long and is straightened down the center of the robe. The overall design size is smaller both vertically and horizontally. All copies have at least one straight edge. (1288B)

**115**

## THE STAMP COLLECTING PYRAMID

How do you begin separating your stamps and putting them where they belong in your album? The answer is in the stamp collecting pyramid — it contains the tools and procedure you need to build a collection that will give you a lifetime of fun, knowledge and satisfaction.

## THE TOOLS

The most basic tools of collecting are stamp albums and they have been designed to fit specific levels of collecting.

**Beginning albums** contain only a selected number of stamps that were issued by any given country. These stamps are usually very common and easily obtainable.

**Intermediate albums** contain a larger percentage of the total number of stamps that have been issued by any given country and usually provide spaces for both common and harder to obtain stamps.

**Advanced albums** provide spaces for the majority of stamps issued by a country and spaces for all but the rarer issues.

**Comprehensive albums** provide spaces for virtually every stamp issued by a particular country and provide spaces for many extremely rare issues.

## IDENTIFICATION TOOLS

These are the basic tools one needs to properly handle and identify stamps — they form the foundation of the collecting pyramid.

Stamp Tongs:   used to pick up and handle stamps. Their proper use will keep you from bending, tearing, or disturbing the gum on your stamps.

Perforation Guage: used to measure the various distances between the holes punched around stamps to make their separation easier.

Watermark Tray and Fluid: used to distinguish between the types of paper on which some stamps have been printed.

Magnifying Glasses: used to observe small engraving marks that distinguish between stamps with the same general appearance.

## IDENTIFICATION

You now have all the essential tools and it's time to identify the building blocks of the pyramid: your stamps. Here is a procedure for you to follow.

1)   Identify the country of issue
2)   Identify the denomination and date of issue
3)   Measure the perforations
4)   Find a watermark, if any
5)   Look for distinguishing marks, if any

**Note:** On difficult to identify stamps the denomination can sometimes help you narrow the search for issue date, as postal rates tended to stay stable.

To identify the easier stamps you may only need to look at them. Look for the country and any dates — usually the latest date is the date of issue. With this information you can go directly to the appropriate space in your album. (Note: in beginning albums not all stamps are pictured, but you can still place them in their logical date of issue position.)

# HOW TO COLLECT STAMPS

Stamps that are harder to identify will have the country plainly visible, yet no date as a reference. In this case go to your catalog and look for a picture that matches your stamp. The catalog will list the catalog number and date of issue. With this information you can go to the appropriate place in your album.

Country name
no date

Match in
catalog to
find date

Place in album

Difficult to identify stamps include stamps that look alike but may have different perforations, watermarks, or special markings. To identify these stamps you must first gather information using your stamp collecting tools.

Perforations:   To measure the perforations of a stamp place it on a perf guage as shown below. Be sure the perf guage lines up properly or you will have a wrong piece of information. Remember to measure the perfs both across (horizontal) and up and down (verticle) — they can be different measurements.

Correct Reading
(perf. 11) All in line

Wrong Reading
(Not perf. 11-1/2) Out of line

**118**

# HOW TO COLLECT STAMPS

Watermarks: Place the stamp face down in a black watermark tray. Place a few drops of watermark fluid on the stamp — observe and note what you see.

Plain—No Watermark

Special
markings: Some stamps that look alike have only slight line or "secret mark" differences. Refer to the identification section of your catalog.

Once you have gathered this information, match your stamp with the pictures in the catalog. When you find a match, look for the catalog numbers (in Harris) listed underneath or (in Scott) under description type. These are all the possible varieties. Match you list against each catalog number until you find a match.

Scott's Catalog

Harris Catalog

This should enable you to identify even the most difficult stamps.

The more stamps you try to identify the easier it becomes. Don't get disappointed — it takes thinking, observing, and practice. The reward is the satisfaction of building your collection block by block. It's a hobby that can be enjoyed for a lifetime.

# GLOSSARY OF TERMS COMMONLY USED IN IDENTIFYING U.S. STAMPS

**BOOKLET PANES** are small sheets of stamps sold by the Post Office in booklet form. Most United States postage and airmail panes consist of a block of 6 stamps, or 5 stamps plus a label; that is straight-edged on all four sides but perforated between the stamps as illustrated. Booklet panes are usually collected unused, with the tab, or binding edge, attached. On recent issues, the tab is glued to the booklet and, in those cases, the booklet panes are collected without tabs.

**COIL STAMPS** are stamps which come in long rolled strips, especially for use in vending machines, automatic affixing machines, etc. They have straight edges on two opposite sides and perforated edges on the other two sides. If the straight edges run up and down, the stamps are called "endwise coils"; if they run from side to side, they are called "sidewise coils". Coils are generally collected in singles or pairs. They are also collected in Line Pairs with a "line" separating the two stamps. More recent issues also have a plate number under every 20-25 stamps — these are collected in strips of 3 with the number under the center stamp. These are called "Plate Number Coils".

**GRILLS** are raised impressions made in a stamp by pointed metal rollers, resembling the impressions made in a waffle by a waffle iron. The theory behind the grills used on the United States postage issues of 1867-71 was that the cancelling ink would soak into the broken fibers of the paper, thus preventing the stamp from being washed clean and used over again. If the grill impression is made from behind, so that the points show on the face of the stamp, the grill is said to be "points up". If done the opposite way, the grill is said to be "points down". Grills are further classified as "Grill A", "Grill B", etc., according to the type and size of the grill marks on the stamp. It should be remembered that a complete grill is not always found on any one stamp. Major varieties with grills are 79-101, 112-122 and 134-144.

Regular Grill     Continuous Marginal Grill     Split Grill

**PERFORATIONS** around the edges of a stamp are measured by the number of perforation holes in a space of two centimeters, as "Perf. 11", "Perf 12", etc. This sounds complicated but actually collectors use a simple measuring device called a perforation guage which readily gives this information about any stamp. Where a stamp is identified by only one perforation number, it is perforated the same on all four sides; if two numbers are shown (e.g., Perf 11 x 10 1/2), the first number indicates the top and bottom; the second the sides.

Perforation Gauge *(NOT ACTUAL SIZE)*

# HOW TO COLLECT STAMPS

*Double line watermark*
PERIOD OF USE
Postage 1895-1910

*Single line watermark*
PERIOD OF USE
Postage 1910-1916

**WATERMARKS** are faint markings impressed into the paper during manufacture to help detect counterfeiting. Practically all United States postage stamps issued between the years 1895-1916 are watermarked "USPS" (United States Postal Service), either in single line or double line letters, as illustrated. Before 1895 and since 1916, all postage issues, except for Scott's #519 and some copies of the $1 "Presidential" — an error — are unwatermarked.

To see a watermark, place the stamp on a "watermark detector" and add a few drops of watermark fluid. The watermark — if there is one — will usually show clearly. From the illustrations it can be seen that frequently only a part of a letter will appear.

---

## HOW TO DISTINGUISH BETWEEN FLAT, ROTARY AND OFFSET PRINTINGS

**FLAT PLATE** means printed from flat metal plates or engravings.

**Left:** *rotary press issue slightly taller than corresponding flat press design.*
**Right:** *rotary press stamp slightly wider than the same design printed from flat plates.*

**ROTARY PRESS** means printed from plates that are curved to fit around a cylinder. In the curving process, the designs of the stamp stretch slightly in the direction that the plate is curved, so that rotary press stamps issued prior to 1954 are always either slightly wider or slightly taller than the same designs printed from flat plates. Also, on rotary printings, one or more ridges have been forced into the paper to keep it from curling, and these usually show across the back of a stamp. No such ridges are found in flat press stamps.

**OFFSET** is a method of printing in which the plate transfers or "offsets" the design onto a rubber blanket which, in turn, transfers it to the paper. On stamps printed from flat press or rotary press plates (that is, engraved stamps), a relatively large amount of ink is deposited on the paper, giving the stamps a "rough" feeling. If you run a fingernail or metal edge lightly across the lines on such stamps, you can actually feel the ridges of ink. Offset stamps, on the other hand, have a smooth or "soapy" feeling. The ink lies down uniformly on the surface of the paper, and no ridges can be felt.

**SPECIAL PRINTINGS** are reprints, either from the original or from new engravings, of stamps previously issued. They are usually printed in limited quanities and for specific purposes, and can almost always be distinguished form the originals by differences in color, perforations, gum,. type of paper, etc. The larges single group — the Special Printings of 1875 — consist of a complete set of all designs issued up to that date. They were prepared for display by the government at the Philadelphia Centennial Exposition of 1876. Another good example of a Special Printing is the 1947 "CIPEX" souvenir sheet, shown at the front of this U.S. IDENTIFIER, which was printed as a souvenir of the Centenary International Philatelic Exposition held in New York in May, 1947.

# COLLECTOR'S DICTIONARY

**Acknowledgment of Receipt Stamp.** A stamp used to pay the extra fee that is sometimes required when the sender of a postal item requests a receipt, signed by the addressee, acknowledging the item's safe delivery.

**Adhesives.** All stamps intended to be affixed to postal matter, as distinguished from postage printed or hand-stamped directly on cards or covers.

**Aerogramme.** The official Universal Postal Union name for air lettersheets, which are usually carried for less than the normal airmail rates.

**Aero-Philately.** The collecting of airmail stamps and other air-borne mail items; one of the most popular collecting specialties.

**Air Cover.** See **Flight or Flown Cover.**

**Airmail.** Postal matter carried by aircraft.

**Airmail Stamp.** A stamp intended specifically for use on airmail items.

**Albino**. the uncolored impression of a stamp (usually embossed on the envelope).

**Aniline Inks.** Extremely bright water-soluble inks derived from coal-tar. Used extensively in stamp printing because they are easily damaged by rubbing and run when wet, thus discouraging attempts to remove cancellations or other markings.

**Approval Selections or "Approvals".** Stamps sent by dealers to collectors, usually in sheets, books, envelopes, or cards, for free examination. The collector selects the stamps he wishes to purchase and returns the balance to the dealer along with his payment for the stamps he has kept. One of the easiest, quickest, and most popular ways to build a collection.

**Arc or Serrated Roulette.** A roulette in which the slit is curved in a semi-circle.

**124**

**Arms Types.** Stamps bearing coats-of-arms or other heraldic devices; a popular subject among typical collectors.

**Arrow Block.** A block of stamps containing the arrow-shaped markings used to guide the pane-separator and perforator.

**"As is."** A term used when selling stamps to indicate that there is no guarantee of condition. Such items should always be carefully inspected before buying, as they are usually non-returnable.

**Auction.** A public sale at which various lots of stamps are sold to the highest bidder. When the sale is an important one, an Auction Catalog describing the various lots is printed and distributed in advance, so collectors at distant points may submit bids on a stamp.

**Backprint.** Any printing on the back of a stamp.

**Backstamp.** A postmark applied to the back of an envelope to indicate the date of arrival at the post office of destination, the location of the post office, and sometimes the exact time of receipt.

**Bank Mixture.** Mixed stamps, usually still on paper, collected from the incoming mail of banks and other financial institutions. Usually a reliable source of a wide range of foreign stamps.

**Bantams**. The name given to miniature stamps, especially the war-economy and war-tax issues of South Africa.

**Bars**. Bars or parallel lines are sometimes used to cancel stamps to indicate that they are invalid, especially in the case of government remainders. They may also be used to obliterate the face value or other details when overprinting.

**Bicentennial**. A two-hundredth anniversary or its celebration.

**Bicolor**. A stamp printed in two colors. See **Duty Plate.**

**Bilingual**. A stamp inscribed in two languages (Canada, Belgium, etc.).

**Bilingual Pair.** Two joined stamps identical to each other, except that the inscription is in a different language on each stamp (South Africa, South West Africa, etc.).

**Bisect.** A stamp cut in half vertically, horizontally, or diagonally to be used as two separate stamps, each equal to one-half the value of the whole stamp. Often used in emergencies when stamps of lower denominations are unavailable.

**Block.** Four or more unseparated stamps forming a square or rectangle; generally understood to consist of four stamps unless otherwise specified, as "block of six," etc.

**Bogus Stamps.** Imaginary stamps from real or imaginary countries, counterfeited and circulated by swindlers who hope unwary collectors will purchase them as genuine postal issues.

**Booklets.** Small convenient books containing stamps of one or more denominations. They are often sold through vending machines.

**Booklet Pane.** A block of stamps, usually six, which originally formed a page in one of the small booklets of stamps sold by the post office.

**Border.** The outer part or edge of a stamp design.

**Bourse.** An organized meeting of stamp dealers and/or collectors, at which stamps are sold or traded.

**Branding.** See **Perforated Initials.**

**Broken or Incomplete Set.** A group of stamps containing some, but not all, of the stamps in a particular issue or series.

**"Bulls-Eye" or "Socked-on-the-Nose."** A colloquialism used to indicate a stamp with a perfectly-centered and completely legible postmark, usually one with a full town and date cancel.

**Bureau Prints or Precancels.** Stamps printed or precanceled at the United States Bureau of Engraving and Printing in Washington, D.C., where most U.S. issues have been printed since 1894.

**Burelage.** A pattern of fine dots or lines on the face (under the design) or back of a stamp to discourage removal of the cancellation or counterfeiting.

**Burr.** A raised bit of metal on an engraving plate, caused by the engraving tool. If it is not smoothed out or removed, a burr can appear on a sheet of stamps as a printing flaw.

**Cachet.** A picture, design, or inscription printed or rubber-stamped on an envelope to describe or explain the occasion on which the envelope was mailed, such as the first flight over a new airmail route, first day of issue of a new stamp, the event being commemorated by the new stamp, etc.

**Canceled-to-Order or C.T.O.** Canceled without having been used for postal purposes. Government remainders are often C.T.O. before sale to dealers, as are many speculative issues.

**Cancellation.** The ink mark or other defacement (cuts, holes, etc.) on a stamp to show that it has been used once and may not be used again.

**Carrier's Stamps.** Used in the United States from 1851-63 to pay the delivery fee on postal items from the postal receiving station to the addressee, or from one address to another within the same postal delivery zone, as during those years ordinary stamps only paid the postage from one post office to another.

**Catalog Number.** The identifying number assigned to each individual stamp of a country by the publisher of a postage stamp catalog.

**Catalog Value.** The value or "price" assigned to a stamp by the publisher of a postage stamp catalog, usually based on current market conditions.

**Centenary or Centennial.** A one-hundredth anniversary or its celebration.

**Centering.** The placement or location of a stamp design with reference to the piece of paper on which it is printed. If the design is squarely in the center, as shown by equal margins of paper on all sides, it is said to be perfectly centered. If one or more margins are much larger than the others, the stamp is said to be **Off-Center,** and is generally regarded as less desirable and valuable than a well-centered copy.

**Center Line Blocks.** Blocks of stamps with horizontal and vertical lines intersecting the middle of the block.

**Centimeter or cm.** A unit of measurement in the metric system. 2.54 centimeters equal one inch; 100 centimeters equal one meter.

**Certified Mail.** First class mail for which the sender is given a receipt certifying that the item has been mailed. If desired, a receipt signed by the addressee can also be requested, as proof of safe delivery. There is no compensation for loss of Certified Mail, thus distinguishing it from **Registered Mail.**

**Chalky or Coated Paper.** A highly-surfaced chalk-coated paper designed to make it impossible to clean off the postmark without removing the stamp design; also used in some humid countries to prevent sheets of stamps from sticking together.

**Charity Stamps.** See **Semi-Postal Stamps.**

**"Chop."** Japanese characters overprinted, hand-stamped, or handwritten on stamps of territories occupied by Japanese troops during World War II; used until official Japanese occupation stamps became available.

**Classic.** A stamp, chiefly one issued before 1870, which has gained universal popularity and reputation through widespread philatelic acceptance.

**Cleaned.** In philately, the term implies that a stamp has had a cancellation or other marking removed for fraudulent re-use or resale as an unused item.

**Coarse Perforation.** A perforation with large holes and the teeth far apart.

**Coil Line Pair.** A pair of stamps from a rotary coil showing a colored line caused by a gap where the curved printing plate is joined. Coil line pairs are a favorite specialty item. Also called **Joint Line Pair** or **Line-Gap Pair.**

**Coil Stamps.** Stamps which are issued in long, coiled strips, especially for use in vending or affixing machines. Coil stamps have straight edges on two opposing sides, and perforations on the other two. If the straight edges run up and down, the stamps are called "endwise coils"; if they run from side to side, the stamps are called "sidewise coils."

**Collateral Materials.** Relevant literature and illustrations exhibited with a stamp display to provide additional background information about the stamps in the display.

**Color Changeling.** A stamp whose color has been altered, either accidentally or intentionally, by chemicals, heat, sunlight, or moisture.

**Column.** A complete vertical row of stamps from a sheet.

**Comb Perforation.** A perforation made by a machine which perforates three sides of each stamp in a row at the same time.

**Combination Cover.** A cover bearing stamps from two countries **(Mixed Postage);** necessary when mail travels between two non-U.P.U. nations. The first stamp pays postage within the country of origin, the second within the country of destination.

**Commemorative Stamp.** A stamp issued in remembrance of an event, or as a memorial to some person.

**Complete Set.** A group of stamps including all the stamps in a particular series or issue.

**Compound Perforations.** Perforations of two different measurements on the same stamp. A stamp, for example, which is Perf.

12 on the top and bottom, and Perf. 11 on the sides is described as Perf. 12 x 11. See **Perforations.**

**Condition.** The state of being, character, or quality of a stamp, as determined by centering, cancellation marks, cleanliness, etc. Generally recognized grades are: 1. Superb; 2. Very Fine; 3. Fine; 4. Average; 5. Second Grade; 6. Damaged.

**Condominium.** A territory ruled by more than one power. Condominium issues may be bilingual, or they may be separate issues of the same design, printed in different languages (Anglo-French New Hebrides, Anglo-Egyptian Sudan, etc.).

**Constant.** The term used to describe a minor variety which appears in the same place on the sheet throughout multiple printing runs of a stamp.

**Control Mark.** A letter or numeral placed in the sheet margin, or overprinted on the front or back of a stamp for accounting purposes.

**Copyright Block.** Beginning in 1978, the U. S. Postal Service replaced the "Mail Early" slogan with the standard copyright inscription as seen in copyrighted publications, etc. This was a legal move to protect the design from copyright infringement. Copyright Blocks are collected as blocks of four.

**Corner Block.** A block of stamps originally located at one of the four corners of a sheet or pane of stamps, and having intact sheet margins on two adjacent sides.

**Counterfeit.** See **Forgery.**

**Counterfoil.** Some European stamps, especially parcel post issues (Italy, San Marino, etc.), are printed in two parts, one to be affixed to the item being mailed, and the other, known as a counterfoil, being kept by the sender as a receipt.

**Coupon.** A postally invalid label or tag attached to a postage stamp, usually carrying a slogan, propaganda matter, or design related to the stamp.

**Cover.** A complete envelope or card with stamp(s) and cancellation intact.

**"Crash" Cover.** A cover which has been salvaged from a wreck or crash and delivered to the addressee, usually containing an official inscription explaining the delay.

**Crease.** A line or mark on a stamp, caused by folding or wrinkling.

**Current.** The term used to describe stamps which are presently available at the post office.

**Cut Cancellation.** A cancellation which cuts through the stamp.

**Cut Close.** A stamp —usually imperforate— with one or more edges trimmed close to the design, leaving an inadequate margin.

**Cut Square or Envelope Square Cut.** An embossed or printed envelope, postcard, wrapper, lettercard, or lettersheet stamp cut in a squared shape (allowing ample margin) from the entire piece for the sake of convenience. Cut squares are worth more than the same items cut to their exact shape, but are not worth as much as the entire envelope or piece.

**Dead Country.** A country which no longer issues stamps, either because it has ceased to exist or because it has changed its name.

**Dedication Covers.** Covers that are mailed from a place where a special event has occurred such as inaugural covers.

**Definitives.** Stamps used for ordinary postage, and kept in general circulation for a number of years, as distinguished from provisionals, commemoratives, or special purpose stamps. Also called **General** or **Regular Issues.**

**Demonetized.** A stamp is demonetized when it has been declared no longer postally valid by the issuing authority.

**Denomination.** The monetary and postal value of a stamp, as "1 cent," "2 shillings," etc.

**Departmental Stamps.** Official stamps intended for use by one particular government office alone.

**Design.** The printed portion of a stamp, as distinguished from the surrounding margin of blank paper.

**Diamond or Lozenge Roulette.** A roulette in which the slits are X-shaped, thus creating a diamond-shaped space between them.

**Die.** The piece of metal or other material on which the original engraving of a stamp design is made. Multiple reproductions are then taken of the die and put together to form the plate used to print a complete sheet of stamps.

**Documentaries.** Revenue stamps, formerly used on numerous types of documents (mortgages, wills, bills of lading, etc.) in payment of a government tax.

**Double Impression or Double Transfer.** The term used when a stamp shows a second impression of the design distinctly overlapping part or all of the first impression.

**Dry Printing.** A printing method developed in the United States in the 1950's, in which special inks and greater printing pressure allow the use of heavier, stiffer paper with a low moisture content, creating a whiter, high-sheen printing surface which makes the stamp design stand out sharply.

**Dues.** See **Postage Due Stamps.**

**Dumb Cancellation.** A postmark which gives neither the date nor the place of cancellation. The term "dumb" is also used to describe stamps which do not outwardly indicate the country or place of origin, and sometimes even the face value.

**Duplex Cancellation.** A cancellation given in two parts — a cancellation, and a postmark — to ensure the legibility of the date and place name on the postmark.

**Duplicate.** An additional copy of a stamp. Duplicates should be carefully examined to make sure they are not actually minor varieties.

**Duty Plate.** One of the two plates used in printing bi-colored stamps. The duty plate prints the changing part of the design, usually the value alone, but sometimes other elements as well. The unchanging part of the design is printed by the **Key Plate.**

**Electrotype.** A method of producing replicas of a die for printing, by applying a coating of copper to a mold taken from the die.

**Elusive.** The term given to a stamp which is not generally considered to be rare or scarce, but which nonetheless is hard to find.

**Embossed stamps.** Stamps in which part or all of the design is raised above the surface of the paper on which they are printed, most commonly used on pre-stamped envelopes.

**Engraving.** Method of printing using a metal plate into which the stamp design has been cut or etched.

**Entire.** A stamped envelope, wrapper, postcard, or other postal stationery in its entirety, as sold by the post office.

**Envelope Stamp.** A stamp printed directly on an envelope, as distinguished from the separately-printed or "adhesive" stamp.

**Errors.** Stamps with wrong designs, colors, printing, paper, perforations, or over-printing, unwittingly issued by the post office.

**Expertize.** To make an expert examination of a stamp and render an opinion as to its genuineness.

**Express.** Special Delivery.

**Face Value.** The postal value of a stamp as indicated by the figures, words, or abbreviations in the design or surcharge.

**Facsimile.** An exact imitation or close likeness of a genuine stamp, often created so many collectors can have souvenir or specimen copies of a very rare stamp. Unlike forgeries, facsimiles are openly acknowledged as being only imitations (usually by an inscription on the back), and are not intended to deceive or defraud.

**Fake.** An originally genuine stamp that has been illegitimately altered by adding or removing perforations, surcharges, overprints, or cancellations, or by changing the color or the value, etc., to increase its philatelic value.

**Fine Perforation.** A perforation with small holes and the teeth close together.

**First Day Cover.** An envelope bearing a cancellation date representing the first day of issue of the stamp affixed thereon, and which is usually mailed from the postal station where the stamp was first put into circulation.

**First Flight Cover.** A cover carried on the inaugural flight over a new airmail route, or an extension of an existing route.

**Fiscal.** See **Revenue Stamps.**

**Flat Plate.** A stamp printed on a press with flat plates, as opposed to those printed on a rotary press with curved plates.

**Flaw.** See **Freak**.

**Flight or Flown Cover.** An airmail cover.

**Forgery.** An imitation of a genuine postage stamp, made with intent to deceive or defraud.

**Format.** The general physical characteristics of a stamp: size, shape, dimensions, etc.

**Frame.** The outer part or border of a stamp design.

**Frank.** A mark or label indicating that postage either has been paid or is free. Most often associated with government or military mail.

**Freak.** A stamp which shows a production flaw which is not a constant error, such as an ink smudge, a fold or crease in the paper, crooked or off-center perforations, etc. An inconstant minor variety.

**Fugitive Inks.** Generally aniline inks, used to discourage fakes, forgeries, and fraudulent erasures. They run when wet and become easily damaged by rubbing, so great care is necessary when dealing with such stamps.

**General Collector.** One who collects all kinds of stamps from different countries, as opposed to a **Specialist.**

**General Issue.** See **Definitive.**

**Granite Paper.** A type of safety paper, with tiny colored fibers running through it, to deter forgery.

**Grill**. A network of embossed or raised impressions made in a stamp by a metal roll with points. The grill is said to be "points up" if they show on the face of the stamp, and "points down" if they show on the back. Grilling was used on some early United States issues to help the stamp absorb the canceling inks, thus discouraging fraudulent cleaning.

**Groundwork**. The background of a stamp design, against which the principal subject is shown.

**Guide Dots or Lines**. Markings made on the printing plate to guide the pane-separator and perforator.

**Gum**. The adhesive coating on the backs of most unused, adhesive postage stamps.

**Gutter**. The space between panes on a sheet of stamps.

**Handstamped.** Stamped or canceled by hand, usually with a rubber stamp but sometimes hand-written, instead of by a machine.

**Harrow Perforation**. A perforation produced by a machine which perforates the entire sheet of stamps in one operation.

**Heliogravure**. An early type of photogravure still used in some countries for stamp printing.

**Humidor or "Stamplift."** A device used to remove stamps from paper without actually immersing them in water. The stamps are placed on a shelf above the water, then covered. The humidity slowly loosens the paper. Preferable to soaking, especially when dealing with old stamps or fugitive inks.

**Hyphens**. Rectangular-shaped perforations used on some stamps.

**Imperforate or "Imperf."** Printed without perforations.

**Imprint Blocks**. A block of stamps with a portion of the sheet margin bearing the printer's inscription, usually his name or initials, but sometimes technical data or other notations.

**Inconstant**. The term used to describe a minor variety which does not appear in the same place on the sheet through multiple printing runs of a stamp.

**Inscription**. The letters, characters, or words appearing on a stamp as an integral part of the overall design.

**Inscription Block**. A block of stamps bearing a marginal inscription relating either to the stamps or to general postal matters, such as "Use Zip Code" or "Mail Early in the Day."

**Insured Mail**. See **Registered Mail**.

**Intaglio**. Line-engraving, or recess-printing, so-called because the design is cut into the printing plate and thus is recessed below the surface of the plate. The ink which collects in the recessed design is then transferred to the paper. Line-engraved stamps are easily discernible by feeling with the fingers for the raised ridges caused by the ink making up the design.

**Interleaves**. Translucent tissue on thin plastic sheets placed between the pages of an album to prevent rubbing. Necessary in albums with stamps mounted on both sides of the pages.

**Interrupted or Syncopated Perforations.** Used by some countries on stamps intended for use in coil-vending machines. One or more of the hole punches in the perforation machine are removed leaving a paper "bridge" between the stamps for added strength.

**Interverted**. The term used to describe a pair of stamps, or a stamp and counterfoil or label, printed or cut in the wrong sequence.

**Invalidated**. No longer valid for postal use.

**Invert**. A stamp which has part of the design (usually the central portion) upside down in relation to the rest of the design.

**Irregular Perforation**. The term used when the perforations on any one side of a stamp are not evenly lined up, or are of different sizes, etc.

**Issue**. A stamp; also, a related series of stamps, released by a government post office at one time or during a certain period of time.

**Journal Stamps**. Stamps used to pay bulk postage and sometimes tax on newspapers, magazines, and other periodicals.

**Jubilee**. A 25th (silver), 50th (golden), or 60th (diamond) anniversary of a ruler's reign or a country's independence, usually the occasion for issuance of a commemorative set.

**Key Plate. See Duty Plate.**

**Keytype**. A stamp design used in two or more colonies, with only the name and sometimes the value being changed, either by using a different duty plate, or by overprinting. So-called because the common elements of the design are the ones on the key plate.

**"Killer" Cancellation**. A cancellation which is very heavy and/or covers most of the stamp, effectively disfiguring or obliterating the design.

**Label Coupon**. Also used as a disparaging term to describe stamps of dubious philatelic value, as many speculative issues.

**Laid Paper**. One of the two principal types of paper used for printing stamps. Distinguished by closely parallel horizontal and/or vertical lines created during the paper's manufacture.

**Last Day Cancellation**. A cancellation made at a discontinued post office on the last day of operation.

**Late Fee Stamps**. Stamps used to pay the additional postage which is sometimes required when an item is mailed after normal postal hours.

**Letterpress. Typography**, or relief-printing. The stamp design or a photograph of it (**Photo-Engraving**) is transferred onto a metal plate with a greasy ink; the rest of the plate is etched away, leaving only the raised design. Letterpress-printed stamps can be detected by an impression of the design "standing out" on the back, the result of the raised portions of the plate being pressed into the paper.

**Lettersheet**. A sheet of writing paper with a stamp already printed on it, so that the sheet can be folded, addressed, and mailed without the necessity for a separate envelope.

**Line-Engraving**. See **Intaglio.**

**Line Pair**. A pair of stamps showing a line of color between them, usually the guide line. See **Coil Line Pair.**

**Line Perforation**. A perforation made by a machine which only perforates one line at a time.

**Line Roulette**. The most common type of roulette, consisting of ordinary straight slits.

**Lithography**. A flat-surface printing method in which the design is drawn, photographed (**Photo-Lithography**) or otherwise transferred to a stone or metal plate, and fixed there via treatment with acid to accept a greasy ink, the rest of the plate being kept damp to reject the ink. Lithographed stamps are distinguished by their generally flat surface.

**Local Stamps.** Stamps issued for use only in a certain city, town, or district; not good for postage elsewhere.

**Local Precancels.** Stamps intended for bulk mailings, precanceled at a local post office to speed mail processing.

**Luminescent Stamps.** Stamps treated with a phosphorescent substance (**Phosphor Tagged**) or printed on fluorescent paper or with fluorescent ink. Used with electronic machines to speed mail processing.

**Maiden Voyage Covers.** Covers transported on a ship's first voyage and so designated by a special postmark.

**"Mail Early" Inscription Block**. A block of U.S. stamps containing the "Mail Early in the Day" inscription on the sheet margin.

**Major Varieties**. Stamps differing in one or more major respects — design, color, denomination, shape, size, paper, perforations, watermarks, imprints, inscriptions, etc. — either in the same issue or in different issues.

**Manuscript Cancellation**. See **Pen Cancellation.**

**Margin**. The unprinted paper surrounding the design of a stamp; also, the blank paper bordering a sheet of stamps, sometimes called the **Selvedge.**

**Marginal**. The term used to describe a stamp taken from the extreme top, bottom, left, or right rows of stamps in a sheet, i.e., the rows which directly adjoin the sheet margins.

**Master Plate.** A printing plate kept as a "master" from which additional printing plates may be made.

**Maximum Card.** A pictorial postcard showing a stamp design or other subject, bearing either the stamp pictured or a stamp related to the design, and bearing a postmark related to the stamp or subject.

**Memorials**. Stamps issued to honor prominent persons. The U.S. by policy does not honor persons until after death.

**Meter Cancellation.** A design printed directly on an envelope or strip of gummed paper (for affixing to mail) by postage meter machine, and used as a substitute for postage stamps. Meter postage is paid in advance, and thus differs from a **Permit.**

**Military Stamps.** Issued for use by a country's army and military personnel, usually during time of war only.

**Millimeter or mm.** A unit of measurement in the metric system, equal to one-tenth of a centimeter, and often used in expressing stamp measurements.

**Miniature Sheet.** A smaller-than-regular-size sheet of stamps; often a **Souvenir Sheet.**

**Minor Varieties.** Seemingly similar stamps which differ in minor respects such as shade of color or of paper; imperfections in design, printing, or perforations; positioning of watermark or overprint; etc. See **Major Varieties.**

**Mint or Mint Condition.** A stamp which is in the same physical condition as when it left the mint or printing source or supply;

with full, original gum and never hinged, canceled, soiled, stained, creased, marked, or torn.

**Mirror Print.** An error in which part or all of a stamp is reversed, as in a mirror.

**Mission Mixture.** Mixed stamps, usually still on paper, collected by mission houses and other charitable organizations. Usually a reliable source of a wide variety of foreign stamps, and has come to signify any bulk mixture of unsorted stamps.

**Mixed Postage.** Stamps of two different countries used on the same postal item. See **Combination Cover.**

**Mixture.** A miscellaneous lot of unsorted stamps, usually containing many duplicates and with the stamps frequently on bits of paper, just as torn from envelopes and wrappers.

**Multicolored.** A stamp printed in three or more colors.

**Multiple.** A group of stamps from the same sheet, unseparated, numbering more than two but less than a full sheet.

**Multiple Watermarks.** A popular form of watermarking, in which a design is repeated so frequently on a sheet that partial watermarks may appear several times on a single stamp.

**Mute Cancellation.** See **Dumb Cancellation.**

**Name Block.** A block of stamps on whose margins appears a name rather than a number.

**Net.** Clear of or free from all deductions.

**New Issue.** The latest stamp or series of stamps issued currently by a country.

**Newspaper Stamps.** See **Journal Stamps.**

**New Value.** An additional value (denomination) added to an existing series; also a new value surcharged on a stamp of different original value, creating a "revalued" stamp.

**Oblique Roulette.** A roulette consisting of parallel diagonal slits.

**Obliteration.** An overprint used to blot out unwanted parts of a stamp design. See Bars.

**Obsolete.** No longer in use; a term applied to stamps that are no longer being issued or distributed by the post office.

**Occupation Stamps.** Stamps issued by one country for use in conquered or occupied territory of another country.

**Off Center.** See **Centering.**

**Off Paper.** The term used to describe a used stamp which has been removed from the piece of paper to which it was affixed.

**Official Seal.** See **Post Office Seal.**

**Official Stamps**. Stamps used by some countries for use on official government mail.

**Offset**. A type of lithography in which the design is first transferred from the printing plate to a rubber roller, then from the roller to the paper. See **Lithography.**

**Omnibus Issues.** A group of stamps, usually sharing a common design, issued by a number of different postal authorities to mark the same occasion. Usually issued by all the colonies of one country, or all the countries in a commonwealth or union (British Commonwealth of Nations, EUROPA, etc.)

**On Cover.** A stamp still affixed to the entire piece of mail, usually an envelope, on which it was originally used.

**On Paper**. A stamp still affixed to enough of the paper on which it was originally used, to provide philatelic evidence of authenticity, such as a postmark.

**Original**. A stamp that is not a reprint, forgery, or facsimile.

**Original Gum** or **O.G.** The unimpaired gum with which the stamp was originally issued.

**Overprint**. Any additional printing (surcharging, hand-stamping, overprinting, etc.) on a stamp after the stamp itself has been printed.

**Oxidation**. An unintended chemical process by which the original color of a stamp changes, usually through exposure to the elements.

**Packet**. An envelope or package of stamps, as offered for sale by a dealer. Properly, a packet contains all different stamps; as distinguished from mixtures which usually contain duplicates.

**Packet Cancellation**. A special postmark applied to mail carried on a ship maintained or chartered by a government or post office. Differs from a **Ship Cancellation,** which is a postmark applied to mail carried on a private vessel. Both postmarks usually include the name of the ship and/or shipping line.

**Pair**. Two unseparated stamps; a "vertical pair" when one stamp is above the other, a "horizontal pair" when side by side.

**Pane**. The so-called "sheets" of stamps sold by post offices are more correctly termed "panes." Most stamps are actually printed in much larger-sized sheets, which are then divided into smaller units, or panes, for distribution at post offices.

**Parcel Post.** A class of postal service reserved for the sending of packages or parcels, sometimes requiring special **Parcel Post Stamps.**

**Part-Perforate.** Perforated on two or three sides only. Most coil stamps are perforated on two opposing sides — top and bottom, or left and right; booklet pane stamps are perforated on two or three connecting sides, depending on the location of the stamp in the pane.

**Patriotic Covers**. Covers on which patriotic pictures and slogans appear. These are generally used during a period of war and were prominent on both sides during the Civil War.

**Pen Cancellation**. A cancellation drawn by hand with a pen or pencil. Also called a Manuscript Collection.

**Perforated Initials or Perfins**. Holes punched in a stamp to form letters of a design, used to advertise or to prevent theft. Also called Branding or Punch Perforating.

**Perforations**. The holes punched between the rows of stamps in a sheet to facilitate separation. Usually round, but may be square, rectangular, diamond-shaped, etc.

**Perforation or Perf. Number.** The number of perforated holes in a space of 2 centimeters along the edge of a stamp, determined by using a perforation gauge.

```
Nonprofit
Organization
U.S. Postage
Paid
The American
Film Institute
```

**Permit**. A postal system used to facilitate bulk mailings. The sender is licensed to use a registered permit number on his mail in lieu of stamps. He is then charged for the total number of items on which his permit number appears.

**Philatelic Agency.** A bureau or central point maintained by a government for selling current issues of stamps in quantity to dealers, and in some cases, also to collectors.

**Philatelist**. A person who collects and studies stamps.

**Philately**. The technical name for stamp collecting.

**Phosphor Tagged. See Luminescent Stamps.**

**Photo-Engraving. See Letterpress.**

**Photogravure**. A popular method for printing stamps, in which a photograph of the stamp design is etched into a metal plate, usually for use on a rotary press ( when the process is called

Rotogravure). Photogravure stamps have the general impression of a photograph, with the design made up of fine dots which can be clearly seen with a magnifier.

**Photo-Lithography.** See **Lithography.**

**Pictorials.** Stamps bearing pictures, such as landscapes, animals, flowers, etc., as distinguished from those bearing portraits or symbols.

**Pin Roulette.** A roulette consisting of tiny pin-holes, with no paper removed.

**Plate Number.** A file or index number engraved in a plate from which stamps are printed. This number is used to help keep track of the plates, and is usually found in a corner margin of the sheet.

**Plate Number Block.** A block of stamps with an attached portion of the sheet margin bearing the plate number. A popular collecting specialty.

**Plate Number Coil or Strip**. A strip of three (some collectors prefer five) containing a tiny plate number below the center stamp.

**Position Blocks**. Blocks of four or more stamps which have markings, usually on an attached portion of sheet margin, indicating a position on the sheet, such as plate number blocks, arrow blocks, inscription blocks, etc.

**Post Office Seals**. Postally-invalid adhesive labels used to re-seal letters or parcels damaged in transit or opened for inspection, or to seal registered items to prevent tampering.

**Postage and Revenue**. An inscription meaning that the stamps so inscribed can be used for either postage or revenue purposes.

**Postage Due Stamps**. Special stamps affixed by postal clerks to mail on which the postage was underpaid by the sender. The amount indicated by the stamps is then collected from the addressee upon delivery.

**Postal Cancellations**. Cancellations showing that a stamp has been used for postal rather than revenue purposes.

**Postal-Fiscal.** See **Revenue Stamps.**

**Postal Stationery**. Envelopes, postcards, lettersheets, wrappers, lettercards, etc. with stamps officially printed or embossed on them.

**Postally Used**. Used for postage, as distinguished from stamps used for non-mail purposes, or canceled-to-order.

**Postmark**. A cancellation which usually gives the place and date, and sometimes the exact time of cancellation.

**Postmasters' Provisionals**. Stamps issued by individual postmasters in various towns and cities, with or without official Post Office sanction, and used locally before general postal issues were made available.

**Pre-Adhesive.** A postal item dating from the period prior to the use of adhesive stamps in a particular country.

**Precancels**. Stamps canceled in advance of use, usually with the name of the place where they are to be used, to facilitate the handling of large mailings.

**Printed on Both Sides**. An error which occurs when a sheet of stamps is accidentally turned over and run through the printing press a second time, so that both sides are "correctly" printed. Not to be confused with **Set-Off,** in which the impression on the back of the stamp is a reverse, or "mirror" image.

**Printing**. The four most common methods used in printing stamps are: Line-engraving (**Intaglio,** or recess-printing); **Lithography** (usually **Offset** photo-lithography); **Photogravure;** and **Typography** (**Letterpress**, usually photo-engraving). See separate listings.

**Proof**. A trial impression taken at various stages of the printing process to make sure that the colors are correct, design is satisfactory, etc. before the actual printing run begins.

**Protectorate**. A country governed, guided, or protected by a larger, stronger country.

**Provisionals or Provisional Issues**. Stamps issued or overprinted for temporary use until regular issues are available.

**Punch perforating**. See Perforated Initials.

**Quadrille**. Paper containing intersecting vertical and horizontal lines forming small squares or rectangles.

**Quartz Lamp**. See **Ultraviolet Lamp**.

**Railroad Cancellation**. A cancellation used on a railway mail car, usually while the mail is in transit.

**Recut or Re-Engrave**. To remake part or all of a printing plate, to make additions or alterations without materially changing the design.

**Redrawn**. A redrawn stamp design usually retains all the main characteristics and essential elements of its type, but exhibits minor variations.

**Registered Mail**. First class mail for which the sender is given a numbered receipt by the post office, ascribing a specific monetary value to the item being mailed (for purposes of compensation in event of loss). A signed receipt is also required of the addressee, certifying safe delivery of the item. Insured Mail is similar, but is sent third class.

**Registration Stamps**. Stamps issued by some countries exclusively for use on registered mail.

**Regular Issue**. See **Definitives.**

**Reissue**. A stamp which has been withdrawn from circulation may later be reprinted and reissued by postal authorities.

**Remainders**. The stamps left on hand in government offices after an issue of stamps has been discontinued. Remainder stocks are usually destroyed, but are sometimes canceled-to-order and sold to stamp dealers.

**Repaired or Mended.** Stamps that are damaged (thin spots, creases, tears, etc.) are sometimes very cleverly repaired to hide the damage, usually for fraudulent resale as better-quality items.

**Reprint**. A stamp printed from the original plates (usually after an issue has become obsolete) but not intended for postal use.

**Retouching**. Minor repairs made to a printing plate, to mend damaged or worn portions. Usually involves less severe alterations than does recutting.

**Revenue Stamps or Fiscals.** Stamps affixed to playing cards, tobacco, wines and other spirits, documents, stock certificates, patent medicines, etc., to show that the required government tax on these items has been paid. Revenue stamps used for regular postage are called **Postal-Fiscals;** regular stamps used for revenue purposes are called **Fiscal-Postals.**

**Rotary Press.** A printing method using curved plates; stamps printed on a rotary press are slightly higher or wider than those printed with flat plates on a flat-bed press, due to the plates stretching slightly when they are being curved.

**Rough Perforation**. A perforation with jagged holes.

**Rouletting**. A method of stamp-separation in which slits or pin-holes of various sizes and shapes are made between the rows of stamps without removing any of the paper, thus differing from perforating. See **Arc (Serrated), Diamond (Lozenge), Line, Oblique, Pin, Sawtooth, Serpentine,** and **Zigzag (Point) Roulette** listings.

**Safety or Security Paper**. Special paper used to make forgery or fraudulent alterations of a stamp more difficult. See **Chalky** and **Granite Papers.**

**Sawtooth Roulette.** A roulette which leaves angular pointed edges.

**Se-tenant**. A term applied to two or more unseparated stamps having different values, overprints, or designs, and printed that way intentionally (usually as part of the same set) rather than through an error.

**Seals**. Postally-invalid adhesive labels usually sold to raise money for various charities. Not to be confused with **Post Office Seals.**

**Secret Marks.** Microscopic or hidden marks placed in a stamp design by the artist or engraver for identification or reference.

**Selvedge.** See **Margin.**

**Semi-Postal Stamps**. Stamps surcharged, overprinted, or inscribed (as above) to obtain funds for various charities, in addition to the usual postal fee.

**Separation**. See **Perforations** and **Rouletting.**

**Series**. All the denominations of stamps belonging to a certain issue, as the United States Bicentennial Era Series, often released at different times over a period of months or years.

**Serpentine Roulette**. A roulette consisting of wavy lines.

**Service**. When surcharged on a stamp, usually means "on government services," and indicates that the stamp is for use only by a government official.

**Sesquicentennial**. A 150th anniversary or its celebration.

**Set**. A number of stamps belonging to a particular issue or series.

**Set-Off.** A reverse impression on the back of a sheet of stamps, occurring when the sheet has been laid on another sheet whose ink is still wet. Also, reverse impression transferred to the back of an album page by the stamps on the following page, occurring when the album has been kept for a long time under great pressure. Avoidable through the use of interleaves.

**Shade**. Slight variations of colors; in philately, taken to mean any variation from the normal color of a stamp.

**153**

**Sheet of Stamps**. The complete sheet as it comes off the printing press. See **Pane.**

**Ship Cancellation.** See **Packet Cancellation.**

**Short Set.** A group of stamps from a particular issue or series, usually including all the stamps except for the higher values.

**"Sleeper."** An unexpectedly elusive or otherwise surprisingly desirable issue.

**Soaking**. The process of immersing a stamp in water to remove any attached bits of paper; somewhat fallen into disfavor now with the growing use of fugitive inks. If soaking is unavoidable, salt should be added to the water to help retard any running of colors.

**"Socked-on-the-Nose."** See **"Bullseye."**

**Souvenir Sheet**. A sheet of one or more stamps specifically printed by a government for a specific event or purpose; the margins are usually extra-wide, carrying inscriptions describing the purpose of the issue, and the stamps may be perforate or imperforate.

**Space Filler.** An inferior copy of a stamp, used to fill an album space only until a better copy can be obtained.

**Special Delivery Stamps.** For use when the sender of a postal item wants it delivered immediately by special messenger, upon its arrival at the post office.

**Special Handling Stamps.** Stamps for use on fourth class mail, entitling it to the same priority given first class mail.

**Specialist.** One who collects stamps in a restricted field, such as United States or German stamps only, airmail or revenue stamps only, sports or floral stamps only, etc.

**"Specimen" or "Sample."** An overprint or perfin applied to postally-invalid samples of a new stamp issue, for distribution to postmasters, philatelic agencies, etc.

**Speculative Issues.** Many countries today issue stamps less for any legitimate postal use they may see, than for the revenue they will generate through sales to collectors. These stamps are known as speculative issues.

**Split.** A stamp which has been cut into two or more pieces, each piece to be used as a separate stamp. See **Bisect.**

**Split Grille.** The term used when a stamp shows parts of two separate grills.

**Spurious.** A term used to describe items that are not completely genuine and are used to defraud, such as **Fakes, Forgeries, Bogus Stamps,** etc. **Facsimiles** are generally excluded, as they are not issued for fraudulent purposes.

**Stampless Covers.** Envelopes, or sheets folded into envelope form with the written message on the inside, which were sent through the mails in the early days before stamps came into use. These covers usually bear postal markings indicating the date the item was mailed and the post office from which it was mailed.

**Straight Edge.** A stamp with one or two adjacent sides without perforations, caused by cutting the sheet into panes.

**"Strike."** The impression of a handstamp on an envelope or cover.

**Strip**. Three or more unseparated stamps in a row, either side by side ("horizontal strip") or one above the other ("vertical strip").

**Stuffed Cover**. An envelope which has had a card or other stiffening material inserted for protection during cancellation and while in transit.

**Subject Collecting**. See **Topical Collecting.**

**Surcharge.** An overprinted revaluation of a stamp, which may include blocking out the original denomination (face value).

**Surtax**. The added fee on **Semi-Postal Stamps.**

**Syncopated Perforations.** See **Interrupted Perforations.**

**Tab.** See **Coupon.**

**Teeth.** The projections between perforation holes on a stamp.

**Telegraph Stamps**. Stamps used to pay telegraph charges or tolls.

**Tercentenary**. A three-hundredth anniversary or its celebration.

**Tete-Beche**. The term used to describe a pair of unseparated stamps arranged so that one is printed upside-down in relation to the other. The usual method of printing triangular stamps.

**Thematic Collecting**. See **Topical Collecting.**

**"Tied To" or "On Cover."** A stamp affixed to an envelope, card, or wrapper, with a postmark extending over the stamp onto the cover to prove that cover and stamp belong together, and that the stamp was not affixed at another time in a fraudulent attempt to increase its value.

**Topical Collecting**. The increasingly popular practice of collecting only stamps relating to a single subject or theme, such as Sports, Flowers, Animals, etc.

**Torn Stamps**. Slightly-torn stamps are generally acceptable as space-fillers, but should otherwise be rejected. An exception are certain issues of Afghanistan, which were canceled by having the post office clerk tear off a piece of the stamp.

**Town** or **Office Cancellation**. The most common type of postmark, giving the name of the post office where (and usually also the date when) the item was mailed.

**Typeset stamps**. Stamps printed from regular printer's type, rather than from engraved designs.

**Typography.** See **Letterpress.**

**Ultraviolet, UV** or **Quartz Lamp**. A lamp producing strong ultraviolet rays, used by experts to check for tampering, aniline inks, or phosphor tags in postage stamps.

**Underprints**. As an anti-forgery measure, a light color tint or fine repeat design or pattern is sometimes applied underneath the main design of a stamp. See **Burelage.**

**Ungummed.** Some countries with hot, humid climates issue stamps without gum, as gummed stamps would be too prone to stick together. Other ungummed stamps are normally-gummed issues which have, for one reason or another, lost their adhesive, and usually much of their philatelic desirability as well.

**Universal Postal Union** or **U.P.U.** An international organization formed in 1874, and of which virtually all countries are members. The purpose of the U.P.U. is to regulate international postal matters and facilitate cooperation on such issues as worldwide mail distribution, international postal rates, etc.

**Unperforated**. Imperforate.

**Unused**. Not canceled or otherwise defaced, but not necessarily still in mint condition or with original gum.

**Unwatermarked**. A term applied to stamps printed on unwatermarked paper.

**Used**. The term implies a stamp which has been postally-used, as distinguished from canceled-to-order.

**Value. Face Value**, when referring to the amount of money for which the stamp was sold at a post office and for which postal service will be rendered; **Market or Monetary Value,** when referring to its worth as a philatelic commodity.

**Varieties**. Two or more stamps that are not duplicates. See **Major** and **Minor Varieties.**

**Varnish Bars.** Lines or bars of clear varnish, sometimes applied to the face of a stamp to make fraudulent removal of cancellation difficult.

**Vignette**. The main portion of a stamp design, usually the portrait or picture inside the border.

**"Wallpaper."** A disparaging term used to describe sheets of stamps which have little or no philatelic market value.

**Want List.** One of the most effective ways for a collector to obtain the stamps he needs is to submit a want list to a dealer, specifying the catalog number, country, value, desired condition, and quantity of each item wanted.

**War Tax Stamp**. Stamps issued during wartime by some countries, and required to be used on mail in addition to regular postage, the money thus raised being used to help pay the costs of war.

**Watermark**. A design, characters, letters, numerals, or words impressed into paper during its manufacture, and visible in part or whole on each stamp printed on such paper, though usually only with the aid of a watermark detecting device.

**Wove Paper.** The most popular used for printing stamps. Distinguishable by its finely netted texture, created during the paper's manufacture.

**Wrapper**. A sheet of paper, gummed at one end and printed with a stamp, to be used for wrapping and mailing periodicals.

**Zeppelins**. Stamps issued for use on and more recently to commemorate the German Airship Graf Zeppelin.

**Zig-zag or Point Roulette.** A roulette which leaves evenly shaped pointed teeth along the edges of a stamp.

**"Zip Code" Inscription Block.** A block of U.S. stamps containing the sheet margin inscription, "Use Zip Code."

# HOW TO COLLECT STAMPS

## FOREIGN NUMERICAL TABLES

| CHINESE | | ENGLISH |
|---|---|---|
| SIMPLE | FORMAL | |
| 半 | 半 | 1/2 |
| 一 | 壹 | 1 |
| 二 | 貳 | 2 |
| 三 | 叄 | 3 |
| 四 | 肆 | 4 |
| 五 | 伍 | 5 |
| 六 | 陸 | 6 |
| 七 | 柒 | 7 |
| 八 | 捌 | 8 |
| 九 | 玖 | 9 |
| 十 | 拾 | 10 |
| 百 | 佰 | 100 |
| 千 | 仟 | 1,000 |
| 萬 | 萬 | 10,000 |
| 分 | | Cent |
| 圓 | | Dollar |
| 貳 佰 圓 | | $200. |
| 伍 佰 圓 | | $500. |

(EXAMPLES)

160

# FOREIGN NUMERICAL TABLES

| | ARABIC (ALPHA) | ARABIC (EASTERN) | ARABIC (GOBAR) | ARABIC (HYDERBAD) | ARABIC (TURKEY) | BURMESE |
|---|---|---|---|---|---|---|
| 0 | ڡ | ٠ | ٥ | ٠ | ٠ | ၀ |
| 1 | ١ | ١ | ١ | ١ | ١ | ၁ |
| 2 | ٢ | ٢ | ٢ | ٢ | ٢ | ၂ |
| 3 | ٣ | ٣ | ٣ | ٣ | ٣ | ၃ |
| 4 | ٤ | ٤ | ٤ | ٤ | ٤ | ၄ |
| 5 | ٥ | ٥ | ٥ | ٥ | ٥ | ၅ |
| 6 | ٦ | ٦ | ٦ | ٦ | ٦ | ၆ |
| 7 | ٧ | ٧ | ٧ | ٧ | ٧ | ၇ |
| 8 | ٨ | ٨ | ٨ | ٨ | ٨ | ၈ |
| 9 | ٩ | ٩ | ٩ | ٩ | ٩ | ၉ |
| 10 | | ١٠ | ١٠ | ١٠ | ١٠ | ၁၀ |
| 100 | | ١٠٠ | ١٠٠ | ١٠٠ | ١٠٠ | ၁၀၀ |

# FOREIGN NUMERICAL TABLES

## FOREIGN NUMERICAL TABLES

| | MALAY-PERSIAN | MONGOLIAN | NEPALESE | ROMAN | THAI-LAO | TIBETIAN |
|---|---|---|---|---|---|---|
| 0 | • | 0 | 0 | | 0 | o |
| 1 | ١ | ᠑ | ੧ or ੧ | I | ๑ | ༡ |
| 2 | ٢ | ᠒ | ੨ | II | ๒ | ༢ |
| 3 | ٣ | ᠓ | ੩ | III | ๓ | ༣ |
| 4 | ٤ | ᠔ | ੪ | IV | ๔ | ༤ |
| 5 | ٥ | ᠕ | ੫ or ੫ | V | ๕ | ༥ |
| 6 | ٦ or ٦ | ᠖ | ੬ or ੬ | VI | ๖ | ༦ |
| 7 | ٧ | ᠗ | ੭ or ੭ | VII | ๗ | ༧ |
| 8 | ٨ | ᠘ | ੮ or ੮ | VIII | ๘ | ༨ |
| 9 | ٩ | ᠙ | ੯ or ੯ | IX | ๙ | ༩ |
| 10 | ١ • | ᠑᠐ | ੧੦ | X | ๑๐ | ༧ ༠ |
| 100 | ١ • • | ᠑᠐᠐ | ੧੦੦ | C | ๑๐๐ | ༧ ༠༠ |

163

# PHILATELIC HISTORY

In this section you will find a capsule history of most countries as they affect the issuance of stamps. A title in CAPITAL LETTERS signifies that it was or is a stamp-issuing entity under that name. A name in parentheses ( ) shows the name of the country whose stamps were used during that stated time period. In the back of this section you will find a list of countries, islands, protectorates, etc., that no longer issue stamps under those names, although in some cases the country has gained independence and now issues stamps under its new name (Example: Ceylon, now Sri Lanka.)

## CURRENT STAMP-ISSUING COUNTRIES

**AITUTAKI**
| | |
|---|---|
| Prior to 1903 | Part of Cook Islands |
| 1903-1932 | NEW ZEALAND DEPENDENCY |
| 1932-1972 | Part of Cook Islands |
| 1972- | POSTAL REGION OF COOK ISLANDS |

**AFGHANISTAN**
| | |
|---|---|
| 1871-1973 | KINGDOM |
| 1973-1979 | REPUBLIC |
| 1979- 1992 | COMMUNIST REPUBLIC |
| 1992- | ISLAMIC REPUBLIC |

**ALBANIA**
| | |
|---|---|
| 1913-1920 | PROVISIONAL GOVERNMENTS & OCCUPATION ISSUES |
| 1920-1925 | REGENCY |
| 1925-1928 | REPUBLIC |
| 1928-1939 | KINGDOM |
| 1939-1943 | ITALIAN DOMINION |
| 1943-1944 | GERMAN OCCUPATION |
| 1944-1946 | PROVISIONAL GOVERNMENT |
| 1946-1992 | COMMUNIST REPUBLIC |
| 1992- | DEMOCRATIC REPUBLIC |

**ALGERIA**
| | |
|---|---|
| 1849-1871 | French Colony (France) |
| 1871-1924 | Fr. Overseas Department (France) |
| 1924-1958 | FRENCH OVERSEAS DEPARTMENT |
| 1958-1962 | Fr. Overseas Department (France) |
| 1962- | REPUBLIC |

**ANDORRA**
| | |
|---|---|
| 1877-1928 | Principality (France & Spain) |
| 1928- | PRINCIPALITY (1928-on Spanish Issues) (1931-on French Issues) |

**ANGOLA**
| | |
|---|---|
| 1870-1935 | PORTUGUESE COLONY |
| 1935-1951 | OVERSEAS PART OF PORTUGAL |
| 1951-1975 | PORTUGUESE OVERSEAS PROVINCE |
| 1975- | INDEPENDENT STATE |

**ANGUILLA**
| | |
|---|---|
| Prior to 1967 | Part of St. Kitts-Nevis |
| 1967-1969 | SEMI-AUTONOMOUS STATE |
| 1969-1976 | BRITISH ADMINISTRATION |
| 1976-1980 | SELF-GOVERNING PART OF ST. CHRISTOPHER, NEVIS & ANGUILLA |
| 1980- | SELF-GOVERNING BRITISH COLONY |

**ANTIGUA**
| | |
|---|---|
| 1862-1890 | BRITISH COLONY |
| 1890-1903 | Part of Leeward Islands |
| 1903-1956 | LEEWARD ISLAND PRESIDENCY |
| 1967-1981 | BR. WEST INDIES ASSOCIATED STATE |
| 1981- | INDEPENDENT STATE |

**ARGENTINA**
| | |
|---|---|
| 1858-1862 | CONFEDERATION |
| 1862- | REPUBLIC |
| | **Provences:** |
| 1858-1864 | BUENOS AIRES |
| 1858-1865 | CORDOBA |
| 1856-1880 | CORRIENTES |

**ARMENIA**
| | |
|---|---|
| Prior to 1918 | Part of Russia |
| 1918-1919 | National Republic (Russia) |
| 1919-1921 | NATIONAL REPUBLIC |
| 1921-1922 | SOVIET REPUBLIC |
| 1922-1923 | PART OF TRANSCAUCASIAN F.R. |
| 1923-1991 | Part of T.F.R. / Russia |
| 1991- | REPUBLIC |

**ARUBA**
| | |
|---|---|
| 1986- | INDEPENDENT PART OF NETHERLANDS KINGDOM |

# HOW TO COLLECT STAMPS

**ASCENSION**

| | |
|---|---|
| 1867-1922 | British Colony (Great Britain) |
| 1922- | ST. HELENA DEPENDENCY |

**AUSTRALIA**

| | |
|---|---|
| Prior to 1901 | Separate British Colonies of New South Wales, Queensland, South Australia, Tasmania, Victoria and Western Australia |
| 1901-1913 | INDEPENDENT DOMINION — Postage Due Stamps plus issues of separate states |
| 1913- | INDEPENDENT DOMINION |

**AUSTRIA**

| | |
|---|---|
| 1850-1871 | DUAL MONARCHY: Austria-Hungary |
| 1871-1918 | DUAL MONARCHY: for Austria only |
| 1918-1938 | REPUBLIC |
| 1938-1945 | Part of Germany |
| 1945 | ALLIED & U.S.S.R. OCCUPATION ISSUES |
| 1945-1955 | REPUBLIC — Under Allied Occupation |
| 1955- | REPUBLIC |

**AZERBAIDZHAN**

| | |
|---|---|
| Prior to 1918 | Part of Russia |
| 1918-1919 | National Republic (Russia) |
| 1919-1920 | NATIONAL REPUBLIC |
| 1920-1922 | SOVIET REPUBLIC |
| 1922-1923 | PART OF TRANSCAUCASIAN F.R. |
| 1923-1991 | Part of T.F.R. / Russia |
| 1991- | REPUBLIC |

**BAHAMAS**

| | |
|---|---|
| 1859-1973 | BRITISH COLONY |
| 1973- | INDEPENDENT COMMONWEALTH |

**BAHRAIN**

| | |
|---|---|
| 1884-1933 | BRITISH PROTECTORATE (India) |
| 1933-1948 | BRITISH PROTECTORATE — Indian Postal Administration |
| 1948-1966 | BRITISH PROTECTED SHEIKDOM — Independent Postal Administration |
| 1971- | INDEPENDENT SHEIKDOM |

**BANGLADESH**

| | |
|---|---|
| Prior to 1947 | Part of India |
| 1947-1971 | Part of Pakistan |
| 1971-1975 | INDEPENDENT STATE |
| 1975- | REPUBLIC |

**BARBADOS**

| | |
|---|---|
| 1852-1962 | KINGDOM |
| 1962-1966 | SELF-GOVERNING BRITISH COLONY |
| 1966- | PARLIAMENTARY DEMOCRACY |

**BARBUDA**

| | |
|---|---|
| Prior to 1922 | Part of Antigua |
| 1922 | ANTIGUA DEPENDENCY |
| 1922-1968 | Part of Antigua |
| 1968 | ANTIGUA DEPENDENCY |

**BELARUS**

| | |
|---|---|
| Prior to 1918 | Part of Russia |
| 1918-1919 | National Republic (Russia) |
| 1919-1920 | NATIONAL REPUBLIC |
| 1920-1922 | SOVIET REPUBLIC |
| 1922-1923 | PART OF SOVIET SOCIALIST REPUBLIC |
| 1923-1990 | Part of S.S.R. / Russia |
| 1990- | REPUBLIC |

**BELGIUM**

| | |
|---|---|
| 1849-1915 | KINGDOM |
| 1914-1918 | GOVERNMENT-IN-EXILE/ GERMAN OCCUPATION |
| 1918-1940 | KINGDOM |
| 1940-1944 | GERMAN OCCUPATION |
| 1944- | KINGDOM |

**BELIZE**

| | |
|---|---|
| Prior to 1973 | See British Honduras |
| 1973-1981 | SELF-GOVERNING BRITISH COLONY |
| 1981- | INDEPENDENT COMMONWEALTH |

**BENIN**

| | |
|---|---|
| 1892-1894 | FRENCH PROTECTORATE |
| 1894-1975 | See Dahomey |
| 1975- | PEOPLE'S REPUBLIC |

**BERMUDA**

| | |
|---|---|
| 1848-1865 | BRITISH COLONY — Postmasters Provisionals |
| 1865-1968 | BRITISH COLONY |
| 1968- | SEMI-AUTONOMOUS BRITISH COLONY |

**BHUTAN**

| | |
|---|---|
| 1910-1947 | British Protected Kingdom (India) |
| 1947-1962 | Kingdom (India) |
| 1962- | KINGDOM |

**BOLIVIA**

| | |
|---|---|
| 1867- | REPUBLIC |

**BOSNIA & HERZEGOVINA**
| | |
|---|---|
| Prior to 1879 | Part of Turkey |
| 1879-1908 | PROVINCE OF TURKEY UNDER AUSTRIAN OCCUPATION |
| 1908-1918 | AUSTRIAN PROVINCE |
| 1918-1921 | YUGOSLAV PROVINCE |
| 1921-1992 | Part of Yugoslavia |
| 1992- | REPUBLIC |

**BOTSWANA**
| | |
|---|---|
| Prior to 1966 | See Bechuanaland Protectorate |
| 1966- | REPUBLIC |

**BRAZIL**
| | |
|---|---|
| 1843-1890 | EMPIRE |
| 1890 | REPUBLIC |

**BRITISH ANTARCTIC TERRITORY**
| | |
|---|---|
| Prior to 1963 | Part of Falkland Islands Dependencies |
| 1963- | BRITISH TERRITORY |

**BRITISH INDIAN OCEAN TERRITORY**
| | |
|---|---|
| 1847-1965 | Part of Mauritius & Seychelles |
| 1965-1976 | BRITISH TERRITORY |
| 1976-1990 | British Territory (Great Britain) |
| 1990- | BRITISH TERRITORY |

**BRUNEI**
| | |
|---|---|
| 1877-1906 | Part of Straits Settlement |
| 1906-1942 | BRITISH PROTECTED SULTANATE |
| 1942-1945 | JAPANESE OCCUPATION |
| 1945-1947 | Br. Military Administration (Sarawak; North Borneo, Australia) |
| 1947-1983 | BRITISH PROTECTED SULTANATE |
| 1983- | INDEPENDENT SULTANATE |

**BULGARIA**
| | |
|---|---|
| 1863-1878 | Part of Turkey |
| 1878-1885 | PRINCIPALITY UNDER TURKISH DOMINION |
| 1885-1908 | PRINCIPALITY |
| 1908-1944 | KINGDOM |
| 1944-1946 | PROVISIONAL GOVERNMENT |
| 1946-1991 | COMMUNIST REPUBLIC |
| 1991- | DEMOCRACY |

**BURKINA FASO**
| | |
|---|---|
| 1906-1920 | Part of Upper Senegal & Niger |
| 1920-1933 | COLONY OF FRENCH WEST AFRICA |
| 1933-1958 | Part of Fr. Sudan, Ivory Coast and Niger Terr. |
| 1958-1984 | REPULIC OF UPPER VOLTA |
| 1984- | REPUBLIC |

**BURUNDI**
| | |
|---|---|
| 1924-1962 | Part of Ruanda-Urundi |
| 1962-1966 | MONARCHY |
| 1966- | REPUBLIC |

**CAMBODIA**
| | |
|---|---|
| Prior to 1946 | Part of Indochina |
| 1946-1951 | Autonomous Kingdom (Indochina) |
| 1951-1955 | KINGDOM OF FRENCH UNION |
| 1955-1970 | KINGDOM |
| 1970-1975 | KHMER REPUBLIC |
| 1975-1979 | COMMUNIST REPUBLIC |
| 1979-1991 | KAMPUCHEA REPUBLIC - Vietnamese occupation |
| 1991- | UNDER U.N. MANAGEMENT |

NOTE: Since 1975 it has been illegal to import Cambodian stamps into the United States.

**CAMEROUN**
| | |
|---|---|
| 1897-1915 | GERMAN PROTECTORATE |
| 1915-1919 | FRENCH OCCUPATION |
| 1919-1946 | FRENCH MANDATE |
| 1946-1959 | FRENCH U.N. TRUSTEESHIP |
| 1960-1961 | REPUBLIC |
| 1961-1972 | FEDERAL REPUBLIC |
| 1972- | UNITED REPUBLIC |

Also see Cameroons.

**CANADA**
| | |
|---|---|
| 1851-1867 | British Colony |
| 1867- | INDEPENDENT DOMINION OF BRITISH COMMONWEALTH |

**CAPE VERDE**
| | |
|---|---|
| 1877-1951 | PORTUGUESE COLONY |
| 1951-1975 | PORTUGUESE OVERSEAS PROVINCE |
| 1975- | REPUBLIC |

**CAYMAN ISLANDS**
| | |
|---|---|
| 1889-1900 | Dependency of Jamaica (Jamaica) |
| 1900-1962 | DEPENDENCY OF JAMAICA |
| 1962- | BRITISH COLONY |

# HOW TO COLLECT STAMPS

**CENTRAL AFRICA**
| | |
|---|---|
| Prior to 1958 | See Ubangi-Shari |
| 1958-1959 | Autonomous Republic (Fr. Equatorial Africa) |
| 1959-1960 | AUTONOMOUS REPUBLIC |
| 1960-1976 | REPUBLIC |
| 1976-1979 | EMPIRE |
| 1979- | REPUBLIC |

**CHAD**
| | |
|---|---|
| 1915-1922 | Part of Ubangi-Shari-Chad |
| 1922-1936 | COLONY OF FRENCH EQUATORIAL AFRICA |
| 1936-1958 | Part of Fr. Equatorial Africa |
| 1958-1959 | Autonomous Republic (Fr. Equatorial Africa) |
| 1959-1960 | AUTONOMOUS REPUBLIC |
| 1960- | REPUBLIC |

**CHILE**
| | |
|---|---|
| 1853- | REPUBLIC |

**CHINA: Taiwan**
| | |
|---|---|
| Prior to 1949 | See China |
| 1949- | NATIONALIST REPUBLIC |

**CHINA: People's Republic**
| | |
|---|---|
| Prior to 1949 | See China |
| 1949- | COMMUNIST REPUBLIC |

NOTE: Starting as early as 1929, regional issues were used in Communist-controlled areas of China.

**CHRISTMAS ISLAND**
| | |
|---|---|
| Prior to 1948 | Part of Straits Settlements |
| 1948-1958 | Dependency of Singapore (Singapore) |
| 1958- | AUSTRALIAN TERRITORY |

**COCOS ISLANDS**
| | |
|---|---|
| 1955-1963 | Australian Possession (Australia) |
| 1963- | AUSTRALIAN TERRITORY |

**COLOMBIA**
| | |
|---|---|
| 1859-1861 | GRANADINE CONFEDERATION |
| 1861-1862 | UNITED STATES OF NEW GRANADA |
| 1862-1886 | UNITED STATES OF COLOMBIA |
| 1886- | REPUBLIC |

**States and Departments:**
Antioguia, Boliva, Boyaca, Cauca, Cundinimarca, Panama, Santander, Tolima

**COMOROS**

**Comoro Islands**
| | |
|---|---|
| 1892-1914 | Issues of separate islands (Anjouan, Grand Comoro, Mayotte, Moheli) |
| 1914-1946 | Part of Madagascar |
| 1946-1950 | Fr. Overseas Territory (Madagascar) |
| 1950-1975 | FRENCH OVERSEAS TERRITORY |

**Comoros (without Mayotte)**
| | |
|---|---|
| 1975-1978 | REPUBLIC |
| 1978- | ISLAMIC REPUBLIC |

**CONGO REPUBLIC**
| | |
|---|---|
| Prior to 1958 | BRITISH POSSESSION |
| 1901-1919 | NEW ZEALAND DEPEN-DENCY |
| 1919-1932 | Raratonga - NEW ZEALAND DEPENDENCY |
| 1932-1965 | NEW ZEALAND DEPEN-DENCY |
| 1965- | SELF-GOVERNING STATE WITH NEW ZEALAND ASSOCIATION |

**COSTA RICA**
| | |
|---|---|
| 1863- | REPUBLIC |

**Province Issues:**
| | |
|---|---|
| 1885-1891 | GUANACASTE |

**CROATIA**
| | |
|---|---|
| Prior to 1941 | Part of Yugoslavia |
| 1941-1945 | GERMAN PUPPET REPUBLIC |
| 1945-1991 | Part of Yugoslavia |
| 1991- | REPUBLIC |

**CUBA**

**Cuba and Puerto Rico:**
| | |
|---|---|
| 1855-1873 | SPANISH COLONIES - Joint Issues |

**Cuba:**
| | |
|---|---|
| 1873-1898 | SPANISH COLONY |
| 1898-1899 | U.S. ADMINISTRATION |
| 1899-1902 | REPUBLIC UNDER U.S. RULE |
| 1902-1959 | REPUBLIC |
| 1959- | COMMUNIST REPUBLIC |

NOTE: Since 1962, it has been illegal to import Cuban stamps into the United States.

**CYPRUS**
| | |
|---|---|
| Prior to 1878 | Part of Turkey |
| 1878-1880 | British Administration (Great Britain) |

# HOW TO COLLECT STAMPS

| 1880-1925 | BRITISH ADMINISTRATION |
| 1925-1960 | BRITISH COLONY |
| 1960- | REPUBLIC |

NOTE: Part of Cyprus is under Turkish Occupation and issues local stamps for that region.

**CZECH REPUBLIC**

| Prior to 1918 | Part of Austria-Hungary |
| 1918-1939 | REPUBLIC OF CZECHOSLOVAKIA |
| 1939-1945 | Under German & Hungarian Occupation See Bohemia & Moravia under Vanished Lands and Slovakia under Current Stamp Issuing Countries |
| 1945-1948 | REPUBLIC OF CZECHOSLOVAKIA |
| 1948-1968 | COMMUNIST REPUBLIC |
| 1968-1992 | COMMUNIST FEDERAL REPUBLIC |
| 1993- | REPUBLIC |

**DENMARK**

| 1851-1940 | KINGDOM |
| 1940-1945 | GERMAN OCCUPATION |
| 1945- | KINGDOM |

**DJIBOUTI**

| 1893-1902 | FRENCH POSSESSION |
| 1902-1977 | See Somali Coast; Afars & Issas |
| 1977- | REPUBLIC |

**DOMINICA**

| 1860-1874 | British Colony (Handstamps) |
| 1874-1890 | BRITISH COLONY |
| 1890-1903 | Part of Leewards Islands |
| 1903-1939 | PRESIDENCY OF LEEWARD ISLANDS |
| 1940-1968 | BRITISH COLONY |
| 1968-1978 | BR. WEST INDIES ASSOCIATED STATE |
| 1978- | INDEPENDENT COMMONWEALTH |

**DOMINICAN REPUBLIC**

| | **Santo Domingo:** |
| 1861-1865 | Spanish Colony (Cuba & Puerto Rico) |
| | **Dominican Republic:** |
| 1865- | REPUBLIC |

**ECUADOR**

| 1865- | REPUBLIC |
| | **Territory:** |
| 1957-1959 | GALAPAGOS ISLANDS |

**EGYPT**

| 1866-1882 | TURKISH SUZERAINTY |
| 1882-1914 | NOMINAL TURKISH SUZERAINTY UNDER BRITISH ADMINISTRATION |
| 1914-1922 | BRITISH PROTECTORATE |
| 1922-1953 | KINGDOM |
| 1953-1958 | REPUBLIC |
| 1958-1971 | UNITED ARAB REPUBLIC |
| 1971- | REPUBLIC |

**EQUATORIAL GUINEA**

| Prior to 1968 | See Spanish Guinea |
| 1968- | REPUBLIC |

**ESTONIA**

| Prior to 1918 | Part of Russia |
| 1918 | GERMAN OCCUPATION |
| 1918-1940 | REPUBLIC |
| 1940-1941 | Russian Occupation (Russia) |
| 1941 | GERMAN OCCUPATION |
| 1941-1944 | German Occupation (Russia-Ostland) |
| 1944-1991 | Part of Russia |
| 1991- | INDEPENDENT REPUBLIC |

**ETHIOPIA**

| 1894-1936 | MONARCHY |
| 1936 | ITALIAN OCCUPATION |
| 1936-1938 | DISTRICT OF ITALIAN EAST AFRICA |
| 1938-1941 | Part of Italian East Africa |
| 1941-1942 | British Occupation (Great Britain) |
| 1942-1943 | Monarchy (Middle East Forces) |
| 1943-1974 | MONARCHY |
| 1974- | MARXIST STATE |

**FALKLAND ISLANDS**

| 1878- | BRITISH COLONY |

**FALKLAND IS. DEPENDENCIES**

| Prior to 1946 | Part of Falkland Islands |
| 1946-1963 | DEPENDENCY OF FALKLAND ISLANDS |
| 1963-1980 | Divided between British Antarctic Territory & South Georgia |
| 1980- | DEPENDENCY OF FALKLAND ISLANDS |
| | **Regional Issues:** |
| 1944-1946 | GRAHAM LAND; SOUTH |

# HOW TO COLLECT STAMPS

GEORGIA; SOUTH
ORKNEYS AND SOUTH
SHETLANDS

**FAROE ISLANDS**

| | |
|---|---|
| 1851-1940 | Part of Danish Kingdom (Denmark) |
| 1919 | LOCAL ISSUES |
| 1940-1945 | BRITISH ADMINISTRATION |
| 1945-1975 | Part of Danish Kingdom (Denmark) |
| 1975- | AUTONOMOUS DISTRICT OF DANISH KINGDOM |

**FIJI**

| | |
|---|---|
| 1870-1874 | BRITISH PROTECTED KINGDOM |
| 1874-1970 | BRITISH COLONY |
| 1970- | INDEPENDENT BRITISH DOMINION |

**FINLAND**

| | |
|---|---|
| 1856-1917 | RUSSIAN GRAND DUCHY |
| 1917-1919 | INDEPENDENT STATE |
| 1919- | REPUBLIC |
| | **Regional Issues:** |
| 1984- | ALAND ISLANDS |

**FRANCE**

| | |
|---|---|
| 1849-1852 | REPUBLIC |
| 1852-1870 | EMPIRE |
| 1870-1940 | REPUBLIC |
| 1940-1942 | GERMAN OCCUPATION (North) & VICHY GOVERNMENT (South) |
| 1942-1944 | GERMAN OCCUPATION |
| 1944-1946 | PROVISIONAL GOVERNMENT |
| 1946- | REPUBLIC |

**FRENCH POLYNESIA**

| | |
|---|---|
| | **French Oceania:** |
| 1882-1892 | French Colony (Tahiti) |
| 1892-1958 | FRENCH COLONY |
| | **French Polynesia:** |
| 1958- | FRENCH OVERSEAS TERRITORY |

**FRENCH SOUTHERN & ANTARCTIC TERRITORIES**

| | |
|---|---|
| Prior to 1955 | Dependency of Madagascar (Madagascar) |
| 1955- | FRENCH TERRITORIES |

**GABON**

| | |
|---|---|
| 1886-1891 | FRENCH COLONY |
| 1891-1904 | Part of French Congo |
| 1904-1910 | FRENCH COLONY |
| 1910-1936 | COLONY OF FRENCH EQUATORIAL AFRICA |
| 1936-1958 | Part of French Equatorial Africa |
| 1958-1959 | Autonomous Republic (Fr. Equatorial Africa) |
| 1960- | REPUBLIC |

**GAMBIA**

| | |
|---|---|
| 1869-1888 | DEPENDENCY OF SIERRA LEONE |
| 1888-1965 | BRITISH COLONY |
| 1965-1970 | INDEPENDENT STATE |
| 1970- | REPUBLIC |

**GEORGIA**

| | |
|---|---|
| Prior to 1918 | Part of Russia |
| 1918 | GERMAN OCCUPATION |
| 1918-1940 | REPUBLIC |
| 1940-1941 | Russian Occupation (Russia) |
| 1941 | GERMAN OCCUPATION |
| 1941-1944 | German Occupation (Russia-Ostland) |
| 1944-1991 | Part of Russia |
| 1991- | REPUBLIC |

**GERMANY**

| | |
|---|---|
| | **Germany:** |
| Prior to 1872 | Separate States |
| 1872-1918 | EMPIRE |
| 1918-1933 | REPUBLIC |
| 1933-1945 | NAZI STATE |
| | **West Germany:** |
| 1945-1949 | VARIOUS U.S., BRITISH & FRENCH OCCUPATION ISSUES |
| 1949- | GERMAN FEDERAL REPUBLIC |

**GHANA**

| | |
|---|---|
| Prior to 1957 | See Gold Coast |
| 1957-1960 | INDEPENDENT STATE |
| 1960- | REPUBLIC |

**GIBRALTAR**

| | |
|---|---|
| 1857-1885 | British Colony (Great Britain) |
| 1885- | BRITISH COLONY |

**GREAT BRITAIN**

| | |
|---|---|
| 1840- | CONSTITUTIONAL MONARCHY |
| | **Regional Issues:** |
| 1958-1969 | GUERNSEY |
| 1958-1969 | JERSEY |
| 1958-1973 | MAN, ISLE OF |
| 1958- | NORTHERN IRELAND |
| 1958- | SCOTLAND |

| 1958- | WALES & MONMOUTHSHIRE |
|---|---|

**GREAT BRITAIN: Guernsey**

| 1840-1940 | Part of Great Britain |
|---|---|
| 1940-1945 | GERMAN OCCUPATION |
| 1945-1958 | Part of Great Britain |
| 1958-1969 | REGIONAL ISSUES (Great Britain) |
| 1969- | AUTONOMOUS BAILIWICK OF UNITED KINGDOM |

**GREAT BRITAIN: Jersey**

| 1840-1940 | Part of Great Britain |
|---|---|
| 1940-1945 | GERMAN OCCUPATION |
| 1945-1958 | Part of Great Britain |
| 1958-1969 | REGIONAL ISSUES (Great Britain) |
| 1969- | AUTONOMOUS BAILIWICK OF UNITED KINGDOM |

**GREAT BRITAIN: Isle of Man**

| 1840-1958 | Part of Great Britain |
|---|---|
| 1958-1973 | REGIONAL ISSUES (Great Britain) |
| 1973- | AUTONOMOUS REGION OF UNITED KINGDOM |

**GREECE**

| 1861-1924 | KINGDOM |
|---|---|
| 1924-1935 | REPUBLIC |
| 1935-1941 | KINGDOM |
| 1941-1944 | GERMAN AND ITALIAN OCCUPATION |
| 1944-1946 | REGENCY |
| 1946-1967 | KINGDOM |
| 1967-1963 | MILITARY GOVERNMENT |
| 1973- | REPUBLIC |

**GREENLAND**

| Prior to 1905 | Danish Colony (Denmark) |
|---|---|
| 1905-1937 | DANISH COLONY (Parcel Post Issues plus Denmark) |
| 1938-1940 | DANISH COLONY |
| 1940-1945 | U.S. PROTECTORATE |
| 1945-1953 | DANISH COLONY |
| 1953-1979 | PART OF DANISH KINGDOM |
| 1979- | PART OF DANISH KINGDOM WITH HOME RULE |

**GRENADA**

| 1861-1967 | BRITISH COLONY |
|---|---|
| 1967-1974 | BR. WEST INDIES ASSOCIATED STATE |
| 1974-1979 | INDEPENDENT STATE |
| 1979-1983 | MARXIST STATE |

| 1983- | INDEPENDENT STATE |
|---|---|
| | **Regional Issues:** |
| 1973- | GRENADA GRENADINES |

**GUATEMALA**

| 1871- | REPUBLIC |
|---|---|

**GUINEA**

| Prior to 1958 | See French Guinea |
|---|---|
| 1958-1959 | Republic (French West Africa) |
| 1959- | REPUBLIC |

**GUINEA-BISSAU**

| Prior to 1974 | See Portuguese Guinea |
|---|---|
| 1974- | REPUBLIC |

**GUYANA**

| Prior to 1966 | See British Guiana |
|---|---|
| 1966-1970 | INDEPENDENT STATE |
| 1970- | REPUBLIC |

**HAITI**

| 1881- | REPUBLIC |
|---|---|

**HONDURAS**

| 1866- | REPUBLIC |
|---|---|

**HONG KONG**

| 1862-1942 | BRITISH COLONY |
|---|---|
| 1942-1945 | Japanese Occupation (Japan) |
| 1945 | JAPANESE OCCUPATION |
| 1945- | BRITISH COLONY |

**HUNGARY**

| 1850-1871 | Part of Austria-Hungary |
|---|---|
| 1871-1918 | DUAL MONARCHY - Issues for Hungary only |
| 1918-1919 | PEOPLE'S REPUBLIC |
| 1919 | SOVIET REPUBLIC |
| 1919-1920 | NATIONAL GOVERNMENT |
| 1920-1944 | REGENCY |
| 1944-1946 | PROVISIONAL GOVERNMENT |
| 1946-1990 | COMMUNIST REPUBLIC |
| 1990- | REPUBLIC |

**ICELAND**

| 1870-1873 | Danish Colony (Denmark) |
|---|---|
| 1873-1918 | DANISH ADMINISTRATION |
| 1918-1940 | KINGDOM UNDER DANISH CROWN |
| 1940-1944 | BRITISH & U.S. ADMINISTRATION |
| 1944- | REPUBLIC |

## INDIA

| | |
|---|---|
| 1852-1854 | SCINDE DISTRICT POST |
| 1854-1860 | EAST INDIA COMPANY ADMINISTRATION |
| 1860-1877 | BRITISH COLONY |
| 1877-1947 | EMPIRE UNDER BRITISH CROWN |
| 1957-1950 | INDEPENDENT BRITISH DOMINION |
| 1950- | REPUBLIC |

## INDONESIA

| | |
|---|---|
| Prior to 1958 | See Netherlands Indies |
| 1948-1949 | NETHERLANDS COLONY |
| 1949 | AUTONOMOUS STATE |
| 1949-1950 | UNITED STATES OF INDONESIA |
| 1950- | REPUBLIC |
| | **District:** |
| 1954-1964 | RIOUW ARCHIPELAGO |

## IRAN

| | |
|---|---|
| | **Persia:** |
| 1870-1935 | KINGDOM |
| | **Iran:** |
| 1935-1979 | KINGDOM |
| 1979- | ISLAMIC STATE |

NOTE: Importation prohibited since Oct. 29, 1987.

## IRAQ

| | |
|---|---|
| Prior to 1923 | See Mesopotamia |
| 1923-1932 | BRITISH MANDATE |
| 1932-1958 | KINGDOM |
| 1958- | REPUBLIC |

NOTE: Importation prohibited since 1992.

## IRELAND

| | |
|---|---|
| 1840-1922 | PART OF GREAT BRITAIN |
| | Irish FreeState: |
| 1922 | PROVISIONAL GOVERNMENT |
| 1922-1937 | INDEPENDENT BRITISH DOMINION |
| | **Eire:** |
| 1937-1949 | INDEPENDENT STATE |
| | **Ireland:** |
| 1949- | REPUBLIC |

## ISRAEL

| | |
|---|---|
| Prior to 1948 | See Palestine |
| 1948- | REPUBLIC |

## ITALY

| | |
|---|---|
| Prior to 1861 | Separate States |
| 1861-1862 | Kingdom (Sardinia and Neopolitan Provinces) |
| 1862-1922 | KINGDOM |
| 1922-1943 | FASCIST KINGDOM |
| 1943 | ALLIED MILITARY GOVERNMENT |
| 1943-1946 | KINGDOM |
| 1946- | REPUBLIC |

## IVORY COAST

| | |
|---|---|
| 1892-1895 | FRENCH COLONY |
| 1895-1941 | COLONY OF FRENCH WEST AFRICA |
| 1941-1942 | VICHY FRENCH COLONY |
| 1942-1944 | COLONY OF FRENCH WEST AFRICA |
| 1944-1958 | Part of French West Africa |
| 1958-1959 | Autonomous Republic (Fr. West Africa) |
| 1959-1960 | AUTONOMOUS REPUBLIC |
| 1960- | REPUBLIC |

## JAMAICA

| | |
|---|---|
| 1860-1962 | BRITISH COLONY |
| 1962- | INDEPENDENT STATE |

## JAPAN

| | |
|---|---|
| 1871-1945 | EMPIRE |
| 1945-1948 | U.S. MILITARY RULE |
| 1948- | CONSTITUTIONAL MONARCHY |

## JORDAN

| | |
|---|---|
| | **Trans-Jordan:** |
| 1918-1920 | Part of Palestine |
| 1920-1946 | KINGDOM UNDER BRITISH MANDATE |
| 1946-1949 | KINGDOM |
| | **Jordan:** |
| 1949- | KINGDOM |

## KAZAKHSTAN

| | |
|---|---|
| Prior to 1918 | Part of Russia |
| 1918-1919 | National Republic (Russia) |
| 1919-1921 | NATIONAL REPUBLIC |
| 1921-1922 | SOVIET REPUBLIC |
| 1922-1924 | REPUBLIC OF RUSSIA |
| 1924-1991 | Part of Russia |
| 1991- | REPUBLIC |

## KENYA

| | |
|---|---|
| Prior to 1922 | See British East Africa |
| 1922-1935 | British Colony (Kenya & Uganda) |
| 1935-1963 | British Colony (Kenya, Uganda & Tanganyika) |
| 1963-1964 | INDEPENDENT STATE |

1964-          REPUBLIC
NOTE: From 1963-1977 Kenya also used
stamps of Kenya, Uganda & Tanzania.

## KIRIBATI
Prior to 1979   See Gilbert Islands
1979-          REPUBLIC

## KOREA: South
### Korea:
1884-1897      KINGDOM
1897-1905      EMPIRE
1905-1945      Japanese Rule (Japan)
1945           Divided into North & South
               South Korea:
1945-1946      U.S. Occupation (Japan)
1946-1948      U.S. MILITARY RULE
1948-          REPUBLIC

## KUWAIT
1899-1914      Br. Protected Sheikdom
               (Turkey)
1914-1923      Br. Protected Sheikdom (India)
1923-1948      BRITISH PROTECTED
               SHEIKDOM (Indian Postal
               Administration)
1948-1959      BRITISH PROTECTED
               SHEIKDOM (British Postal
               Administration)
1959-1961      BRITISH PROTECTED
               SHEIKDOM (Independent
               Postal Administration)
1961-          INDEPENDENT SHEIKDOM

## KYRGYZSTAN
Prior to 1918   Part of Russia
1918-1919      National Republic (Russia)
1919-1920      NATIONAL REPUBLIC
1920-1921      SOVIET REPUBLIC
1922-1923      PART OF SOVIET
               SOCIALIST REPUBLIC
1923-1990      Part of S.S.R. / Russia
1991-          REPUBLIC

## LAOS
1899-1947      Part of Indochina
1947-1951      Autonomous Kingdom
               (Indochina)
1951-1956      KINGDOM OF FRENCH
               UNION
1956-1975      KINGDOM
1975-          COMMUNIST REPUBLIC
               (Vietnamese Occupation)

## LATVIA
Prior to 1916   Part of Russia

1918-1919      INDEPENDENT STATE
1919           RUSSIAN OCCUPATION
1919-1940      REPUBLIC
1940           RUSSIAN OCCUPATION
1940-1941      Part of Russia
1941-1944      Part of German Eastern
               Command
1944-1991      Part of Russia
1991-          INDEPENDENT REPUBLIC

## LEBANON
1918-1919      Part of Palestine
1919-1924      Part of Syria
1924-1926      FRENCH MANDATE
1926-1941      AUTONOMOUS REPUBLIC
               UNDER FRENCH MANDATE
1941-          REPUBLIC

## LESOTHO
Prior to 1966   See Basutoland
1966-          KINGDOM

## LIBERIA
1860-          REPUBLIC

## LIBYA
### Libia:
    -1912      Part of Turkey
1912-1939      ITALIAN COLONY
1939-1942      PROVINCES OF ITALY
1942-1951      Divided into various
               Occupation Areas
### Libya:
1951-1952      Kingdom (Separate Areas)
1952-1969      KINGDOM
1969-          ARAB REPUBLIC
NOTE: Importation prohibited since Jan. 7,
1986.

## LIECHTENSTEIN
1866-1912      Principality (Austria)
1912-1920      PRINCIPALITY (Austrian
               Postal Admin.)
1920-1921      PRINCIPALITY (National
               Postal Admin.)
1921-          PRINCIPALITY (Swiss Postal
               Admin.)

## LITHUANIA
Prior to 1916   Part of Russia
1916-1918      GERMAN OCCUPATION
1918-1919      INDEPENDENT STATE
1919-1940      REPUBLIC
1940           RUSSIAN OCCUPATION
1940-1941      Part of Russia

| | | |
|---|---|---|
| 1941-1944 | Part of German Eastern Command | |
| 1944-1991 | Part of Russia | |
| 1991- | INDEPENDENT STATE | |

**LUXEMBOURG**

| | |
|---|---|
| 1852-1914 | GRAND DUCHY |
| 1914-1918 | Part of Germany |
| 1918-1940 | GRAND DUCHY |
| 1940-1941 | GERMAN OCCUPATION |
| 1941-1944 | Part of Germany |
| 1944- | GRAND DUCHY |

**MACAO**

| | |
|---|---|
| 1863-1884 | Portuguese Colony (Hong Kong) |
| 1884-1951 | PORTUGUESE COLONY |
| 1951-1976 | PORTUGUESE OVERSEAS PROVINCE |
| 1976- | AUTONOMOUS PORTU-GUESE PROVINCE |

**MADAGASCAR**

| | |
|---|---|
| 1889-1896 | French Protectorate (Fr. Post Offices in Madagascar) |
| 1896-1958 | FRENCH COLONY |
| 1958-1960 | AUTONOMOUS REPUBLIC |
| 1960-1975 | MALAGASY REPUBLIC |
| 1975- | REPUBLIC |

**MALAWI**

| | |
|---|---|
| Prior to 1964 | See Nyasaland Protectorate |
| 1964-1966 | INDEPENDENT STATE |
| 1966- | REPUBLIC |

**MALAYSIA**

| | |
|---|---|
| Prior to 1963 | See Malaya, North Borneo and Sarawak |
| 1963- | FEDERATED MONARCHY |

**MALDIVES**

| | |
|---|---|
| 1887-1906 | Dependency of Ceylon (Ceylon) |
| 1906-1948 | CEYLON DEPENDENCY |
| 1948-1965 | BRITISH PROTECTED SULTANATE |
| 1965-1968 | INDEPENDENT SULTANATE |
| 1968- | REPUBLIC |

**MALI**

| | |
|---|---|
| Prior to 1958 | See French Sudan |
| 1958-1959 | Autonomous Republic (French West Africa) |
| 1959-1960 | Part of Mali Federation |
| 1960- | REPUBLIC |

**MALTA**

| | |
|---|---|
| 1857-1860 | British Colony (Great Britain) |
| 1860-1964 | BRITISH COLONY |
| 1964-1974 | INDEPENDENT STATE |
| 1974- | REPUBLIC |

**MARSHALL ISLANDS**

| | |
|---|---|
| 1889-1897 | German Protectorate (Germany) |
| 1897-1914 | GERMAN PROTECTORATE |
| 1914-1945 | Japanese Occupation and Mandate (Japan) |
| 1945-1947 | U.S. Occupation (U.S.) |
| 1947-1984 | Part of Trust Territories of the Pacific (U.S.) |
| 1984- | AUTONOMOUS STATE OF TERRITORIES OF THE PACIFIC |

**MAURITIUS**

| | |
|---|---|
| 1847-1968 | BRITISH COLONY |
| 1968- | INDEPENDENT STATE |

**MAURITANIA**

| | |
|---|---|
| 1899-1903 | Part of Fr. West Africa (Fr. Soudan) |
| 1903-1906 | Part of Fr. West Africa (Senegambia & Niger) |
| 1906-1944 | COLONY OF FRENCH WEST AFRICA |
| 1944-1958 | Part of French West Africa |
| 1958-1959 | Autonomous Republic (French West Africa) |
| 1959- | ISLAMIC REPUBLIC |

**MEXICO**

| | |
|---|---|
| 1856-1864 | REPUBLIC |
| 1864-1867 | EMPIRE UNDER BRITISH PROTECTORATE |
| 1867- | REPUBLIC |

**MICRONESIA**

| | |
|---|---|
| Prior to 1977 | Part of Caroline Islands |
| 1977-1984 | State of Trust Territories of the Pacific (U.S.) |
| 1984- | AUTONOMOUS STATE OF U.S. TRUST TERRITORIES OF THE PACIFIC |

**MOLDOVA**

| | |
|---|---|
| Prior to 1918 | Part of Russia |
| 1918-1919 | National Republic (Russia) |
| 1919-1920 | NATIONAL REPUBLIC |
| 1921-1922 | SOVIET REPUBLIC |
| 1922-1923 | PART OF SOVIET SOCIALIST REPUBLIC |
| 1923-1991 | Part of S.S.R. / Russia |

| | |
|---|---|
| 1991- | REPUBLIC |

**MONACO**
| 1851-1860 | Principality (Sardinia) |
| 1860-1885 | Principality (France) |
| 1885- | PRINCIPALITY |

**MONGOLIA**
| Prior to 1912 | Part of China |
| 1912-1924 | Autonomous Republic (China) |
| 1924-1945 | AUTONOMOUS SOVIET REPUBLIC |
| 1945- | COMMUNIST REPUBLIC |

**MONSERRAT**
| 1860-1876 | British Colony (Handstamps) |
| 1876-1890 | BRITISH COLONY |
| 1890-1903 | Part of Leeward Islands |
| 1903-1956 | LEEWARD IS. PRESIDENCY |
| 1956- | BRITISH COLONY |

**MOROCCO**
| 1891-1912 | Kingdom (Various Foreign Post Offices) |
| 1912-1956 | Divided into Fr. Morocco, Sp. Morocco and Tangier |
| 1956-1958 | KINGDOM - Issues for Northern & Southern Zones |
| 1958- | KINGDOM |

**MOZAMBIQUE**
| 1877-1951 | PORTUGUESE COLONY |
| 1951-1975 | PORTUGAL OVERSEAS PROVINCE |
| 1975- | PEOPLE'S REPUBLIC |

**MYANMAR**
| Prior to 1937 | Part of India |
| 1937-1942 | BURMA BRITISH DOMINION |
| 1942 | BURMA INDEPENDENCE ARMY - Japanese controlled areas. |
| 1942-1945 | JAPANESE OCCUPATION |
| 1945-1948 | BRITISH MILITARY ADMINISTRATION |
| 1946-1948 | INTERIM GOVERNMENT |
| 1948-1989 | REPUBLIC OF BURMA |
| 1989- | REPUBLIC OF MYANMAR |

**NAMIBIA**
| 1886-1897 | German Colony (Germany) |
| 1897-1915 | GERMAN COLONY |

| 1915-1923 | S.WEST AFRICA - Union of S. Africa Occup. (Union of South Africa) |
| 1923-1946 | SOUTH AFRICAN MANDATE |
| 1946-1990 | SOUTH AFRICAN ADMINIS-TRATION |
| 1990- | REPUBLIC |

**NAURU**
| 1889-1914 | Part of Marshall Islands |
| 1914-1916 | Part of Northwest Pacific Islands |
| 1916-1920 | BRITISH ADMINISTRATION |
| 1920-1942 | JOINT BRITISH, AUSTRALIAN & NEW ZEALAND ADMINISTRATION |
| 1942-1945 | Japanese Occupation (Japan) |
| 1945-1968 | JOINT BRITISH, AUSTRALIAN, & NEW ZEALAND ADMINISTRATION |
| 1968- | REPUBLIC |

**NEPAL**
| 1854-1881 | Kingdom (India) |
| 1881- | KINGDOM |

**NETHERLANDS**
| 1852-1940 | KINGDOM |
| 1940-1945 | GERMAN OCCUPATION |
| 1945- | KINGDOM |

**NETHERLANDS ANTILLES**
**Curacao:**
| 1873-1948 | NETHERLANDS COLONY |
**Netherlands Antilles:**
| 1948-1954 | NETHERLANDS COLONY |
| 1954- | AUTONOMOUS PART OF NETHERLANDS KINGDOM |

**NEVIS**
| 1861-1890 | BRITISH COLONY |
| 1890-1903 | Part of Leeward Islands |
| 1903-1956 | Part of St. Kitts-Nevis Leeward Isl. |
| 1956-1980 | Part of St. Kitts-Nevis |
| 1980- | PART OF ST. KITTS-NEVIS |

**NEW CALEDONIA**
| 1858-1862 | FRENCH COLONY |
| 1862-1881 | French Colony (French Colonies) |
| 1881-1946 | FRENCH COLONY |
| 1946- | FRENCH OVERSEAS TERRITORY |

# HOW TO COLLECT STAMPS

**NEW ZEALAND**
1855-1907   BRITISH COLONY
1907-   INDEPENDENT BRITISH DOMINION

**NICARAGUA**
1862-1981   REPUBLIC
1981-   SANDINISTA GOVERNMENT

**NIGER**
1862-1921   Part of Upper Senegal & Niger
1921-1922   TERRITORY OF FR. WEST AFRICA
1922-1944   COLONY OF FRENCH WEST AFRICA
1944-1958   Part of French West Africa
1958-1960   Autonomous Republic (Fr. West Africa)
1960   AUTONOMOUS REPUBLIC
1960-   REPUBLIC

**NIGERIA**
-1914   See Northern & Southern Nigeria
1914-1960   BRITISH COLONY & PROTECTORATE
1960-1963   FEDERATED STATE
1963-   FEDERAL REPUBLIC

**NIUE**
1892-1902   Part of Cook Islands
1902-1974   NEW ZEALAND DEPENDENCY
1974-   SELF-GOVERNING STATE WITH NEW ZEALAND ASSOCIATION

**NORFOLK ISLAND**
1914-1947   Australian Dependency (Australia)
1947-   AUSTRALIAN DEPENDENCY

**NORWAY**
1855-1905   KINGDOM UNDER SWEDISH RULE
1905-1940   KINGDOM
1940-1945   GERMAN OCCUPATION
1945-   KINGDOM

**OMAN**
**Muscat & Oman:**
1864-1944   British Protected Sultanate (India)

1944-1947   BRITISH PROTECTED SULTANATE
1947-1948   Br. Protected Sultanate (Pakistan)
1948-1966   BRITISH PROTECTED SULTANATE
1966-1970   SULTANATE
**Oman:**
1970-   SULTANATE

**PAKISTAN**
Prior to 1947   Part of India
1947-1956   INDEPENDENT BRITISH DOMINION
1956-   REPUBLIC

**PALAU**
-1977   Part of Trust Territory of the Pacific (Caroline Islands)
1977-1983   State of Trust Territory of the Pacific
1983-   AUTONOMOUS STATE UNDER U.S. TRUSTEESHIP

**PANAMA**
Prior to 1878   Part of Colombia
1878-1886   STATE OF COLOMBIA
1886-1903   DEPARTMENT OF COLOMBIA
1903-   REPUBLIC

**PAPUA NEW GUINEA**
**Papua & New Guinea:**
Prior to 1952   Separate Territories
1952-1971   AUSTRALIAN TERRITORIES
**Papua New Guinea:**
1971-1975   AUSTRALIAN TERRITORY
1975-   INDEPENDENT STATE

**PARAGUAY**
1870-   REPUBLIC

**PENRHYN ISLAND: Northern Cook Islands**
**Penrhyn Island:**
1892-1902   Part of Cook Islands
1902-1932   NEW ZEALAND DEPENDENCY
1932-1973   Part of Cook Islands
**Northern Cook Islands**
1973-   COOK ISLAND POSTAL REGION

**PERU**

| | |
|---|---|
| 1857- | REPUBLIC |

**PHILIPPINES**

| | |
|---|---|
| 1854-1898 | SPANISH DOMINION |
| 1898-1899 | PROVISIONAL GOVERNMENT |
| 1899-1935 | U.S. ADMINISTRATION |
| 1935-1941 | U.S. COMMONWEALTH |
| 1941-1944 | JAPANESE OCCUPATION |
| 1944-1946 | U.S. COMMONWEALTH |
| 1946- | REPUBLIC |

**PITCAIRN ISLANDS**

| | |
|---|---|
| 1898-1940 | British Colony (Fiji) |
| 1940- | BRITISH COLONY |

**POLAND**

| | |
|---|---|
| 1860-1865 | DUCHY OF RUSSIA |
| 1865-1915 | Duchy of Russia (Russia) |
| 1915-1918 | GERMAN OCCUPATION |
| 1918-1919 | INDEPENDENT STATE |
| 1919-1939 | REPUBLIC |
| 1939-1944 | POLISH GENERAL GOVERNMENT (German Occupation) |
| 1944-1945 | PROVISIONAL GOVERNMENT |
| 1945-1990 | COMMUNIST REPUBLIC |
| 1990- | REPUBLIC |

**PORTUGAL**

| | |
|---|---|
| 1853-1910 | MONARCHY |
| 1910- | REPUBLIC |

**PORTUGAL: Azores**

| | |
|---|---|
| 1868-1931 | PORTUGUESE COLONY |
| 1931-1980 | Part of Portugal |
| 1980- | REGIONAL ISSUES - Part of Portugal |

**PORTUGAL: Madeira**

| | |
|---|---|
| 1868-1881 | PORTUGUESE COLONY |
| 1881-1892 | Port. Colony (Portugal) |
| 1898 | SPECIAL ISSUES |
| 1905-1931 | Port. Colony (Azores) |
| 1925-1928 | SPECIAL ISSUES |
| 1931-1980 | Part of Portugal |
| 1980- | REGIONAL ISSUES - Part of Portugal |

**QATAR**

| | |
|---|---|
| Prior to 1916 | Part of Turkey |
| 1916-1950 | British Protected Sheikdom (India) |
| 1950-1957 | British Protected Sheikdom (Muscat & Oman) |
| 1957-1971 | BRITISH PROTECTED SHEIKDOM |
| 1971- | INDEPENDENT SHEIKDOM |

**ROMANIA**

| | |
|---|---|
| | **Moldavia:** |
| 1858-1861 | PRINCIPALITY |
| | **Moldavia-Wallachia:** |
| 1861-1865 | PRINCIPALITY |
| | **Romania:** |
| 1865-1881 | PRINCIPALITY |
| 1881-1947 | KINGDOM |
| 1948-1991 | COMMUNIST REPUBLIC |
| 1991- | REPUBLIC |

**RUSSIA**

| | |
|---|---|
| 1852-1917 | EMPIRE |
| 1917 | PROVISIONAL GOVERNMENT |
| 1917-1922 | SOVIET REPUBLIC |
| 1922-1992 | COMMUNIST REPUBLIC |
| 1992- | REPUBLIC |

**RWANDA**

| | |
|---|---|
| Prior to 1962 | Part of Rwandi-Urundi |
| 1962- | REPUBLIC |

**ST. HELENA**

| | |
|---|---|
| 1856- | BRITISH COLONY |

**ST. KITTS-NEVIS**

| | |
|---|---|
| | **St. Kitts-Nevis:** |
| Prior to 1903 | Separate Colonies |
| 1903-1952 | LEEWARD ISLAND PRESIDENCY |
| | **St. Christopher, Nevis & Anguilla:** |
| 1952-1956 | LEEWARD ISLAND PRESIDENCY |
| 1956-1967 | BRITISH COLONY |
| 1967-1980 | BRITISH WEST INDIES ASSOCIATED STATE |
| | **St. Kitts-Nevis:** |
| 1980- | Br. West Indies Assoc. (Separate Local Issues for St. Kitts and Nevis) |

**ST. LUCIA**

| | |
|---|---|
| 1869-1967 | BRITISH COLONY |
| 1967-1979 | BRITISH WEST INDIES ASSOCIATED STATE |
| 1979- | INDEPENDENT STATE |

**ST. PIERRE & MIQUELON**

| | |
|---|---|
| 1885-1958 | FRENCH COLONY |
| 1958- | OVERSEAS TERRITORY |

**ST. VINCENT**

| | |
|---|---|
| 1861-1969 | BRITISH COLONY |
| 1969-1979 | BRITISH WEST INDIES ASSOCIATED STATE |
| 1979- | INDEPENDENT COMMONWEALTH |

**ST. VINCENT GRENADINES**

| | |
|---|---|
| 1973 | PART OF ST. VINCENT |
| | **Regional Issues** |
| 1984- | BEQUIA |
| 1984- | UNION ISLANDS |

**SALVADOR, EL**

| | |
|---|---|
| 1867- | REPUBLIC |

**SAMOA: Western Samoa**

| | |
|---|---|
| | **Samoa:** |
| 1877-1899 | KINGDOM |
| 1900 | Divided into Western Samoa and American Samoa |
| | **Western Samoa:** |
| 1900-1914 | GERMAN PROTECTORATE |
| 1914-1920 | NEW ZEALAND OCCUPATION |
| 1920-1962 | NEW ZEALAND MANDATE |
| 1962- | INDEPENDENT STATE |

**SAN MARINO**

| | |
|---|---|
| 1862-1877 | Republic (Italy) |
| 1877-1943 | REPUBLIC |
| 1943-1944 | GERMAN OCCUPATION |
| 1944- | REPUBLIC |

**SAUDI ARABIA**

| | |
|---|---|
| | **Hejaz:** |
| Prior to 1916 | Part of Turkey |
| 1916-1926 | KINGDOM |
| | **Nejd:** |
| 1925-1926 | KINGDOM |
| | **Hejaz-Nejd:** |
| 1926-1932 | KINGDOM |
| | **Saudi Arabia:** |
| 1932- | KINGDOM |

**SENEGAL**

| | |
|---|---|
| 1887-1895 | FRENCH COLONY |
| 1895-1944 | COLONY OF FRENCH WEST AFRICA |
| 1944-1958 | Part of French West Africa |
| 1958-1959 | Autonomous Republic (French West Africa) |
| 1959-1960 | Part of Mali Federation |
| 1960- | REPUBLIC |

**SEYCHELLES**

| | |
|---|---|
| 1861-1890 | Dependency of Mauritius (Mauritius) |
| 1890-1903 | DEPENDENCY OF MAURITIUS |
| 1903-1976 | BRITISH COLONY |
| 1976- | REPUBLIC |
| | **Regional Issues** |
| 1980 | ZIL ELWANNYEN STEEL |

**SIERRA LEONE**

| | |
|---|---|
| 1859-1896 | BRITISH COLONY |
| 1896-1961 | BRITISH COLONY & PROTECTORATE |
| 1961-1971 | INDEPENDENT STATE |
| 1971- | REPUBLIC |

**SINGAPORE**

| | |
|---|---|
| 1867-1946 | Part of Straits Settlements |
| 1946-1948 | British Colony (Straits Settlements) |
| 1948-1959 | BRITISH COLONY |
| 1959-1963 | AUTONOMOUS STATE |
| 1963-1965 | Part of Malaysia |
| 1965- | REPUBLIC |

**SLOVENIA**

| | |
|---|---|
| Prior to 1991 | Part of Yugoslavia |
| 1991- | REPUBLIC |

**SOLOMAN ISLANDS**

| | |
|---|---|
| | **British Soloman Islands:** |
| 1896-1907 | British Protectorate (New South Wales) |
| 1907-1975 | BRITISH PROTECTORATE |
| | **Soloman Islands:** |
| 1975-1978 | BRITISH PROTECTORATE |
| 1978- | INDEPENDENT STATE |

**SOMALIA**

| | |
|---|---|
| | **Italian Somalia:** |
| 1903-1905 | ITALIAN COLONY - Benadir |
| 1905-1936 | ITALIAN COLONY |
| 1936-1938 | DISTRICT OF ITALIAN EAST AFRICA |
| 1938-1941 | Part of Italian East Africa |
| 1941-1950 | British Occupation (Offices in Africa) |
| | **Somalia:** |
| 1950-1960 | ITALIAN TRUSTEESHIP |
| 1960- | REPUBLIC |

**SOUTH AFRICA**

| | |
|---|---|
| | **Union of South Africa:** |
| Prior to 1910 | Separate British Colonies |

# HOW TO COLLECT STAMPS

| | | |
|---|---|---|
| 1910-1961 | INDEPENDENT BRITISH DOMINION | |
| | **South Africa:** | |
| 1961- | REPUBLIC | |
| | **Regional Issues:** | |
| 1977- | BOPHUTHATSWANA Self Governing Homeland | |
| 1981- | CISKEI Self Governing Homeland | |
| 1981- | TRANSKEI Self Governing Homeland | |
| 1979- | VENDA Self Governing Homeland | |

**SPAIN**
| | |
|---|---|
| 1850-1869 | KINGDOM |
| 1868-1869 | PROVISIONAL GOVERNMENT |
| 1869-1870 | DUKE DE LA TORRE REGENCY |
| 1870-1873 | KINGDOM |
| 1873-1875 | REPUBIC |
| 1875-1931 | KINGDOM |
| 1931-1936 | REPUBLIC |
| 1936-1939 | CIVIL WAR ISSUES |
| 1939-1977 | FASCIST MONARCHY |
| 1977- | CONSTITUTIONAL MONARCHY |

**SRI LANKA**
| | |
|---|---|
| Prior to 1972 | Named Ceylon |
| 1972- | REPUBLIC |

**SUDAN**
| | |
|---|---|
| 1867-1889 | British Military Administration (Egypt) |
| 1889-1897 | Mahdi Government (No Stamps) |
| 1897-1956 | ANGLO-EGYPTIAN CONDOMINIUM |
| 1956- | REPUBLIC |

**SURINAM**
| | |
|---|---|
| 1873-1954 | NETHERLANDS COLONY |
| 1954-1975 | PART OF NETHERLANDS KINGDOM |
| 1975- | INDEPENDENT STATE |

**SWAZILAND**
| | |
|---|---|
| 1889-1895 | KINGDOM |
| 1895-1903 | Part of Transvaal |
| 1903-1910 | British Colony (Transvaal) |
| 1910-1933 | British Colony (Union of South Africa) |
| 1933-1968 | BRITISH PROTECTORATE |
| 1968- | KINGDOM |

**SWEDEN**
| | |
|---|---|
| 1855- | KINGDOM |

**SWITZERLAND**
| | |
|---|---|
| 1850- | REPUBLIC |

**SYRIA**
| | |
|---|---|
| Prior to 1918 | Part of Turkey |
| 1918-1919 | Part of Palestine |
| 1919-1923 | FRENCH OCCUPATION |
| 1923-1934 | FRENCH MANDATE |
| 1934-1941 | AUTONOMOUS REPUBLIC UNDER FRENCH |
| 1941-1958 | REPUBLIC |
| 1958-1961 | PART OF UNITED ARAB REPUBLIC - with Egypt |
| 1961- | SYRIAN ARAB REPUBLIC |

**TAJIKISTAN**
| | |
|---|---|
| Prior to 1918 | Part of Russia |
| 1918-1919 | National Republic (Russia) |
| 1919-1920 | NATIONAL REPUBLIC |
| 1921-1922 | SOVIET REPUBLIC |
| 1922-1923 | PART OF SOVIET SOCIALIST REPUBLIC |
| 1923-1991 | Part of S.S.R. / Russia |
| 1991- | REPUBLIC |

**TANZANIA**
| | |
|---|---|
| Prior to 1964 | See Tanganyika |
| | **Tanganyika-Zanzibar:** |
| 1964 | REPUBLIC |
| | **Tanzania:** |
| 1964- | REPUBLIC |

**THAILAND**
| | |
|---|---|
| | **Siam:** |
| 1883-1950 | KINGDOM |
| | **Thailand:** |
| 1950- | KINGDOM |

**TOGO**
| | |
|---|---|
| 1885-1897 | German Protectorate (Germany) |
| 1897-1914 | GERMAN PROTECTORATE |
| 1914-1916 | BRITISH OCCUP. - Western Part |
| 1914-1919 | FRENCH OCCUPATION |
| 1919-1922 | FRENCH ADMINISTRATION |
| 1922-1946 | FRENCH MANDATE |
| 1946-1955 | FRENCH U.N. TRUSTEESHIP |
| 1955-1960 | AUTONOMOUS REPUBLIC |
| 1960- | REPUBLIC |

**TOKELAU ISLANDS**
| | |
|---|---|
| 1911-1925 | Part of Gilbert & Ellice Islands |
| 1925-1948 | Part of Western Samoa |

| | |
|---|---|
| 1948- | NEW ZEALAND TERRITORY |

**TONGA**

| | |
|---|---|
| 1886-1900 | KINGDOM |
| 1900-1970 | BRITISH PROTECTED KINGDOM |
| 1970- | KINGDOM |
| | **Regional Issues:** |
| 1983- | NIUAFO'OU - Tin Can Island |

**TRINIDAD & TOBAGO**

| | |
|---|---|
| Prior to 1913 | Separate Issues for Trinidad & Tobago |
| 1913-1962 | BRITISH COLONY |
| 1962-1976 | INDEPENDENT STATE |
| 1976- | REPUBLIC |

**TRISTAN DA CUNHA**

| | |
|---|---|
| 1867-1938 | British Colony (Great Britain) |
| 1938-1952 | St. Helena Dependency (St. Helena) |
| 1952-1961 | ST. HELENA |
| 1961-1963 | Uninhabited |
| 1963- | ST. HELENA DEPENDENCY |

**TUNISIA**

| | |
|---|---|
| 1863-1881 | Part of Turkey |
| 1881-1888 | French Protectorate (France) |
| 1888-1956 | FRENCH PROTECTORATE |
| 1956-1957 | KINGDOM |
| 1957- | REPUBLIC |

**TURKEY**

| | |
|---|---|
| 1863-1922 | OTTOMAN EMPIRE |
| 1920-1923 | NATIONALIST GOVERNMENT - Turkey in Asia |
| 1923- | REPUBLIC |

**TURKMENISTAN**

| | |
|---|---|
| Prior to 1918 | Part of Russia |
| 1918-1919 | National Republic (Russia) |
| 1919-1920 | NATIONAL REPUBLIC |
| 1921-1922 | SOVIET REPUBLIC |
| 1922-1923 | PART OF SOVIET SOCIALIST REPUBLIC |
| 1923-1990 | Part of S.S.R. / Russia |
| 1991- | REPUBLIC |

**TURKS & CIACOS ISLANDS**

| | |
|---|---|
| Prior to 1900 | See Turks Islands |
| 1900-1959 | DEPENDENCY OF JAMAICA |
| 1959- | BRITISH COLONY |
| | **Regional Issues:** |
| 1981- | CAICOS |

**TUVALU**

| | |
|---|---|
| Prior to 1975 | Part of Gilbert & Ellice Islands |
| 1975-1978 | BRITISH COLONY |
| 1978- | INDEPENDENT STATE |

**UGANDA**

| | |
|---|---|
| 1890-1895 | Part of British East Africa |
| 1895-1903 | BRITISH PROTECTORATE |
| 1903-1922 | Br. Protectorate (East Africa & Uganda) |
| 1922-1935 | Br. Protectorate (Kenya & Uganda) |
| 1935-1962 | Br. Protectorate (Kenya, Uganda & Tanganyika) |
| 1962 | BRITISH PROTECTORATE |
| 1962-1967 | INDEPENDENT STATE |
| 1967- | REPUBLIC |

**UKRAINE**

| | |
|---|---|
| Prior to 1918 | Part of Russia |
| 1918-1919 | NATIONAL REPUBLIC |
| 1919-1920 | PETLYURA DIRECTORATE |
| 1920-1922 | SOVIET REPUBLIC |
| 1922-1924 | PART OF SOVIET SOCIALIST REPUBLIC |
| 1924-1941 | Part of S.S.R. / Russia |
| 1941 | German Occupation (Germany) |
| 1941-1943 | GERMAN PUPPET REPUBLIC |
| 1943-1991 | Part of S.S.R. / Russia |
| 1991- | REPUBLIC |

**UNITED ARAB EMIRATES**

| | |
|---|---|
| Prior to 1971 | See Trucial States |
| 1971-1972 | Federation (Issues of Separate Sheikdoms) |
| 1972- | FEDERATION OF SHEIKDOMS |

**UNITED NATIONS**

| | |
|---|---|
| 1945-1951 | International Organization (United States) |
| 1951- | INTERNATIONAL ORGANIZATION |
| | **Offices Abroad:** |
| 1969- | GENEVA |
| 1979- | VIENNA |

**URUGUAY**

| | |
|---|---|
| 1856-1859 | Republic — Carrier Issues |
| 1859- | REPUBLIC |

**UZBEKISTAN**

| | |
|---|---|
| Prior to 1918 | Part of Russia |
| 1918-1919 | NATIONAL REPUBLIC |

| | |
|---|---|
| 1920-1922 | SOVIET REPUBLIC |
| 1923-1924 | PART OF SOVIET SOCIAL-IST REPUBLIC |
| 1924-1991 | Part of S.S.R. / Russia |
| 1991- | REPUBLIC |

**VANUATU**

| | |
|---|---|
| Prior to 1980 | See New Hebrides |
| 1980- | REPUBLIC |

**VATICAN CITY**

| | |
|---|---|
| 1870-1929 | Part of Italy |
| 1929- | ECCLESIASTIC STATE |

**VENEZUELA**

| | |
|---|---|
| 1859- | REPUBLIC |

**VIETNAM**

| | |
|---|---|
| Prior to 1949 | Part of Indochina |
| 1949-1951 | Autonomous Kingdom (Indochina) |
| 1951-1955 | KINGDOM OF FRENCH UNION |
| 1955 | Divided into North & South Vietnam |

**South Vietnam:**

| | |
|---|---|
| 1955-1956 | INDEPENDENT STATE OF FRENCH UNION |
| 1956-1975 | REPUBLIC |
| 1975- | Part of Vietnam |

NOTE: It is illegal to import Communist issues of Vietnam into the U.S.

**VIRGIN ISLANDS**

| | |
|---|---|
| 1866-1890 | BRITISH COLONY |
| 1890-1899 | Part of Leeward Islands |
| 1899-1956 | PRESIDENCY OF LEEWARD ISLANDS |
| 1956- | BRITISH COLONY |

**WALLIS & FUTUNA ISLANDS**

| | |
|---|---|
| 1888-1920 | French Protectorate (New Caledonia) |
| 1920-1961 | FRENCH PROTECTORATE |
| 1961- | FRENCH OVERSEAS TERRITORY |

**YEMEN**

| | |
|---|---|
| Prior to 1913 | Part of Turkey |
| 1913-1918 | Autonomous Kingdom (Turkey) |
| 1918-1926 | Kingdom (No Stamps) |
| 1926-1962 | KINGDOM |
| 1962-1970 | ROYALIST REGIME (Part) |
| 1962-1990 | YEMEN ARAB REPUBLIC |
| 1990- | REPUBLIC |

**YEMEN PEOPLE'S REPUBLIC**

| | |
|---|---|
| Prior to 1968 | See Aden and South Arabia |
| 1968-1971 | PEOPLE'S REPUBLIC OF SOUTHERN YEMEN |
| 1971- | PEOPLE'S REPUBLIC |

**YUGOSLAVIA**

| | |
|---|---|
| Prior to 1918 | Separate Countries |
| 1918-1921 | Kingdom (Issues of Separate Provinces) |
| 1921-1941 | KINGDOM |
| 1941-1944 | Separate Areas under German and Italian Occupation |
| 1944-1945 | DEMOCRATIC FEDERATION |
| 1945-1992 | COMMUNIST REPUBLIC |
| 1992- | REPUBLIC |

**ZAIRE**

| | |
|---|---|
| Prior to 1971 | See Belgian Congo and Congo Democratic Republic |
| 1971- | REPUBLIC |

**ZAMBIA**

| | |
|---|---|
| Prior to 1964 | See Northern Rhodesia |
| 1964- | REPUBLIC |

**ZIMBABWE**

| | |
|---|---|
| Prior to 1979 | See Rhodesia and Southern Rhodesia |
| 1979- | REPUBLIC |

# VANISHED LANDS
## Stamp-Issuing Entities No Longer Producing Postage Stamps

**ABU DHABI**

| | |
|---|---|
| Prior to 1964 | Part of Trucial States |
| 1964-1971 | BRITISH PROTECTED SHEIKDOM |
| 1971-1972 | STATE OF UNITED ARAB EMIRATES |
| 1973- | Part of United Arab Emirates |

**ADEN**

| | |
|---|---|
| 1854-1937 | British Possession (India) |
| 1937-1963 | BRITISH COLONY & PROTECTORATE |
| 1963-1965 | PART OF SOUTH AFRICA |
| 1965- | Part of South Arabia / Southern Yemen |
| | **States:** |
| 1942-1968 | KATHIRI STATE OF SEIYUN |
| 1942-1955 | QUAITI STATE OF SHIHR & MUKALLA |
| 1955-1968 | QUAITI STATE IN THE HADHRAMAUT |

**AFARS AND ISSAS**

| | |
|---|---|
| Prior to 1967 | Named Somali Coast |
| 1967-1977 | FRENCH OVERSEAS TERRITORY |
| 1977- | Name changed to Djibouti |

**AGUERA, LA**

| | |
|---|---|
| 1901-1920 | Part of Rio de Oro |
| 1920-1924 | SPANISH POSSESSION |
| 1924- | Part of Spanish Sahara / Morocco |

**AJMAN**

| | |
|---|---|
| Prior to 1964 | Part of Trucial States |
| 1964-1971 | BRITISH PROTECTED SHEIKDOM |
| 1971-1972 | STATE OF UNITED ARAB EMIRATES |
| 1973- | Part of United Arab Emirates |

**ALAOUITES**

| | |
|---|---|
| 1919-1924 | Part of Syria |
| 1935-1930 | AUTONOMOUS STATE UNDER FRENCH MANDATE |
| 1930- | Name changed to Latakia |

**ALEXANDRETTA**

| | |
|---|---|
| 1919-1923 | Part of Syria |
| 1923-1938 | French Mandate (Syria) |
| 1938 | FRENCH MANDATE STATE |
| 1939 | Name changed to Hatay |

**ALLENSTEIN**

| | |
|---|---|
| Prior to 1920 | Part of Germany |
| 1920 | PLEBISCITE AREA |
| 1920-1945 | Part of Germany |
| 1945- | Part of Poland |

**ANGRA**

| | |
|---|---|
| Prior to 1892 | District of Azores |
| 1892-1905 | DISTRICT OF AZORES |
| 1905- | District of Azores |

**ANJOUAN**

| | |
|---|---|
| 1892-1898 | FRENCH COLONY |
| 1898-1912 | FRENCH DEPENDENCY |
| 1912-1914 | FRENCH COLONY |
| 1914- | Part of Madagascar / Comoros |

**ANNAM & TONKIN**

| | |
|---|---|
| 1865-1888 | Fr. Protectorate (French Colonies) |
| 1888-1892 | FRENCH PROTECTORATE |
| 1892- | Part of Indochina / Vietnam |

**AUSTRIA: Lombardy-Venetia**

| | |
|---|---|
| 1850-1859 | PROVINCES OF AUSTRIA |
| 1859- | Lombardy - to Sardinia / Italy |
| 1859-1866 | VENETIA — PROVINCE OF AUSTRIA |
| 1866- | Venetia - Part of Italy |

**AZORES**

| | |
|---|---|
| 1853-1868 | Portuguese Colony (Portugal) |
| 1868-1931 | PORTUGUESE COLONY |
| 1931- | Part of Portugal |

**BANGKOK**

| | |
|---|---|
| 1882-885 | BRITISH TREATY PORT |
| 1885- | Part of Thailand |

**BASUTOLAND**

| | |
|---|---|
| 1871-1883 | Part of Cape of Good Hope |
| 1883-1910 | British Colony (Cape of Good Hope) |

| | |
|---|---|
| 1910-1933 | British Colony (Union of S. Afr.) |
| 1933-1966 | BRITISH COLONY |
| 1966- | Name changed to Lesotho |

**BATUM**

| | |
|---|---|
| Prior to 1918 | Part of Russia |
| 1918-1920 | BRITISH OCCUPATION |
| 1920- | Part of Georgia/Russia |

**BECHUANALAND**

| | |
|---|---|
| 1885-1895 | BRITISH COLONY |
| 1895-1897 | DISTRICT OF CAPE OF GOOD HOPE |
| 1897- | Part of Cape of G.H. / South Africa |

**BECHUANALAND PROTECTORATE**

| | |
|---|---|
| 1888-1966 | BRITISH PROTECTORATE |
| 1966- | Name changed to Botswana |

**BELGIAN CONGO**

| | |
|---|---|
| 1886-1908 | Congo: SEMI-INDEPENDENT STATE UNDER BELGIAN CROWN |
| 1909-1960 | BELGIAN COLONY |
| 1960- | Name changed to Congo, then Zaire |

**BRITISH CENTRAL AFRICA**

| | |
|---|---|
| 1891-1907 | BRITISH TERRITORY |
| 1908- | Name changed to Nyasaland, then Malawi |

**BRITISH COLUMBIA & VANCOUVER I.**

| | |
|---|---|
| 1860-1865 | BRITISH COLONIES - Joint Issues |
| 1865-1866 | BRITISH COLONIES - Separate Issues for British Columbia & Vancouver I. |
| 1866-1868 | BRITISH COLONY - Unified but with separate issues |
| 1868-1871 | BRITISH COLONY OF BRITISH COLUMBIA |
| 1871- | Part of Canada |

**BRITISH EAST AFRICA**

| | |
|---|---|
| 1890-1895 | BRITISH EAST AFRICA COMPANY ADMINISTRATION |
| 1895-1903 | BRITISH PROTECTORATE |
| 1903-1922 | Part of East Africa & Uganda |
| 1922- | Name changed to Kenya |

**BRITISH GUIANA**

| | |
|---|---|
| 1850-1966 | BRITISH COLONY |
| 1966- | Name changed to Guyana |

**BRITISH HONDURAS**

| | |
|---|---|
| 1866-1884 | JAMAICA DEPENDENCY |
| 1884-1964 | BRITISH COLONY |
| 1964-1973 | SELF-GOVERNING BRITISH COLONY |
| 1973- | Name changed to Belize |

**BRITISH INDIAN OCEAN TERRITORY**

| | |
|---|---|
| 1847-1965 | Part of Mauritius & Seychelles |
| 1965-1976 | BRITISH TERRITORY |
| 1976- | British Territory (Great Britain) |

**BURMA**

| | |
|---|---|
| Prior to 1937 | Part of India |
| 1937-1942 | BRITISH DOMINION |
| 1942- | BURMA INDEPENDENCE ARMY - Japanese controlled areas |
| 1942-1945 | JAPANESE OCCUPATION |
| 1945-1948 | BRITISH MILITARY ADMINISTRATION |
| 1946-1948 | INTERIM GOVERNMENT |
| 1948- | REPUBLIC |

**BUSHIRE**

| | |
|---|---|
| Prior to 1915 | Part of Persia |
| 1915 | BRITISH OCCUPATION |
| 1915- | Part of Persia/Iran |

**CAMEROONS**

| | |
|---|---|
| Prior to 1915 | Part of Cameroun |
| 1915-1916 | BRITISH OCCUPATION |
| 1916-1922 | British Occupation (Nigeria) |
| 1922-1960 | Part of Nigeria |

**Southern Cameroons:**

| | |
|---|---|
| 1960-1961 | BRITISH MANDATE |
| 1961- | Part of Cameroon |

**CANAL ZONE**

| | |
|---|---|
| Prior to 1903 | Part of Colombia |
| 1903-1980 | U.S. LEASED TERRITORY |
| 1980- | Part of Panama - Joint U.S. and Panamanian Administration |

**CABE JUBY**

| | |
|---|---|
| Prior to 1916 | Part of French Morocco |
| 1916-1917 | SPANISH POSSESSION |
| 1917-1919 | Spanish Possession (Rio de Oro and Spanish Morocco) |
| 1919-1949 | SPANISH POSSESSION |

# HOW TO COLLECT STAMPS

| 1949-1950 | PART OF SP. WEST AFRICA |
| 1950- | Part of Sp. Sahara/Morocco |

**CAPE OF GOOD HOPE**
| 1853-1910 | BRITISH COLONY |
| 1910-1913 | PROVINCE OF UNION OF SOUTH AFRICA |
| 1913- | Part of South Africa |

**CAROLINE ISLANDS**
| 1899-1914 | GERMAN PROTECTORATE |
| 1914-1945 | Japanese Occupation & Mandate (Japan) |
| 1945-1977 | Part of Trust Territory of Pacific (U.S.) |
| 1977- | Divided into Palau and Micronesia |

**CASTELLORIZO**
| Prior to 1915 | Part of Turkey |
| 1915-1920 | French Occupation (Fr. Post Offices in Turkey) |
| 1920 | FRENCH OCCUPATION |
| 1920-1922 | Italian Dominion (Italy) |
| 1922-1932 | ITALIAN DOMINION |
| 1932- | Part of Aegean Is./Greece |

**CENTRAL LITHUANIA**
| 1918-1920 | Part of Lithuania |
| 1920-1922 | POLISH OCCUPATION |
| 1922-1939 | Part of Poland |
| 1939-1940 | Part of Lithuania |
| 1940- | Part of Russia |

**CEYLON**
| 1857-1948 | BRITISH COLONY |
| 1948-1972 | INDEPENDENT BRITISH DOMINION |
| 1972- | Name changed to Sri Lanka |

**CHINA**
| 1878-1912 | EMPIRE |
| 1912-1949 | REPUBLIC |

**CILICIA**
| 1863-1918 | Part of Turkey |
| 1918-1919 | Part of Palestine |
| 1919-1921 | FRENCH OCCUPATION |
| 1921- | Part of Turkey |

**COCHIN-CHINA**
| 1865-1886 | French Colony (French Colonies) |
| 1886-1892 | FRENCH COLONY |
| 1892- | Part of Indochina/Vietnam |

**CONFEDERATE STATES**
| Prior to 1861 | Part of United States |
| 1861 | CONFEDERACY — Provisional Issues |
| 1861-1865 | CONFEDERACY |
| 1865- | Part of United States |

**CONGO DEMOCRATIC REPUBLIC**
| Prior to 1960 | Belgian Congo |
| 1960-1971 | REPUBLIC |
| 1971- | Name changed to Zaire |

**CORFU**
| Prior to 1923 | Part of Greece |
| 1923 | ITALIAN OCCUPATION |
| 1923-1941 | Part of Greece |
| 1941-1944 | Italian & German Occupation |
| 1944- | Part of Greece |

**CRETE**
| Prior to 1898 | Part of Turkey |
| 1898-1900 | Joint Administration by Great Britain, France, Italy & Russia — DISTRICT ISSUES |
| 1900-1913 | AUTONOMOUS STATE |
| 1913- | Part of Greece |

**CYRENAICA**
| Prior to 1923 | Part of Libia |
| 1923-1927 | DISTRICT OF LIBIA |
| 1927-1934 | ITALIAN COLONY |
| 1934-1942 | Part of Libia |
| 1943-1950 | British Administration (G.B. - Mid-East Forces) |
| 1950-1951 | AUTONOMOUS STATE |
| 1951- | Part of Libya |

**CZECHOSLOVAKIA**
| Prior to 1918 | Part of Austria-Hungary |
| 1918-1939 | REPUBLIC |
| 1939-1945 | Divided into various regions under German and Hungarian occupation — see Bohemia & Moravia, Slovakia. |
| 1945-1948 | REPUBLIC |
| 1948-1968 | COMMUNIST REPUBLIC |
| 1968- | COMMUNIST FEDERAL REPUBLIC |

**CZECHOSLOVAKIA: Bohemia & Moravia**
| 1918-1939 | Part of Czechoslovakia |
| 1939-1945 | GERMAN PROTECTORATE |
| 1945- | Part of Czechoslovakia |

## CZECHOSLOVAKIA: Slovakia

| | |
|---|---|
| 1918-1939 | Part of Czechoslovakia |
| 1939-1945 | GERMAN PUPPET REPUBLIC |
| 1945- | Part of Czechoslovakia |

## DAHOMEY

| | |
|---|---|
| Prior to 1894 | Called Benin |
| 1894-1899 | French Colony (Benin) |
| 1899-1944 | COLONY OF FRENCH WEST AFRICA |
| 1944-1958 | Part of French West Africa |
| 1858-1960 | Autonomous Republic (French West Africa) |
| 1960 | AUTONOMOUS REPUBLIC |
| 1960-1975 | REPUBLIC |
| 1975- | Name changed to Benin |

## DALMATIA

| | |
|---|---|
| Prior to 1918 | Part of Austria |
| 1919-1922 | ITALIAN OCCUPATION |
| 1922- | Part of Yugoslavia |

## DANISH WEST INDIES

| | |
|---|---|
| 1855-1917 | DANISH COLONY |
| 1917- | U.S. Territory (United States) — U.S. Virgin Islands |

## DANZIG

| | |
|---|---|
| Prior to 1920 | Part of Germany |
| 1920-1939 | FREE CITY |
| 1939 | GERMAN OCCUPATION |
| 1939-1944 | Part of Germany |
| 1944- | Part of Poland |

## DIEGO-SUAREZ

| | |
|---|---|
| 1890-1898 | FRENCH COLONY |
| 1898- | Part of Madagascar |

## DUBAI

| | |
|---|---|
| Part to 1963 | Part of Trucial States |
| 1963-1971 | BRITISH PROTECTED SHEIKDOM |
| 1971-1972 | STATE OF UNITED ARAB EMIRATES |
| 1973- | Part of United Arab Emirates |

## EAST AFRICA & UGANDA

| | |
|---|---|
| 1895-1903 | Separate issues for Uganda and British East Africa |
| 1903-1922 | BRITISH COLONY & PROTECTORATE |
| 1922- | Name changed to Kenya & Uganda |

## EASTERN RUMELIA

| | |
|---|---|
| 1863-1880 | Part of Turkey |
| 1880-1885 | TURKISH PROVINCE |
| 1885 | BULGARIAN PROVINCE - South Bulgaria |
| 1885- | Part of Bulgaria |

## EASTERN SILESIA

| | |
|---|---|
| Prior to 1918 | Part of Austria |
| 1918-1920 | Czechoslovak Occupation (Czechoslovakia) |
| 1920 | PLEBISCITE AREA |
| 1920- | Divided between Czechoslovakia & Poland |

## EGYPT: Palestine Issues - Gaza Area

| | |
|---|---|
| Prior to 1948 | Part of Palestine |
| 1948-1956 | EGYPTIAN OCCUPATION |
| 1956-1957 | Israeli Occupation (Israel) |
| 1957-1967 | EGYPTIAN OCCUPATION |
| 1967- | Israeli Occupation (Israel) |

## ELOBEY, ANNOBON & CORISCO

| | |
|---|---|
| 1885-1903 | Part of Fernando Po |
| 1903-1909 | SPANISH POSSESSION |
| 1909-1960 | Part of Spanish Guinea |
| 1960-1968 | Divided between Fernando Po & Rio Muni |
| 1968- | Part of Equatorial Guinea |

## EPIRUS

| | |
|---|---|
| Prior to 1913 | Part of Turkey |
| 1914 | PROVISIONAL GOVERN-MENT |
| 1914-1916 | GREEK OCCUPATION |
| 1916-1919 | Italian Occupation (Italy) |
| 1919- | Part of Albania |

## ERITREA

| | |
|---|---|
| 1893-1936 | ITALIAN COLONY |
| 1936-1938 | DISTRICT OF ITALIAN EAST AFRICA |
| 1938-1941 | Part of Italian East Africa |
| 1941-1942 | British Occupation (Great Britain) |
| 1942-1948 | British Administration (G. Br. - Middle Eastern Forces) |
| 1948-1951 | British Administration (G. Br. - Eritrea) |
| 1952- | Part of Ethiopia |

## FAR EASTERN REPUBLIC

| | |
|---|---|
| Prior to 1920 | Part of Russia |
| 1920-1922 | BOLSHEVIK REPUBLIC |
| 1922-1923 | REPUBLIC OF RUSSIA |
| 1923- | Part of Russia |

# HOW TO COLLECT STAMPS

### Priamur & Maritime Districts
| | |
|---|---|
| 1921-1922 | ANTI-BOLSHEVIK GOVERNMENT |

### FERNANDO PO
| | |
|---|---|
| 1868 | SPANISH COLONY |
| 1868-1879 | Spanish Colony (Cuba & Puerto Rico) |
| 1879-1909 | SPANISH COLONY |
| 1909-1960 | Part of Spanish Guinea |
| 1929 | SPECIAL ISSUE |
| 1960-1968 | SPANISH OVERSEAS PROVINCE |
| 1968- | Part of Equatorial Guinea |

### FIUME
| | |
|---|---|
| Prior to 1918 | Part of Austria |
| 1918-1919 | ALLIED OCCUPATION |
| 1919-1920 | ITALIAN OCCUPATION — D'Annunzio |
| 1920-1924 | FREE STATE - Italian Protectorate |
| 1924 | PART OF ITALY |
| 1924-1945 | Part of Italy |
| 1945- | Part of Yugoslavia |

### FRANCE: Alsace-Lorraine
| | |
|---|---|
| Prior to 1870 | Part of France |
| 1870-1871 | NORTH GERMAN CONFEDERATION OCCUPATION |
| 1872-1918 | Part of Germany |
| 1918-1940 | Part of France |
| 1940-1941 | GERMAN OCCUPATION |
| 1942-1944 | Part of Germany |
| 1944- | Part of France |

### FRENCH COLONIES
| | |
|---|---|
| 1859-1906, 1943-1945 | GENERAL ISSUE FOR USE IN VARIOUS FRENCH COLONIES |

### FRENCH CONGO
| | |
|---|---|
| 1891-1906 | FRENCH COLONY |
| 1906- | Divided into separate colonies |

### FRENCH EQUATORIAL AFRICA
| | |
|---|---|
| 1910-1936 | French Administrative Unit (Separate Colonies) |
| 1936-1958 | FRENCH COLONIAL ADMINISTRATIVE UNIT |
| 1958-1960 | POSTAL SERVICE FOR SEPARATE AUTONOMOUS REPUBLICS |

### FRENCH GUIANA
| | |
|---|---|
| 1886-1946 | FRENCH COLONY |
| 1946-1947 | FRENCH OVERSEAS DEPARTMENT |
| 1947- | French Overseas Dept. (France) |

### FRENCH GUINEA
| | |
|---|---|
| 1892-1895 | FRENCH COLONY |
| 1895-1944 | COLONY OF FRENCH WEST AFRICA |
| 1944-1958 | Part of French West Africa |
| 1958- | Name changed to Guinea |

### FRENCH INDIA
| | |
|---|---|
| 1854-1892 | French Possession (India) |
| 1892-1954 | FRENCH TERRITORY |
| 1954- | Part of India |

### FRENCH MOROCCO
| | |
|---|---|
| Prior to 1912 | Part of Morocco |
| 1912-1914 | French Protectorate (French Post Offices in Morocco) |
| 1914-1956 | FRENCH PROTECTORATE |
| 1956- | Part of Morocco |

### FRENCH SUDAN
| | |
|---|---|
| 1894-1895 | FRENCH COLONY |
| 1895-1899 | COLONY OF FRENCH WEST AFRICA |
| 1899-1906 | Colony dissolved |
| 1906-1920 | Part of Upper Senegal & Niger |
| 1920-1921 | Colony of French West Africa (Upper Senegal & Niger) |
| 1921-1944 | COLONY OF FRENCH WEST AFRICA |
| 1944-1958 | Part of French West Africa |
| 1958- | Name changed to Sudanese Republic, then Mali |

### FRENCH WEST AFRICA
| | |
|---|---|
| 1895-1944 | French Administration Unit (Issues of Separate Colonies) |
| 1944-1958 | FRENCH ADMINISTRATIVE UNIT |
| 1958-1959 | POSTAL SERVICE FOR SEPARATE AUTONOMOUS REPUBLICS |

### FUJEIRA
| | |
|---|---|
| Prior to 1964 | Part of Trucial States |
| 1964-1971 | BRITISH PROTECTED SHEIKDOM |
| 1971-1972 | STATE OF UNITED ARAB EMIRATES |
| 1972- | Part of United Arab Emirates |

**FUNCHAL**

| | |
|---|---|
| Prior to 1892 | Part of Madeira |
| 1892-1905 | PORTUGUESE COLONY — All of Madeira |
| 1905- | Part of Madeira/Portugal |

**GERMAN EAST AFRICA**

| | |
|---|---|
| 1888-1893 | German Protectorate (Germany) |
| 1893-1918 | GERMAN PROTECTORATE |
| 1918- | Divided between Britain, Belgium & Portugal |

**GERMAN NEW GUINEA**

| | |
|---|---|
| 1888-1898 | German Protectorate (Germany) |
| 1898-1914 | GERMAN PROTECTORATE |
| 1914- | New Britain/N.W. Pacific Is./ New Guinea |

**GERMAN SOUTH-WEST AFRICA**

| | |
|---|---|
| 1886-1897 | Germany Colony (Germany) |
| 1897-1915 | GERMAN COLONY |
| 1915- | Name changed to South West Africa |

**GERMAN STATES**

**Baden:**

| | |
|---|---|
| 1851-1871 | GRAND DUCHY |
| 1872-1945 | Part of Germany/Ger. Fed. Rep. |

**Bavaria:**

| | |
|---|---|
| 1849-1871 | KINGDOM |
| 1872-1918 | KINGDOM OF GERMAN EMPIRE |
| 1919-1920 | AUTONOMOUS REPUBLIC |
| 1920 | PART OF GERMANY |
| 1920- | Part of Germany/German Fed. Rep. |

**Bergedorf:**

| | |
|---|---|
| 1861-1867 | JOINT HAMBURG & LUBECK POSSESSION |
| 1867- | Part of Hamburg/German Fed. Rep. |

**Bremen:**

| | |
|---|---|
| 1855-1867 | FREE CITY |
| 1868- | Part of Nth German Conf./Ger. Fed. Rep. |

**Brunswick:**

| | |
|---|---|
| 1852-1867 | GRAND DUCHY |
| 1868- | Part of Nth German Conf./Ger. Fed. Rep. |

**Hamburg:**

| | |
|---|---|
| 1852-1859 | Free City (Thurn & Taxis) |
| 1859-1867 | FREE CITY |
| 1868- | Part of Nth German Conf./Ger. Fed. Rep. |

**Hanover:**

| | |
|---|---|
| 1850-1866 | KINGDOM |
| 1866-1867 | Part of Prussia |
| 1868- | Part of Nth German Conf./Ger. Fed. Rep. |

**Lubeck:**

| | |
|---|---|
| 1852-1858 | Free City (Thurn & Taxis) |
| 1859-1867 | FREE CITY |
| 1868- | Part of Nth German Conf./Ger. Fed. Rep. |

**Mecklenburg-Schwerin:**

| | |
|---|---|
| 1856-1867 | GRAND DUCHY |
| 1868- | Part of Nth German Conf./Ger. Fed. Rep. |

**Mecklenburg-Strelitz:**

| | |
|---|---|
| 1864-1867 | GRAND DUCHY |
| 1868- | Part of Nth German Conf./Ger. Fed. Rep. |

**North German Confederation:**

| | |
|---|---|
| Prior to 1867 | Issues of separate states |
| 1868-1871 | CONFEDERATION OF NORTHERN GERMAN STATES |
| 1872- | Part of Germany |

**Oldenburg:**

| | |
|---|---|
| 1852-1867 | GRAND DUCHY |
| 1868- | Part of Nth German Conf./Ger. Fed. Rep. |

**Prussia:**

| | |
|---|---|
| 1850-1867 | KINGDOM |
| 1868-1945 | Part of Nth German Conf./ Germany |
| 1945- | Divided by Ger. Fed. Rep., Ger. Dem. Rep., Poland and Russia |

**Saxony:**

| | |
|---|---|
| 1850-1867 | KINGDOM |
| 1868- | Part of Nth German Conf./Ger. Fed. Rep. |

**Schleswig-Holstein:**

| | |
|---|---|
| 1850-1851 | PROVISIONAL GOVERNMENT |
| 1851-1864 | Autonomous Duchies (Denmark) |
| 1864-1865 | Schleswig — AUSTRO-PRUSSIAN OCCUPATIONS |
| 1864-1865 | Holstein — GERMAN FEDERAL ADMINISTRATION |
| 1865 | AUSTRO-PRUSSIAN OCCUPATION |
| 1865-1867 | Schleswig — PRUSSIAN ADMINISTRATION |
| 1865-1867 | Holstein — AUSTRIAN ADMINISTRATION |

| | |
|---|---|
| 1867 | Provinces of Prussia |
| 1868- | Part of Nth German Conf./Ger. Fed. Rep. |
| | **Thurn & Taxis** |
| 1852-1867 | PRINCELY POSTAL SYSTEM FOR VARIOUS GERMAN STATES |
| 1868- | Service dissolved |
| | **Wurttemberg:** |
| 1851-1871 | KINGDOM |
| 1872-1902 | KINGDOM OF GERMAN EMPIRE |
| 1902-1918 | KINGDOM OF GERMAN EMPIRE — Officials only plus German stamps |
| 1918-1919 | PROVISIONAL GOVERNMENT (plus Germany) |
| 1919-1924 | PART OF GERMANY — Officials only |
| 1924- | Part of Germany/Ger. Fed. Rep. |

**GERMANY: Berlin (West)**

| | |
|---|---|
| Prior to 1945 | Part of Germany |
| 1945-1948 | British, French & U.S. Occupation (Issues of General German Occupation) |
| 1948-1950 | JOINT BRITISH, FRENCH & U.S. OCCUPATION |
| 1950- | LAND OF GERMAN FEDERAL REPUBLIC UNDER U.S., BR. & FR. PROTECTION |

**GERMANY: German Democratic Republic**

| | |
|---|---|
| Prior to 1945 | Part of Germany |
| 1945-1949 | U.S.S.R. OCCUPATION — Local & General Issues |
| 1949- | COMMUNIST REPUBLIC |

**GERMANY: Occupation Issues**
**Rhineland Area:**

| | |
|---|---|
| 1919-1921 | BELGIAN OCCUPATION |
| | **British & U.S. Zones:** |
| 1945-1946 | ALLIED MILITARY GOVERNMENT |
| 1946-1948 | JOINT ISSUES WITH RUSSIA |
| 1948-1949 | JOINT U.S. & BR. ISSUES |
| | **Russian Zone:** |
| 1945-1946 | Russian Occupation (Local issues) |
| 1946-1948 | JOINT ISSUES WITH US. & BR. |
| 1948-1949 | RUSSIAN OCCUPAITION |

**French Zone:**

| | |
|---|---|
| 1945-1947 | FRENCH OCCUPATION |
| 1947-1949 | French Occupation (Separate Issues for Baden, Rheinland Palatinate & Wurttemberg) |

**GILBERT ISLANDS**

| | |
|---|---|
| Prior to 1975 | Part of Gilbert & Ellice Islands |
| 1975-1979 | BRITISH COLONY |
| 1979- | Name changed to Kiribati |

**GILBERT & ELLICE ISLANDS**

| | |
|---|---|
| 1901-1911 | British Protectorate (New South Wales) |
| 1911-1915 | BRITISH PROTECTORATE |
| 1915-1975 | BRITISH COLONY |
| 1975- | Divided into Gilbert Islands & Tuvalu |

**GOLD COAST**

| | |
|---|---|
| 1875-1957 | BRITISH COLONY |
| 1957- | Name changed to Ghana |

**GRAND COMORO ISLAND**

| | |
|---|---|
| 1897-1898 | FRENCH COLONY |
| 1898-1912 | FRENCH DEPENDENCY |
| 1912-1914 | FRENCH COLONY |
| 1914- | Part of Madagascar/Comoros |

**GRIQUALAND WEST**

| | |
|---|---|
| 1871-1874 | British Administration (Cape of Good Hope) |
| 1874-1880 | BRITISH COLONY |
| 1880- | Part of Cape of Good Hope/ South Africa |

**GUADELOUPE**

| | |
|---|---|
| 1884-1946 | FRENCH COLONY |
| 1947 | FRENCH OVERSEAS DEPARTMENT |
| 1947- | Fr. Overseas Dept. (France) |

**GUAM**

| | |
|---|---|
| Prior to 1899 | Part of Marianna Islands |
| 1899-1901 | U.S. POSSESSION |
| 1901-1941 | U.S. Navy Administration (U.S.) |
| 1941-1944 | Japanese Occupation (Japan) |
| 1944- | U.S. Territory (U.S.) |

**HATAY**

| | |
|---|---|
| Prior to 1939 | Named Alexandretta |

| | |
|---|---|
| 1939 | AUTONOMOUS REPUBLIC UNDER FRENCH PROTECTORATE |
| 1939- | Part of Turkey |

**HAWAII**

| | |
|---|---|
| 1851-1893 | KINGDOM |
| 1893-1894 | PROVISIONAL GOVERNMENT |
| 1894-1898 | REPUBLIC |
| 1899-1900 | U.S. ADMINISTRATION |
| 1900-1959 | U.S. Territory (U.S.) |
| 1959- | State of United States |

**HELIGOLAND**

| | |
|---|---|
| Prior to 1867 | Part of Hamburg |
| 1867-1890 | BRITISH POSSESSION |
| 1890- | Part of Germany/Ger. Fed. Rep. |

**HUNGARY: Occupation Issues**

| | |
|---|---|
| 1919-1920 | Arad: FRENCH OCCUPATION |
| 1919-1920 | Banat, Bacska: SERBIAN OCCUPATION |
| 1919-1920 | Baranya: SERBIAN OCCUPATION |
| 1919-1920 | Debrecen: ROMANIAN OCCUPATION |
| 1919 | Szeged: ANTI-SOVIET GOVERNMENT |
| 1919 | Temesvar: SERBIAN OCCUPATION |
| 1919-1920 | Temesvar: ROMANIAN OCCUPATION |
| 1919-1920 | Transylvania: ROMANIAN OCCUPATION |

**IFNI**

| | |
|---|---|
| 1860-1941 | Spanish Colony (Handstamps) |
| 1941-1949 | SPANISH COLONY |
| 1949-1951 | PART OF SPANISH WEST AFRICA |
| 1951-1969 | SPANISH COLONY |
| 1969- | Part of Morocco |

**INDIAN STATES**

**Convention States:**

| | |
|---|---|
| 1886-1950 | CHAMBA |
| 1886-1901 | FARIDKOT |
| 1885-1950 | GWALIOR |
| 1885-1950 | JIND |
| 1885-1950 | NABHA |
| 1884-1950 | PATIALA |

**Feudatory States:**

| | |
|---|---|
| 1877-1902 | ALWAR |
| 1888-1894 | BAMRA |
| 1921-1948 | BARWANI |
| 1876-1950 | BHOPAL |
| 1879-1902 | BHOR |
| 1935-1939 | BIJAWAR |
| 1894-1949 | BUNDI |
| 1895-1901 | BUSSAHIR |
| 1894-1950 | CHARKHARI |
| 1892-1949 | COCHIN |
| 1897-1901 | DHAR |
| 1893-1921 | DUTTIA |
| 1879-1886 | FARIDKOT |
| 1869-1950 | HYDERABAD |
| 1939-1944 | IDAR |
| 1886-1950 | INDORE |
| 1904-1949 | JAIPUR |
| 1866-1894 | JAMMU & KAHSMIR |
| 1942-1949 | JASDAN |
| 1887-1900 | JHALAWAR |
| 1874-1885 | JIND |
| 1899-1949 | KISHANGARH |
| 1931-1949 | MORVI |
| 1891-1895 | NANDGAON |
| 1877-1895 | NOWANUGGUR |
| 1913-1950 | ORCCHA |
| 1876-1894 | POONCH |
| 1948-1950 | RAJASTHAN |
| 1880-1886 | RAJPEEPLA |
| 1923-1950 | SAURASHTRA |
| 1879-1902 | SIRMOOR |
| 1864-1923 | SORUTH |
| 1888-1949 | TRAVANCORE |
| 1949-1951 | TRAVANCORE-COCHIN |
| 1888-1895 | WADHWAN |

**INDOCHINA**

| | |
|---|---|
| 1887-1892 | French Colonies & Protectorates (French Colonies) |
| 1889-1941 | FRENCH COLONY & PROTECTORATE |
| 1941-1945 | JAPANESE OCCUPATION |
| 1945-1949 | FRENCH COLONY & PROTECTORATE |
| 1949-1951 | FOR USE IN SEPARATE STATES |
| 1951- | Divided into Cambodia, Laos & Vietnam |

**INHAMBANE**

| | |
|---|---|
| Prior to 1895 | Part of Mozambique |
| 1895-1920 | DISTRICT OF MOZAMBIQUE |
| 1920- | Part of Mozambique |

**ININI**

| | |
|---|---|
| Prior to 1932 | Part of French Guiana |

| | |
|---|---|
| 1932-1946 | FRENCH TERRITORY |
| 1946- | Part of French Guiana |

## IONIAN ISLANDS

| | |
|---|---|
| 1859-1864 | BRITISH PROTECTORATE |
| 1864-1941 | Part of Greece |
| 1941-1943 | ITALIAN OCCUPATION |
| 1943-1944 | GERMAN OCCUPATION |
| 1944- | Part of Greece |

## ITALIAN COLONIES

| | |
|---|---|
| 1932-1934 | GENERAL ISSUES FOR USE IN ITALIAN COLONIES |

## ITALIAN EAST AFRICA

| | |
|---|---|
| Prior to 1936 | Ethiopia, Eritrea and Italian Somaliland |
| 1936-1938 | Italian Colony — Issues of Ethiopia, Eritrea & Italian Somaliland |
| 1938-1941 | ITALIAN COLONY |
| 1941- | Divided after British Occupation |

## ITALIAN STATES

**Modena:**

| | |
|---|---|
| 1852-1859 | GRAND DUCHY |
| 1859-1860 | PROVISIONAL GOVERNMENT |
| 1860- | Part of Sardinia/Italy |

**Parma:**

| | |
|---|---|
| 1852-1859 | GRAND DUCHY |
| 1859-1860 | PROVISIONAL GOVERNMENT |
| 1860- | Part of Sardinia/Italy |

**Romagna:**

| | |
|---|---|
| 1852-1859 | Part of Roman States |
| 1859-1860 | PROVISIONAL GOVERNMENT |
| 1860- | Part of Sardinia/Italy |

**Roman States:**

| | |
|---|---|
| 1852-1870 | ECCLESIASTIC STATE |
| 1870- | Part of Italy |

**Sardinia:**

| | |
|---|---|
| 1851-1861 | KINGDOM |
| 1861-1862 | PART OF ITALY |
| 1862- | Part of Italy |

**Tuscany:**

| | |
|---|---|
| 1851-1859 | GRAND DUCHY |
| 1860 | PROVISIONAL GOVERNMENT |
| 1860- | Part of Sardinia/Italy |

**Two Sicilies:**

| | |
|---|---|
| 1858-1860 | Naples - PART OF TWO SICILIES KINGDOM |
| 1859-1860 | Sicily - PART OF TWO SICILIES KINGDOM |
| 1860-1861 | PROVISIONAL GOVERNMENT |
| 1861-1862 | Neopolitan Provinces - PART OF ITALY |
| 1862- | Part of Italy |

## ITALY: Aegean Islands

| | |
|---|---|
| Prior to 1912 | Part of Turkey |
| 1912 | PROVISIONAL GOVERNMENT |
| 1912 | ITALIAN OCCUPATION |
| 1912-1920 | Italian Occupation: Issues of separate islands |
| 1920-1929 | Italian Dominion - Issues of separate islands |
| 1929-1943 | ITALIAN DOMINION |
| 1943-1944 | GERMAN OCCUPATION |
| 1944-1947 | British Occupation (Middle East Forces) |
| 1947 | GREEK OCCUPATION |
| 1947- | Part of Greece |

**Issues of Separate Islands:**

| | |
|---|---|
| 1912-1932 | CALCHI; CALINO; CASO; COO; LERO; LISSO; NISIRO; PATMOS; PISCOPI; SCARPANTO; SIMI & STAMPALIA |
| 1912-1945 | RHODES - Used in all Aegean Islands from 1932-1945 |

## ITALY: Italian Social Republic

| | |
|---|---|
| 1943-1945 | REPUBLIC NORTH ITALY UNDER GERMAN OCCUPATION |
| 1945- | Part of Italy |

## ITALY: Venzia-Guilia

| | |
|---|---|
| 1919-1945 | Part of Italy |
| 1945 | YUGOSLAV OCCUPATION |
| 1945-1947 | ALLIED MILITARY GOVERNMENT |
| 1947- | Divided between Italy & Trieste - Zone A |

## JORDAN: Palestine Issues - West Bank

| | |
|---|---|
| Prior to 1948 | Part of Palestine |
| 1948-1950 | JORDANIAN OCCUPATION |
| 1950-1967 | Part of Jordan |
| 1967- | Israeli Occupation (Israel) |

## KARELIA

| | |
|---|---|
| Prior to 1922 | Part of Russia |
| 1922 | AUTONOMOUS REPUBLIC |

| | |
|---|---|
| 1922-1941 | Part of Russia |
| 1941-1944 | Eastern Karelia: FINNISH OCCUPATION |
| 1944- | Part of Russia |

**KENYA & UGANDA**

| | |
|---|---|
| Prior to 1922 | Called East Africa & Uganda |
| 1922-1935 | BRITISH COLONY & PROTECTORATE |
| 1935- | Separated - stamps of Kenya, Uganda & Tanganyika |

**KENYA, UGANDA & TANZANIA**

| | |
|---|---|
| Prior to 1935 | Issues for Tanganyika & Kenya-Uganda |

**Kenya, Uganda, & Tanganyika:**

| | |
|---|---|
| 1935-1961 | BRITISH POSTAL UNIT |
| 1961-1964 | EAST AFRICAN POSTAL UNION - Kenya, Uganda & Tanzania |
| 1964-1976 | EAST AFRICAN POSTAL UNION |
| 1976- | Postal Union Dissolved |

**KIAUCHAU**

| | |
|---|---|
| Prior to 1897 | Part of China |
| 1898-1900 | German Leased Territory (Germany) |
| 1900-1914 | GERMAN LEASED TERRITORY |
| 1914-1922 | Japanese Occupation (Japan) |
| 1922- | Part of China |

**KIONGA**

| | |
|---|---|
| Prior to 1916 | Part of German East Africa |
| 1916-1919 | PORTUGUESE OCCUPATION |
| 1919- | Part of Mozambique |

**LABUAN**

| | |
|---|---|
| 1860-1867 | British Colony (India) |
| 1867-1879 | British Colony (Straits Settlements) |
| 1879-1889 | DEPENDENCY OF STRAITS SETTLEMENTS |
| 1890-1906 | BRITISH NORTH BORNEO COMPANY ADMINISTRATION |
| 1906-1942 | Part of Strait Settlements |
| 1942- | Part of North Borneo/Malaysia |

**LAGOS**

| | |
|---|---|
| 1861-1874 | Dependency of Sierra Leone (Sierra Leone) |
| 1874-1886 | DEPENDENCY OF GOLD COAST |

| | |
|---|---|
| 1886-1899 | ROYAL NIGER CO. ADMINISTRATION |
| 1899-1906 | BRITISH PROTECTORATE |
| 1906- | Part of Southern Nigeria/ Nigeria |

**LATAKIA**

| | |
|---|---|
| Prior to 1930 | Called Alouites |
| 1930-1937 | AUTONOMOUS REPUBLIC UNDER FRENCH MANDATE |
| 1937- | Part of Syria |

**LEEWARD ISLANDS**

| | |
|---|---|
| Prior to 1890 | Separate British Colonies of Antigua, Dominica, Montserrat, Nevis, St. Christopher & Virgin Is. |
| 1890-1956 | BRITISH COLONY |
| 1956- | Separate British Colonies |

**LIBIA: Fezzan-Ghadames**

| | |
|---|---|
| 1943-1949 | FRENCH MILITARY ADMINISTRATION |
| 1948-1950 | Fezzan - FRENCH MILITARY ADMINISTRATION |
| 1950-1951 | Fezzan - FRENCH CIVIL ADMINISTRATION |
| 1949-1951 | Ghadames - FRENCH MILITARY ADMINISTRATION |

**LOURENCO MARQUES**

| | |
|---|---|
| Prior to 1893 | Part of Mozambique |
| 1893-1921 | DISTRICT OF MOZAMBIQUE |
| 1921- | Part of Mozambique |

**MADIERA**

| | |
|---|---|
| 1853-1868 | Portuguese Colony (Portugal) |
| 1868-1881 | PORTUGUESE COLONY |
| 1881-1892 | Portuguese Colony (Portugal) |
| 1892-1905 | Portuguese Colony ( Funchal) |
| 1905-1931 | Portuguese Colony (Azores) |
| 1931- | Part of Portugal |

**MALAYA**

| | |
|---|---|
| Prior to 1943 | Issues of Separate States and Sultanates |
| 1943 | SIAMESE OCCUPATION - Northern Portion |
| 1943-1945 | JAPANESE OCCUPATION - Major Portion |
| 1945-1957 | Separate States & Sultanates |
| 1957-1963 | INDEPENDENT FEDERATION |

# HOW TO COLLECT STAMPS

| | |
|---|---|
| 1963- | Part of Malaysia |

**MALAYAN STATES**
**Federated Malay States:**
| | |
|---|---|
| Prior to 1900 | Separate States |
| 1900-1935 | BRITISH PROTECTED SULTANATES |
| 1935- | Separate States |

**Johore:**
| | |
|---|---|
| 1876-1914 | SULTANATE |
| 1914-1942 | BRITISH PROTECTED SULTANATE |
| 1942-1943 | JAPANESE OCCUPATION |
| 1943-1945 | Japanese Occupation (Malaya) |
| 1945-1948 | Br. Protected Sultanate (Straits Settlements) |
| 1948-1957 | BRITISH PROTECTED SULTANATE |
| 1957-1963 | STATE OF MALAYA |
| 1963-1965 | Part of Malaysia |
| 1965- | STATE OF MALAYSIA |

**Kedah:**
| | |
|---|---|
| Prior to 1909 | Part of Siam |
| 1909-1912 | Br. Protected Sultanate (Fed. Malay States) |
| 1912-1942 | BRITISH PROTECTED SULTANATE |
| 1942-1943 | JAPANESE OCCUPATION |
| 1943 | Siamese Occupation (Siam) |
| 1943-1945 | Br. Protected Sultanate (Straits Settlements) |
| 1948-1957 | BRITISH PROTECTED SULTANATE |
| 1957-1963 | STATE OF MALAYA |
| 1963-1965 | Part of Malaysia |
| 1965- | STATE OF MALAYSIA |

**Malacca:**
| | |
|---|---|
| Prior to 1942 | Part of Straits Settlements |
| 1942 | JAPANESE OCCUPATION |
| 1942-1945 | Japanese Occupation (Malaya/ Straits Sett.) |
| 1945-1949 | British Protectorate (Straits Settlements) |
| 1948-1957 | BRITISH PROTECTORATE |
| 1957-1963 | STATE OF MALAYA |
| 1963-1965 | Part of Malaysia |
| 1965- | STATE OF MALAYSIA |

**Negri Sembilan:**
| | |
|---|---|
| 1891-1900 | FEDERATION OF BRITISH PROTECTED SULTANATES |
| 1900-1935 | Part of Fed. Malay States |
| 1935-1942 | FEDERATION OF BRITISH PROTECTED SULTANATES |
| 1942-1943 | JAPANESE OCCUPATION |
| 1943-1945 | Japanese Occupation (Malaya) |
| 1945-1949 | Federation of Br. Prot. Sultanates (Straits Settlements) |
| 1948-1957 | FEDERATION OF BRITISH PROTECTED SULTANATES |
| 1957-1963 | STATE OF MALAYA |
| 1963-1965 | Part of Malaysia |
| 1965- | STATE OF MALAYSIA |

**Pahang:**
| | |
|---|---|
| 1889-1900 | BRITISH PROTECTED SULTANATE |
| 1900-1935 | Part of Fed. Malay States |
| 1935-1942 | BRITISH PROTECTED SULTANATE |
| 1942-1943 | JAPANESE OCCUPATION |
| 1943-1945 | Japanese Occupation (Malaya) |
| 1945-1950 | Br. Prot. Sultanate (Straits Settlements) |
| 1948-1957 | BRITISH PROTECTED SULTANATE |
| 1957-1963 | STATE OF MALAYA |
| 1963-1965 | Part of Malaysia |
| 1965- | STATE OF MALAYSIA |

**Penang:**
| | |
|---|---|
| Prior to 1942 | Part of Straits Settlements |
| 1942 | JAPANESE OCCUPATION |
| 1942-1945 | Japanese Occupation (Malaya/ Straits Sett.) |
| 1945-1949 | British Protectorate (Straits Settlements) |
| 1948-1957 | BRITISH PROTECTORATE |
| 1957-1963 | STATE OF MALAYA |
| 1963-1965 | Part of Malaysia |
| 1965- | STATE OF MALAYSIA |

**Perak:**
| | |
|---|---|
| 1867-1878 | Br. Protected Sultanate (Straits Settlements) |
| 1878-1900 | BRITISH PROTECTED SULTANATE |
| 1900-1935 | Part of Fed. Malay States |
| 1935-1942 | BRITISH PROTECTED SULTANATE |
| 1942-1943 | JAPANESE OCCUPATION |
| 1943-1945 | Japanese Occupation (Malaya) |
| 1945-1950 | Br. Prot. Sultanate (Straits Settlements) |
| 1948-1957 | BRITISH PROTECTED SULTANATE |
| 1957-1963 | STATE OF MALAYA |
| 1963- | STATE OF MALAYSIA |

**Perlis:**
| | |
|---|---|
| Prior to 1943 | Part of Kedah |
| 1943-1945 | Part of Siam |
| 1945-1951 | Br. Protected Sultanate (Straits Settlements) |

# HOW TO COLLECT STAMPS

| | |
|---|---|
| 1948-1857 | BRITISH PROTECTED SULTANATE |
| 1957-1963 | STATE OF MALAYA |
| 1963-1965 | Part of Malaysia |
| 1965- | STATE OF MALAYSIA |

**Selangor:**

| | |
|---|---|
| 1874-1878 | Br. Protected Sultanate (Straits Settlements) |
| 1878-1900 | BRITISH PROTECTED SULTANATE |
| 1900-1935 | Part of Fed. Malay States |
| 1935-1942 | BRITISH PROTECTED SULTANATE |
| 1942-1943 | JAPANESE OCCUPATION |
| 1943-1945 | Japanese Occupation (Malaya) |
| 1945-1949 | Br. Prot. Sultanate (Straits Settlements) |
| 1948-1957 | BRITISH PROTECTED SULTANATE |
| 1957-1963 | STATE OF MALAYA |
| 1963-1965 | State of Malaysia |
| 1965- | STATE OF MALAYSIA |

**Sunjei Ujong:**

| | |
|---|---|
| 1878-1895 | BRITISH PROTECTED SULTANATE |
| 1895- | Part of Negri Sembilan/ Malaysia |

**Trengganu:**

| | |
|---|---|
| Prior to 1909 | Part of Siam |
| 1909-1910 | Br. Protected Sultanate (Straits Settlements) |
| 1910-1942 | BRITISH PROTECTED SULTANATE |
| 1942-1943 | JAPANESE OCCUPATION |
| 1943 | Siamese Occupation (Siam) |
| 1943-1945 | Part of Siam |
| 1945-1949 | Br. Protected Sultanate (Straits Settlements) |
| 1948-1957 | BRITISH PROTECTED SULTANATE |
| 1957-1963 | STATE OF MALAYA |
| 1963-1965 | Part of Malaysia |
| 1965- | STATE OF MALAYSIA |

## MANCHUKUO

| | |
|---|---|
| Prior to 1932 | Part of China |
| 1932-1934 | JAPANESE OCCUPATION |
| 1934-1945 | JAPANESE PUPPET REPUBLIC |
| 1945- | Part of China |

## MARIANNA ISLANDS

| | |
|---|---|
| Prior to 1899 | Spanish Colony (Philippines) |
| 1899-1900 | SPANISH COLONY |
| 1900-1914 | GERMAN PROTECTORATE |
| 1914-1945 | Japanese Occupation & Mandate (Japan) |
| 1945-1947 | U.S. Occupation (U.S.) |
| 1947-1977 | Part of Trust Territory of Pacific (U.S.) |
| 1977- | Northern Marianna - Commonwealth of Trust Territories of Pacific (U.S.) |

## MARIENWERDER

| | |
|---|---|
| Prior to 1920 | Part of Germany |
| 1920 | PLEBISCITE AREA |
| 1920-1945 | Part of Germany |
| 1945- | Part of Poland |

## MARTINIQUE

| | |
|---|---|
| 1886-1946 | FRENCH COLONY |
| 1947 | FRENCH OVERSEAS DEPARTMENT |
| 1947- | Fr. Overseas Dept. (France) |

## MAYOTTE

| | |
|---|---|
| 1892-1898 | FRENCH COLONY |
| 1898-1912 | FRENCH DEPENDENCY |
| 1912-1914 | FRENCH COLONY |
| 1914-1976 | Part of Madagascar/Comoros |
| 1976- | French Overseas Dept. (France) |

## MEMEL

| | |
|---|---|
| Prior to 1918 | Part of Germany |
| 1918-1920 | Allied Occupation (Germany) |
| 1920-1923 | ALLIED (FRENCH) ADMINISTRATION |
| 1923-1924 | LITHUANIAN OCCUPATION |
| 1924-1939 | Part of Lithuania |
| 1939-1944 | Part of Germany |
| 1944- | Part of Russia |

## MESOPOTAMIA

| | |
|---|---|
| 1863-1917 | Part of Turkey |
| 1917-1918 | British Occupation (India) |
| 1917-1918 | Baghdad - BRITISH OCCUPATION |
| 1918-1921 | Iraq - BRITISH OCCUPATION |
| 1918-1921 | Mosul - BRITISH OCCUPATION |
| 1921- | Name changed to Iraq |

## MIDDLE CONGO

| | |
|---|---|
| Prior to 1904 | Part of French Congo |
| 1904-1907 | French Colony (French Congo) |
| 1907-1910 | FRENCH COLONY |
| 1910-1937 | COLONY OF FR. EQUATORIAL AFRICA |
| 1937-1958 | Part of Fr. Equatorial Africa |

| 1958- | Name changed to Congo Republic |
|-------|---------------|

**MOHELI**

| 1906-1912 | FRENCH DEPENDENCY |
|-----------|-------------------|
| 1912-1914 | FRENCH COLONY |
| 1914- | Part of Madagascar/Comoros |

**MONTENEGRO**

| 1874-1910 | PRINCIPALITY |
|-----------|-------------|
| 1910-1916 | KINGDOM |
| 1916 | GOVERNMENT-IN-EXILE |
| 1917-1918 | AUSTRIAN OCCUPATION |
| 1918-1941 | Part of Serbia/Yugoslavia |
| 1941-1943 | ITALIAN OCCUPATION |
| 1943-1944 | GERMAN OCCUPATION |
| 1944- | Part of Yugoslavia |

**MOZAMBIQUE COMPANY**

| Prior to 1892 | Part of Mozambique |
|---------------|--------------------|
| 1892-1942 | MOZAMBIQUE COMPANY ADMINISTRATION |
| 1942- | Part of Mozambique |

**NATAL**

| 1857-1910 | BRITISH COLONY |
|-----------|----------------|
| 1910-1913 | PROVINCE OF UNION OF SOUTH AFRICA |
| 1913- | Part of South Africa |

**NETHERLANDS INDIES**

| 1864-1942 | NETHERLANDS COLONY |
|-----------|--------------------|
| 1942-1945 | Japanese Occupation (Separate Districts) |
| 1945-1948 | NETHERLANDS COLONY |
| 1948- | Name changed to Indonesia |

**Japanese Occupation Districts:**

| 1943-1945 | JAVA & MADURA |
|-----------|---------------|
| 1943-1945 | SUMATRA |
| 1943-1945 | EASTERN INDONESIA |

**NETHERLANDS NEW GUINEA**

| Prior to 1950 | Part of Netherlands Indies |
|---------------|---------------------------|
| 1950-1962 | NETHERLANDS OVERSEAS TERRRITORY |
| 1962- | Name changed to West Irian |

**NEVIS**

| 1861-1890 | BRITISH COLONY |
|-----------|----------------|
| 1890-1903 | Part of Leeward Islands |
| 1903- | Part of St. Kitts-Nevis |

**NEW BRITAIN**

| Prior to 1914 | Part of German New Guinea |
|---------------|---------------------------|
| 1914-1915 | AUSTRALIAN OCCUPATION |
| 1915- | Part of N.W. Pacific Is./Papua New Guinea |

**NEW BRUNSWICK**

| 1851-1867 | BRITISH COLONY |
|-----------|----------------|
| 1867- | Province of Canada |

**NEWFOUNDLAND**

| 1857-1933 | SELF-GOVERNING BRITISH DOMINION |
|-----------|--------------------------------|
| 1933-1949 | BRITISH COLONY |
| 1949- | Province of Canada |

**NEW GUINEA**

| Prior to 1925 | German New Guinea/ N.W. Pacific Is. |
|---------------|------------------------------------|
| 1925-1942 | AUSTRALIAN TERRITORY |
| 1942-1944 | Japanese Occupation (Japan) |
| 1944-1952 | Australian Territory (Australia) |
| 1952- | Part of Papua New Guinea |

**NEW HEBRIDES**

| 1887-1908 | British & French Protectorate (New Caledonia) |
|-----------|----------------------------------------------|
| 1908-1980 | BRITISH & FRENCH CONDOMINIUM - British & French Currency Issues |
| 1980- | Name changed to Vanuatu |

**NEW REPUBLIC**

| 1881-1886 | Part of Natal |
|-----------|---------------|
| 1886-1888 | BOER REPUBLIC |
| 1888-1903 | Part of South African Rep. |
| 1903- | Part of Natal/South Africa |

**NEW SOUTH WALES**

| 1850-1901 | BRITISH COLONY |
|-----------|----------------|
| 1901-1913 | STATE OF AUSTRALIA |
| 1913- | State of Australia |

**NIGER COAST PROTECTORATE**

| 1892-1893 | Oil River Prot. - BRITISH PROTECTORATE |
|-----------|---------------------------------------|
| 1893-1900 | BRITISH PROTECTORATE |
| 1900- | Part of Southern Nigeria/ Nigeria |

**NORTH BORNEO**

| 1883-1941 | BRITISH NORTH BORNEO COMPANY ADMINISTRATION |
|-----------|--------------------------------------------|
| 1942-1945 | JAPANESE OCCUPATION |
| 1945-1946 | BRITISH MILITARY ADMINISTRATION |
| 1946-1963 | BRITISH COLONY |

1963-          Name changed to Sabah

## NORTH INGERMANLAND
Prior to 1920   Part of Russia
1920           PROVISIONAL GOVERN-
               MENT
1920-          Part of Russia

## NORTHERN NIGERIA
1900-1913      BRITISH PROTECTORATE
1914-          Part of Nigeria

## NORTHERN RHODESIA
Prior to 1924   Part of Rhodesia
1925-1953      BRITISH PROTECTORATE
1954-1963      Part of Rhodesia & Nyasaland
1963-1964      BRITISH PROTECTORATE
1964-          Name changed to Zambia

## NORTHWEST PACIFIC ISLANDS
Prior to 1915   German New Guinea/New
               Britain
1915-1924      AUSTRALIAN MILITARY
               GOVERNMENT
1952-          Name changed to New Guinea

## NOSSI-BE
1889-1894      DEPENDENCY OF
               DIEGO-SUAREZ
1894-1901      FRENCH COLONY
1901-          Part of Madagascar

## NOVA SCOTIA
1851-1867      BRITISH COLONY
1867-          Province of Canada

## NYASALAND PROTECTORATE
Prior to 1908   was called British Central
               Africa
1908-1954      BRITISH PROTECTORATE
1954-1963      Part of Rhodesia & Nyasaland
1963-1964      BRITISH PROTECTORATE
1964-          Name changed to Malawi

## NYASSA
Prior to 1908   Part of Mozambique
1898-1929      NYASSA COMPANY
               ADMINISTRATION
1929-          Part of Mozambique

## OBOCK
1892-1893      FRENCH POSSESSION
1893-1903      USED ONLY IN DJIBOUTI
1903-          Part of Somali Coast/Djibouti

## OLTRE GUIBA
Prior to 1925   Part of Kenya & Uganda
1925-1926      ITALIAN PROTECTORATE
1926-          Part of Somalia

## ORANGE RIVER COLONY
1868-1900      Orange Free State - BOER
               REPUBLIC
1900           Orange Free State - BRITISH
               OCCUPATION
1900-1910      BRITISH COLONY
1910-1913      PROVINCE OF UNION OF
               SOUTH AFRICA
1913-          Part of South Africa

## PAKISTAN: Native States
1945-1949      Bahawalpur: FEUDATORY
               STATE
1897-1907      Las Bela: FEUDATORY
               STATE

## PALESTINE
Prior to 1918   Part of Turkey
1918-1920      BRITISH MILITARY
               ADMINISTRATION
1920-1923      BRITISH ADMINISTRATION
1923-1948      BRITISH MANDATE
1948-          Divided into Israel, Gaza &
               West Bank Areas

## PONTA DELGADA
Prior to 1892   Part of Azores
1892-1905      DISTRICT OF AZORES
1905-          Part of Azores/Portugal

## PORTUGUESE AFRICA
1898, 1919,    SPECIAL ISSUES FOR
1945           PORTUGUESE COLONIES

## PORTUGUESE CONGO
1870-1894      Part of Angola
1894-1920      PORTUGUESE COLONY
1920-          Part of Angola

## PORTUGUESE GUINEA
1877-1881      Dependency of Cape Verde
               (Cape Verde)
1881-1951      PORTUGUESE COLONY
1951-1974      PORTUGUESE OVERSEAS
               PROVINCE
1974-          Name changed to Guinea-
               Bissau

## PORTUGUESE INDIA
1871-1951      PORTUGUESE COLONY

| 1951-1961 | PORTUGUESE OVERSEAS PROVINCE |
| 1961- | Part of India |

## PRINCE EDWARD ISLAND
| 1861-1873 | BRITISH COLONY |
| 1873- | Province of Canada |

## PUERTO RICO
| 1855-1873 | Spanish Colony (Cuba & Puerto Rico) |
| 1873-1898 | SPANISH COLONY |
| 1898-1900 | U.S. ADMINISTRATION |
| 1900-1917 | U.S. Civil Administration (U.S.) |
| 1917-1952 | U.S. Territory (U.S.) |
| 1952- | Autonomous U.S. Common-wealth (U.S.) |

## QUEENSLAND
| 1850-1859 | Part of New South Wales |
| 1859-1901 | BRITISH COLONY |
| 1901-1913 | STATE OF AUSTRALIA |
| 1913- | State of Australia |

## QUELIMANE
| Prior to 1893 | Part of Mozambique |
| 1893-1913 | Part of Zambezia |
| 1913-1914 | DISTRICT OF MOZAMBIQUE |
| 1914-1920 | Part of Zambezia/Mozambique |

## RAS AL KHAIMA
| Prior to 1964 | Part of Trucial States |
| 1964-1971 | BRITISH PROTECTED SHEIKDOM |
| 1971-1972 | STATE OF UNITED ARAB EMIRATES |
| 1973- | Part of United Arab Emirates |

## REUNION
| 1852-1946 | FRENCH COLONY |
| 1946-1975 | FRENCH OVERSEAS DEPARTMENT |
| 1975- | Fr. Overseas Department (France) |

## RHODESIA
| 1890-1909 | British South Africa - BRITISH TERRITORY |
| 1909-1924 | BRITISH TERRITORY |
| 1924- | Divided into Nthn. & Sthn. Rhodesia |

## RHODESIA & NYASALAND
| Prior to 1953 | Separate Colonies & Protectorates |
| 1954-1963 | BRITISH FEDERATED STATE |
| 1963- | Separate Countries |

## RIO DE ORO
| 1901-1905 | Spanish Colony (Spain) |
| 1905-1924 | SPANISH COLONY |
| 1924- | Name changed to Spanish Sahara |

## RIO MUNI
| Prior to 1909 | Called Spanish Guinea |
| 1909-1960 | Part of Spanish Guinea |
| 1960-1968 | SPANISH OVERSEAS PROVINCE |
| 1968- | Part of Equatorial Guinea |

## ROUAD, ILE
| Prior to 1916 | Part of Turkey |
| 1916-1920 | FRENCH OCCUPATION |
| 1920- | Part of Syria |

## RUANDA-URUNDI
| Prior to 1916 | Part of German East Africa |
| 1916-1924 | Belgian Occupation (Ger. East Africa - Belgian Occupation) |
| 1924-1968 | BELGIAN TRUSTEESHIP |
| 1968- | Divided into Burundi & Rwanda |

## RUSSIA: Union of Soviet Socialist Republics
**Russian Socialist Federated Soviet Republics:**
| 1917-1922 | SOVIET REPUBLIC |

**Union of Soviet Socialist Republics:**
| 1922- | COMMUNIST REPUBLIC |

## RUSSIA: Occupation Issues
| 1916-1918 | Baltic Provinces - GERMAN OCCUPATION |
| 1919 | Aunus - FINNISH OCCUPATION |
| 1941-1944 | German Eastern Command - GERMAN OCCUPATION |

## RYUKYU ISLANDS
| Prior to 1879 | Part of China |
| 1879-1945 | Part of Japan |
| 1945-1951 | U.S. MILITARY GOVERN-MENT |
| 1951-1972 | SEMI-AUTONOMOUS UNDER U.S. ADMINISTRA-TION |
| 1972- | Part of Japan |

# HOW TO COLLECT STAMPS

## SAAR
| | |
|---|---|
| Prior to 1920 | Part of Germany |
| 1920-1935 | LEAGUE OF NATIONS ADMINISTRATION |
| 1935-1945 | Part of Germany |
| 1945-1947 | Part of French Occupation Zone |
| 1947-1948 | FRENCH ADMINISTRATION |
| 1948-1951 | FRENCH PROTECTORATE |
| 1951-1957 | SEMI-INDEPENDENT STATE UNDER FRENCH PROTECTORATE |
| 1957-1959 | GER. FEDERAL REP. ADMINISTRATION |
| 1959- | Part of German Federal Republic |

## SABAH
| | |
|---|---|
| Prior to 1963 | Called North Borneo |
| 1963- | STATE OF MALAYSIA |

## ST. CHRISTOPHER
| | |
|---|---|
| 1860-1870 | British Colony (Handstamps) |
| 1870-1890 | BRITISH COLONY |
| 1890-1903 | Part of Leeward Islands |
| 1903- | Part of St. Kitts-Nevis |

## STE. MARIE DE MADAGASCAR
| | |
|---|---|
| 1890-1894 | Part of Diego-Suarez |
| 1894-1898 | FRENCH COLONY |
| 1898- | Part of Madagascar |

## ST. PIERRE & MIQUELON
| | |
|---|---|
| 1885-1946 | FRENCH COLONY |
| 1946-1976 | FRENCH OVERSEAS TERRITORY |
| 1976- | French Overseas Department (French) |

## SARAWAK
| | |
|---|---|
| 1869-1888 | INDPENDENT STATE |
| 1888-1942 | BRITISH PROTECTORATE |
| 1942-1945 | JAPANESE OCCUPATION |
| 1945-1946 | BRITISH MILITARY ADMINISTRATION |
| 1946-1963 | BRITISH COLONY |
| 1963- | STATE OF MALAYSIA |

## SASENO
| | |
|---|---|
| 1914-1923 | Italian Occupation (Italy) |
| 1923 | ITALIAN POSSESSION |
| 1923-1943 | Part of Italy |
| 1943- | Part of Albania |

## SCHLESWIG
| | |
|---|---|
| 1868-1920 | Part of Nth. German Conf./ Germany |
| 1920 | PLEBISCITE AREA |
| 1920- | Zone 1 to Denmark, Zone 2 to Germany |

## SENEGAMBIA & NIGER
| | |
|---|---|
| Prior to 1899 | Part of French Sudan |
| 1899-1903 | Protectorate of Fr. West Africa (French Sudan) |
| 1903-1904 | PROTECTORATE OF FR. WEST AFRICA |
| 1904- | Name changed to Upper Senegal & Niger |

## SERBIA
| | |
|---|---|
| 1866-1878 | AUTONOMOUS PRINCIPALITY |
| 1878-1882 | PRINCIPALITY |
| 1882-1916 | KINGDOM |
| 1916-1918 | GOVERNMENT IN EXILE On Corfu |
| 1916-1918 | AUSTRALIAN OCCUPATION |
| 1918-1921 | YUGOSLAV PROVINCE |
| 1921-1941 | Part of Yugoslavia |
| 1941-1944 | GERMAN OCCUPATION |
| 1944- | Part of Yugoslavia |

## SHANGHAI
| | |
|---|---|
| 1865-1898 | CITY OF CHINA - EUROPEAN POST OFFICES |
| 1898- | City of China |

## SHARJAH
| | |
|---|---|
| Prior to 1963 | Part of Trucial States |
| 1963-1971 | BRITISH PROTECTED SHEIKDOM |
| 1971-1972 | STATE OF UNITED ARAB EMIRATES |
| 1973- | Part of United Arab Emirates |

## SIBERIA
| | |
|---|---|
| Prior to 1919 | Part of Russia |
| 1919-1920 | CZECH LEGION POST |
| 1919 | ADMIRAL KOLCHAK ISSUES |
| 1920 | AMUR - Communist Government |
| 1920 | TRANSBAIKAL - Ataman Semyenou Government |
| 1920- | Part of Russia |

## SOMALI COAST
| | |
|---|---|
| Prior to 1902 | Called Djibouti |

| 1902-1947 | FRENCH COLONY |
| 1947-1967 | FRENCH OVERSEAS TERRITORY |
| 1967- | Name changed to Afars & Issas |

**SOMALILAND PROTECTORATE**

| 1887-1903 | British Somaliland - Br. Protectorate (India) |
| 1903-1904 | British Somaliland - BRITISH PROTECTORATE |
| 1904-1940 | BRITISH PROTECTORATE |
| 1940-1941 | ITALIAN OCCUPATION |
| 1941-1942 | British Protectorate (Aden) |
| 1942-1960 | BRITISH PROTECTORATE |
| 1960 | REPUBLIC |
| 1960- | United with Somalia |

**SOUTH ARABIA**

| Prior to 1959 | Aden & States |
| 1959-1963 | British Federated State (Aden & States) |
| 1963-1967 | BRITISH PROTECTED FEDERATION |
| 1968- | Name changed to Southern Yemen |

**SOUTH AUSTRALIA**

| 1855-1901 | BRITISH COLONY |
| 1901-1913 | STATE OF AUSTRALIA |
| 1913- | State of Australia |

**SOUTH GEORGIA**

| Prior to 1944 | Falkland Islands |
| 1944-1946 | FALKLAND IS. DEPENDENCY |
| 1946-1963 | Part of Falkland Is. Dependency |
| 1963-1980 | FALKLAND IS. DEPENDENCY |
| 1980- | Name changed to Falkland Is. Dependency |

**SOUTH RUSSIA**

| Prior to 1918 | Part of Russia |
| 1919-1920 | GENERAL DENEKIN ISSUES |
| 1919 | Crimea - REGIONAL GOVERNMENT |
| 1918-1920 | Kuban Area - COSSACK GOVERNMENT |
| 1920 | GENERAL WRANGEL ISSUES |
| 1920- | Part of Russia |

**SOUTHERN NIGERIA**

| Prior to 1900 | Niger Coast Protectorate |
| 1900-1901 | British Protectorate (Niger Coast Prot.) |
| 1901-1906 | BRITISH PROTECTORATE |
| 1906-1913 | BRITISH COLONY & PROTECTORATE |
| 1914- | Part of Nigeria |

**SOUTHERN RHODESIA**

| 1909-1924 | Part of Rhodesia |
| 1924-1953 | SELF-GOVERNING BRITISH COLONY |
| 1954-1963 | Part of Rhodesia & Nyasaland |
| 1964-1965 | BRITISH COLONY |
| 1965-1979 | Rhodesia - INDEPENDENT STATE |
| 1979- | Name changed to Zimbabwe |

**SPANISH GUINEA**

| 1885-1902 | Part of Fernando Po |
| 1902-1960 | SPANISH COLONY |
| 1960-1968 | Divided into Rio Muni & Fernando Po |
| 1968- | Name changed to Equatorial Guinea |

**SPANISH MOROCCO**

| Prior to 1912 | Part of Morocco |
| 1912-1914 | Spanish Protectorate (Spanish P. Offices) |
| 1914-1956 | SPANISH PROTECTORATE |
| 1956- | Part of Morocco |

**SPANISH MOROCCO - Tetuan**

| 1908-1912 | SPANISH POSSESSION |

**SPANISH SAHARA**

| Prior to 1924 | Rio de Oro |
| 1924-1949 | SPANISH COLONY |
| 1949-1951 | PART OF SPANISH WEST AFRICA |
| 1951-1958 | SPANISH COLONY |
| 1958-1976 | SPANISH OVERSEAS PROVINCE |
| 1976-1979 | Divided between Morocco & Mauritania |
| 1979- | Moroccan Occupation |

**SPANISH WEST AFRICA**

| Prior to 1949 | Separate Spanish Colonies |
| 1949-1951 | SPANISH ADMINISTRATIVE UNIT |
| 1951- | Divided between Ifni & Spanish Sahara |

**STELLALAND**

| 1884-1885 | BOER REPUBLIC |
| 1885-1897 | Part of British Bechuanaland |

# HOW TO COLLECT STAMPS

| 1897- | Part of Cape of Good Hope/ South Africa |

**STRAITS SETTLEMENTS**
| 1867-1942 | BRITISH COLONY |
| 1942-1943 | JAPANESE OCCUPATION |
| 1943-1945 | Japanese Occupation (Malaya) |
| 1945-1948 | BRITISH MILITARY ADMINISTRATION |
| 1948-1950 | BRITISH POSTAL AREA |
| 1950- | Separate States/Malaya |

**TAHITI**
| 1882-1893 | FRENCH COLONY |
| 1903,1915 | SPECIAL ISSUES |
| 1893- | Part of French Polynesia |

**TANGANYIKA**
| Prior to 1921 | Part of German East Africa |
| 1921-1935 | BRITISH MANDATE |
| 1935-1961 | British Mandate (Kenya, Uganda & Tanganyika) |
| 1961-1962 | INDEPENDENT STATE |
| 1962-1964 | REPUBLIC |
| 1964- | Name changed to Tanzania |

**TANNA TUVA**
| 1878-1912 | Part of China |
| 1912-1926 | Autonomous Republic (Russia) |
| 1926-1945 | AUTONOMOUS SOVIET REPUBLIC |
| 1945- | Part of Russia |

**TASMANIA**
| 1853-1901 | BRITISH COLONY |
| 1901-1913 | STATE OF AUSTRALIA |
| 1913- | State of Australia |

**TETE**
| Prior to 1893 | Part of Mozambique |
| 1893-1913 | Part of Zambezia |
| 1913-1914 | DISTRICT OF MOZAMBIQUE |
| 1914- | Part of Zambezia/Mozambique |

**THRACE**
**Eastern Thrace:**
| Prior to 1920 | Part of Turkey |
| 1920 | GREEK OCCUPATION |
| 1920-1923 | Part of Greece |
| 1923- | Part of Turkey |
**Western Thrace:**
| Prior to 1913 | Part of Turkey |
| 1913 | GREEK OCCUPATION |

| 1913 | AUTONOMOUS GOVERNMENT |
| 1913-1919 | Part of Bulgaria |
| 1919-1920 | ALLIED OCCUPATION |
| 1920 | GREEK OCCUPATION |
| 1920- | Part of Greece |

**TIBET**
| Prior to 1911 | Part of China |
| 1911-1921 | CHINESE POST OFFICES |
| 1912-1951 | AUTONOMOUS THEOCRACY |
| 1951- | Part of China |

**TIMOR**
| 1884-1896 | DEPENDENCY OF MACAO |
| 1896-1951 | PORTUGUESE COLONY |
| 1951-1975 | PORTUGUESE OVERSEAS PROVINCE |
| 1975-1976 | INDONESIAN OCCUPATION |
| 1976- | Part of Indonesia |

**TOBAGO**
| 1860-1879 | British Colony (Handstamps) |
| 1879-1889 | BRITISH COLONY |
| 1889-1896 | WARD OF TRINIDAD |
| 1896- | Part of Trinidad/Trinidad & Tobago |

**TRANSCAUCASIAN FEDERATED REPUBLICS**
| Prior to 1922 | Separate Republics |
| 1922-1923 | Soviet Republic (Armenia, Azerbaijan & Georgia) |
| 1923 | SOVIET REPUBLIC |
| 1923-1924 | PROVINCES OF RUSSIA |
| 1924- | Part of Russia |

**TRANSVAAL**
| 1869-1877 | South African Rep. - BOER REPUBLIC |
| 1877-1878 | BRITISH OCCUPATION |
| 1878-1882 | BRITISH COLONY |
| 1882-1901 | South African Rep. - BOER REPUBLIC |
| 1900-1902 | South African Rep. - BRITISH OCCUPATION |
| 1902-1910 | BRITISH COLONY |
| 1910-1913 | PROVINCE OF UNION OF SOUTH AFRICA |
| 1913- | Part of South Africa |

**TRIESTE - Zone A**
| Prior to 1947 | Part of Italy (Venezia - Guilia) |

| 1947-1954 | ALLIED MILITARY GOVERNMENT |
| 1954- | Part of Italy |

**TRIESTE - Zone B**

| Prior to 1947 | Istria & Slovene Coast |
| 1947-1954 | YUGOSLAV MILITARY ADMINISTRATION |
| 1954- | Part of Yugoslavia |

**TRINIDAD**

| 1851-1913 | BRITISH COLONY |
| 1913- | Name changed to Trinidad & Tobago |

**TRIPOLITANIA**

| 1912-1923 | Part of Libia |
| 1923-1927 | DISTRICT OF LIBIA |
| 1927-1934 | ITALIAN COLONY |
| 1934-1942 | Part of Libia |
| 1943-1948 | British Occupation (Middle East Forces) |
| 1948-1950 | BRITISH MILITARY ADMINISTRATION |
| 1950-1951 | BRITISH ADMINISTRATION |
| 1951- | Part of Libya |

**TRUCIAL STATES**

| Prior to 1961 | Separate Sheikdoms using stamps of Oman, India, etc. |
| 1961-1963 | UNION OF BRITISH PROTECTED SHEIKDOMS |
| 1963-1971 | Issues of separate Sheikdoms |
| 1971- | Name changed to United Arab Emirates |

**TURKS ISLANDS**

| 1867-1873 | BRITISH COLONY |
| 1873-1900 | DEPENDENCY OF JAMAICA |
| 1900- | Name changed to Turks & Caicos Is. |

**UBANGI-SHARI**

| Prior to 1906 | Part of French Congo (Ubangi-Shari-Chad) |
| 1906-1910 | French Colony (French Congo) |
| 1910-1915 | Colony of Fr. Equa. Africa (French Congo) |
| 1915-1922 | COLONY OF FRENCH EQUATORIAL AFRICA (Ubangi-Shari) |
| 1922-1936 | COLONY OF FRENCH EQUATORIAL AFRICA |
| 1936-1958 | Part of French Equatorial Africa |

| 1958- | Name changed to Central African Republic |

**UMM AL QIWAIN**

| Prior to 1964 | Part of Trucial States |
| 1964-1971 | BRITISH PROTECTED SHEIKDOM |
| 1971-1972 | STATE OF UNITED ARAB EMIRATES |
| 1973- | Part of United Arab Emirates |

**UPPER SENEGAL & NIGER**

| Prior to 1904 | Senegambia & Niger |
| 1904-1906 | Colony of Fr. West Africa (Senegambia & Niger) |
| 1906-1920 | COLONY OF FRENCH WEST AFRICA |
| 1920- | Colony dissolved |

**UPPER VOLTA**

| 1906-1920 | Part of Upper Senegal & Niger |
| 1920-1933 | COLONY OF FRENCH WEST AFRICA |
| 1933-1947 | Divided by Niger, French Sudan and Ivory Coast |
| 1947-1958 | Part of French West Africa |
| 1958-1959 | Autonomous Republic (Fr. West Africa) |
| 1959-1960 | AUTONOMOUS REPUBLIC |
| 1960-1986 | REPUBLIC |
| 1986- | Name changed to Boukina Faso |

**VICTORIA**

| 1850-1901 | BRITISH COLONY |
| 1901-1913 | STATE OF AUSTRALIA |
| 1913- | State of Australia |

**WESTERN AUSTRALIA**

| 1854-1901 | BRITISH COLONY |
| 1901-1913 | STATE OF AUSTRALIA |
| 1913- | State of Australia |

**WESTERN UKRAINE**

| Prior to 1918 | Part of Austria-Hungary |
| 1918-1919 | AUTONOMOUS STATE |
| 1919 | ROMANIAN OCCUPATION |
| 1919-1939 | Part of Poland |
| 1939-1941 | Russian Occupation (Russia) |
| 1941-1943 | Part of Ukraine |
| 1943- | Part of Russia |

**WEST IRIAN**

| Prior to 1962 | Netherlands New Guinea |

| | |
|---|---|
| 1962-1963 | West New Guinea - UNITED NATIONS EXECUTIVE AUTHORITY |
| 1963-1970 | INDONESIAN ADMINISTRATION |
| 1970- | Part of Indonesia |

**YUGOSLAVIA: Ljubijana**

| | |
|---|---|
| Prior to 1941 | Part of Yugoslavia |
| 1941 | PROVINCE OF ITALY |
| 1941-1944 | Province of Italy (Italy) |
| 1944-1945 | GERMAN OCCUPATION |
| 1945- | Part of Yugoslavia |

**YUGOSLAVIA: Istria & Slovene Coast**

| | |
|---|---|
| Prior to 1945 | Part of Italy |
| 1945-1947 | YUGOSLAV MILITARY ADMINISTRATION |
| 1947- | Divided by Yugoslavia & Trieste - Zone B |

**ZAMBEZIA**

| | |
|---|---|
| Prior to 1893 | Part of Mozambique |
| 1893-1913 | DISTRICT OF MOZAMBIQUE |
| 1913-1914 | Divided into Quelimane & Tete |
| 1914-1920 | DISTRICT OF MOZAMBIQUE |
| 1920- | Part of Mozambique |

**ZANZIBAR**

| | |
|---|---|
| 1875-1890 | Sultanate (India) |
| 1890-1895 | British Protected Sultanate (India) |
| 1895-1963 | BRITISH PROTECTED SULTANATE |
| 1963-1964 | INDEPENDENT SULTANATE |
| 1964 | REPUBLIC |
| 1964-1968 | PART OF TANZANIA |
| 1968- | Part of Tanzania |

**ZULULAND**

| | |
|---|---|
| 1881-1887 | Part of Natal |
| 1887-1888 | British Occupation (Natal) |
| 1888-1898 | BRITISH COLONY |
| 1898- | Part of Natal/South Africa |

# MAP INDEX

# HOW TO COLLECT STAMPS

**Map No.**                    **Map No.**

**Map No.**                                    **Map No.**

# HOW TO COLLECT STAMPS

**206**

# KEY MAP

Map No. 12
Australia & Pacific Ocean

Map No. 11
The Far East

Map No. 10
Indian Ocean

Map No. 6
German States

Map No. 8
The Near East

Map No. 9
Africa

Map No. 5
Europe

Map No. 7
Italian States

Map No. 4
Atlantic Ocean

Map No. 2
Caribbean & West Indies

Map No. 3
South America

Map No. 1
North America

Antarctica 47 130

SEE PAGE 201 FOR MAP INDEX

# Map No. 1: North & Central AmericaMap No. 2: Caribbean Sea & West Indies

# Map No. 2: Caribbean Sea & West Indies

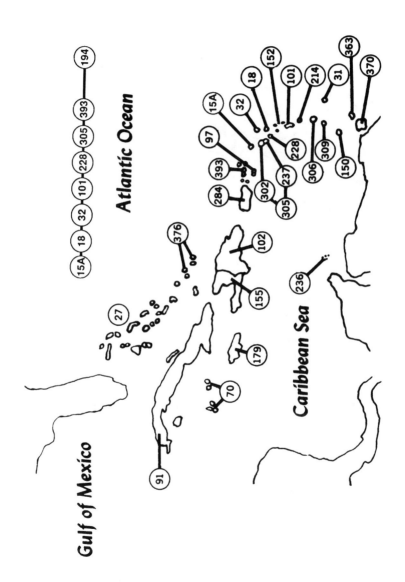

## Map No. 3: South America

## Map No. 4: Atlantic Ocean

## Map No. 5: Europe

## Map No. 6: German States

*(detail of Map No. 5)*

## Map No. 7: Italian States

*(detail of Map No. 5)*

214

## Map No. 8: The Near East

## Map No. 9: Africa

## Map No. 10: West Indian Ocean & Arabian Sea

## Map No. 11: The Far East

# Map No. 12: Australia & South Pacific Ocean

# What's the value of that stamp?

Our US/BNA catalog is the DEFINITIVE guide for United States, United Nations and British North America (Canada and Provinces) stamps.

• *STAMP IDENTIFIER*–explains, with illustrations, how to distinguish between rare and common look-alike issues.

• *COLLECTOR'S GUIDE*–discusses design variet- ies, stamp categories, grading and condition criteria, printing methods, postal markings.

• *PRICE LISTINGS*–current market prices of virtu- ally all US, UN and BNA issues with sections for Plate Blocks, First Day Covers, Booklet Panes, Postal Stationery, and more.

• *SPIRAL BOUND*–easy to use...pages lie flat.

• *REVISED AND UPDATED ANNUALLY*

## ONLY $7.95
### POST-PAID

Order by mail with payment by check or money order to:

*H.E. Harris/ Co.*®

**Dept. HTC**
**P.O. Box 817 • Florence, AL 35631**